Mutual Hierarchy

Mutual Hierarchy

A New Approach to Social Trinitarianism

JEFFREY A. DUKEMAN

WIPF & STOCK · Eugene, Oregon

MUTUAL HIERARCHY
A New Approach to Social Trinitarianism

Copyright © 2019 Jeffrey A. Dukeman. All rights reserved. Except for brief quotations in critical publications or reviews, no part of this book may be reproduced in any manner without prior written permission from the publisher. Write: Permissions, Wipf and Stock Publishers, 199 W. 8th Ave., Suite 3, Eugene, OR 97401.

Wipf & Stock
An Imprint of Wipf and Stock Publishers
199 W. 8th Ave., Suite 3
Eugene, OR 97401

www.wipfandstock.com

PAPERBACK ISBN: 978-1-5326-6425-0
HARDCOVER ISBN: 978-1-5326-6426-7
EBOOK ISBN: 978-1-5326-6427-4

Manufactured in the U.S.A.   FEBRUARY 21, 2019

Scripture quotations, unless otherwise stated, are from *The Holy Bible English Standard Version.* Wheaton, IL: Crossway, 2002.

The original version of chapter 5 appeared as "Mutual Hierarchy as a Framework for Ecclesiology," *Lutheran Mission Matters* 25 (2017) 317–29. Used with permission.

For my loving and supportive family:
my wife Sarah and our children Maria, Ana, Matthew, and Jonathan

Contents

Acknowledgements | ix
Introduction | xi

1. Identifying Themes and a Tension in Social Trinitarianism | 1
2. A Mutual Hierarchy Critique of Traditional Trinitarian Models | 20
3. A Mutual Hierarchy Approach to the Economic Trinity | 53
4. A Mutual Hierarchy Approach to the Immanent Trinity | 88
5. Mutual Hierarchy as a Framework for Ecclesiology | 116
6. Mutual Hierarchy amid the Triadic Macrostructure of the Gospel of Matthew | 130
7. Mutual Hierarchy and Discipleship in the Gospel of Matthew | 163
   Conclusion | 181

Glossary | 187
Bibliography | 191
Index of Names | 199
Index of Scripture | 201

Acknowledgements

THIS STUDY THAT LOOKS at the divine persons as a community truly would not have been possible without the community on earth called the church. I have been a member of numerous Lutheran congregations in my life and have been blessed through fellowship with many of God's children in them. I would like to thank the church of my youth, Pilgrim Lutheran Church, Decatur, Illinois, for helping provide me with a foundation in my life. I also would like to extend my heartfelt thanks to the pastors and members of Timothy Lutheran Church, St. Louis, Missouri, for providing my family a church home during my doctoral studies. Thanks also to the following churches for all that they have done for my family and me: Zion Lutheran Church, Fort Wayne, Indiana; Bethany Lutheran Church, Fort Wayne, Indiana; Immanuel Lutheran Church, Terre Haute, Indiana; and Trinity Lutheran Church, Decatur, Illinois. Thank you also to the various churches and pastors of the Southern District of the Lutheran Church—Missouri Synod, who have provided tremendous fellowship for my family. And I continually thank God for the fellowship I share with the people of St. Matthew Lutheran Church, Gulfport, Mississippi, where I have served as pastor since 2010. The members of St. Matthew have played a huge part in forming me as a pastor and helping me develop the ideas present in my dissertation so that it could be greatly expanded and become the current book.

I am also grateful for the hard work of the faculties of the two seminaries of the LCMS. Among the faculty of Concordia Theological Seminary, I thank especially David Scaer for his bold and faithful instruction that helped inspire me to pursue doctoral studies. Thanks also to William Weinrich for showing me the riches of the early church and for being a mentor during my year as his graduate assistant. Among the faculty of Concordia Seminary, my thanks to Charles Arand, Kent Burreson,

Reed Lessing, David Maxwell, Joel Okamoto, Jeffrey Oschwald, Paul Raabe, William Schumacher, and James Voelz for providing input on my initial proposal for my dissertation. Thanks also to Kent Burreson and William Schumacher for graciously dedicating their time to serve as my final readers. I am also grateful for the work of Reed Lessing, Bruce Schuchard, and the graduate school for supporting me during my years at Concordia Seminary. Thanks also to the staff of the weight room and library (and especially Eric Stancliff) on the campus of Concordia Seminary for providing me with the opportunity for part-time employment and for encouraging me during my studies.

My doctoral advisor Leopoldo Sánchez has done so much to help me that I will not be able to do justice to him here. I have learned from his instruction in classes, benefited from his writings, talked extensively about theology with him, discussed the philosophy of teaching theology with him, taught classes under his guidance, spent time with his family, worked under his supervision at the Center for Hispanic Studies, and benefited from his continued friendship and collaboration since the beginning of our time together in 2005. In so many ways he has been an agent of the Holy Spirit that he studies in teaching me about the selfless love of Christ.

Thanks also to my father, Harold, and my mother, Lynette, without whose selfless love and support, studying for a doctorate probably would not have been possible for me. My father-in-law and mother-in-law, Richard and Sharon Carlson, have also been overwhelmingly supportive of my studies and have been quick to take me into their family as one of their own. Thanks also to my extended family for all of the love and emotional support that you have given to my family.

Finally, thank you to my wife, Sarah, and my children Maria, Ana, Matthew, and Jonathan. It is especially from my time with you that I have learned what a Christian community should be like. I am unworthy of but so grateful for all of your love. Rare was the time when I heard any complaints from you about the sacrifices that you have made for my sake. And overflowing have been your generosity, understanding, and love. I love you all very much. How grateful I am to have you with me as we walk together in the way of Christ and look with hope to the fellowship of heaven.

Introduction

SOCIAL TRINITARIANS HAVE NOT been shy about positing community as the chief ontological category for trinitarian discourse. As beneficial as this is, Social Trinitarians have typically been less helpful in advocating the sort of human community for the trinitarian analogy that most people would probably find desirable. To use the example of a marriage, one has often been forced to choose between a fully egalitarian view where the spouses supposedly have no differences from each other and a hierarchical view where a husband exercises a unilateral and oppressive power over his wife. This book advocates a third alternative for the sort of community present in the Trinity. Just as genuine teamwork is generally desirable in various human communities, the divine persons have a mutual hierarchical relationship with each other. Here each divine person has a unique hierarchy over the others, and yet each uses this hierarchy to serve the others in a dignified way. Recognizing this mutual hierarchy of the divine persons fosters a view of the Trinity that is maximally social, in keeping with the name Social Trinitarianism. In proceeding thus, this book will attempt to show the harmony between systematic theology, exegesis, and practice in a unique way.

The waning years of the twentieth century witnessed the rise of Social Trinitarianism. Here a foundational work in Social Trinitarianism was Jürgen Moltmann's *The Trinity and the Kingdom*, where Moltmann argued that community should be the ultimate ontological category in trinitarian discourse.[1] In the time that has passed since the publication of Moltmann's book, a social model of the Trinity has become a major force in theology. Even though those who utilize it often differ greatly

---

1. Moltmann, *Trinity and the Kingdom*, viii. The original German was entitled *Trinität und Reich Gottes*.

from one another in their theological convictions,[2] they nevertheless are in basic agreement with Moltmann in seeing community as fundamental to the Trinity.[3]

The present book will be a critical survey and constructive proposal in contemporary Social Trinitarianism. Critically, I will attempt to show that there is a tendency in social trinitarian thought toward a *hierarchy-equality polarity* or *tension* in the doctrine of the Trinity where a false alternative of hierarchy versus equality among the divine persons is present and then "resolved" by giving logical priority to either the hierarchical pole or the equality pole of the system. In the book I will argue that this hierarchy-equality tension can be seen in the following three basic areas of tension: (1) the critique of other trinitarian models; (2) the understanding of the economic Trinity with particular emphasis on the relations among the divine persons during Jesus' life; and (3) the understanding of the immanent Trinity.

I will argue that the hierarchy-equality tension that is present in Social Trinitarianism in each of the three areas of tension leads Social Trinitarians with an overall egalitarian trinitarian trajectory to not account adequately for the *uniqueness* of each divine person. I will also argue that this hierarchy-equality tension leads Social Trinitarians with an overall hierarchical trinitarian trajectory to not account adequately for the *dignity* of the divine persons, especially as hierarchy is conceived of in an oppressive manner.

To the extent that a Social Trinitarian does not account adequately for *both* the uniqueness and dignity of each divine person, he or she does not consistently account for the *sociality* of the divine persons. In other words, there are elements present in this case that detract from thinking of the divine persons as a community so that a particular social model of the Trinity does not fully live up to its name. Thus, sociality requires both the uniqueness of the divine persons, which hierarchical Social Trinitarians tend to account for but not egalitarian Social Trinitarians, as well as

---

2. On this point see Brink, "Social Trinitarianism," 333–39; Thompson, "Trinitarianism Today," 26; Horrell, "Toward a Biblical Model of the Social Trinity," 408. Thompson's article is largely a summary of parts of his dissertation entitled *Imitatio Trinitatis*. Gresham makes a similar point in "The Social Model of the Trinity and Its Critics," 325–43. See also Kim, *Relational God and Salvation*, 18–19.

3. See Brink, "Social Trinitarianism," 331–336; Thompson, "Trinitarianism Today," 26; Horrell, "Toward a Biblical Model of the Social Trinity," 404; and Horrell, "Eternal Son of God in the Social Trinity," 54–55, for example lists of some major works in Social Trinitarianism.

the dignity of the divine persons, which egalitarian Social Trinitarians tend to account for but not hierarchical social Trinitarians.

More constructively, I will argue for a mutual hierarchy social model of the Trinity in order to address the areas of hierarchy-equality tension or polarity present in social trinitarian proposals.[4] Here a mutual hierarchy framework aims to uphold both the uniqueness and the dignity of the divine persons. To this end, my proposal will associate the uniqueness of each divine person with his *hierarchy* over the other divine persons in connection with his vocation in the economic Trinity and in connection with his personal properties in the immanent Trinity. Positing a hierarchy of each divine person over the others differs especially from the proposals by egalitarian Social Trinitarians, which do not account adequately for the uniqueness of the divine persons. On the other hand, my proposal will assert that the divine persons exercise their hierarchy over one another in a *mutual* manner by seeking to foster the dignity of the other divine persons. Positing this mutuality of the divine persons differs especially from hierarchical social trinitarian proposals, which tend to conceive of a unilateral and oppressive hierarchy of the Father over the Son and the Spirit. My mutual hierarchy proposal thus will more consistently account for the sociality of the divine persons than other social trinitarian proposals by accounting more adequately for both the uniqueness and the dignity of each divine person.

To better illuminate the three areas of tension in Social Trinitarianism as well as to help guide my own constructive proposal, I will critically engage two significant Social Trinitarians. The first is the now-deceased Roman Catholic theologian Hans Urs von Balthasar, a widely-known and key trinitarian figure who had close ties with the Vatican and represents a

---

4. A few Social Trinitarians have mentioned something like mutual hierarchy among the divine persons. For example, Gruenler speaks of each divine person being a servant and disposable to the others in the "mutual and voluntary subordination among the persons of the Triune Family" (*Trinity in the Gospel of John*, xvi). However, Gruenler's proposal differs significantly from my own, especially due to his tendency to view equality and hierarchy among the divine persons as opposites and choose equality over hierarchy. For example, Gruenler says that any biblical statements suggesting subordination between the divine persons is limited to the time of the economy of salvation, and even these statements must be interpreted within the Son's claims to equality with the Father (ibid., xiv-xvii). See also Erickson, *God in Three Persons*, 310, 331, where Erickson cites Gruenler and speaks of a "mutual submission" of the divine persons to one another but, like Gruenler, says that the subordination of one member of the Trinity to the other in the economy is temporary, functional, and subordinate to their equality.

hierarchical social trinitarian trajectory. A notable strength of Balthasar's hierarchical trinitarian proposal is his stress on the uniqueness of the divine persons. The second is Miroslav Volf, a former doctoral student of Moltmann and an heir of the free church tradition who is a prominent Social Trinitarian known for his egalitarian social trinitarian trajectory. A notable strength of Volf's egalitarian trinitarian proposal is his stress on the dignity of each divine person. These two Social Trinitarians are helpful for representing the three areas of tension present in Social Trinitarianism.

The three areas of tension identified in Social Trinitarianism will be central to the structure of the book. Chapter 1 will set the stage for the following three core chapters. It will look at some key themes and the hierarchy-equality tension in Social Trinitarianism and will also look at how the social trinitarian proposals by Balthasar and Volf evidence these themes and the associated areas of tension. In this chapter I will also argue that studying Balthasar and Volf together is helpful since they represent, respectively, hierarchical and egalitarian trajectories in Social Trinitarianism.

Chapter 2 will look at the question "How does a social model of the Trinity deal with the concerns of person-oriented and unity (substance)-oriented trinitarian models?" Briefly put, a person-oriented trinitarian model teaches that the relative independence of the divine hypostases (in particular, the person of the Father as cause) is the ultimate ontological category in trinitarian discourse. And a substance (unity)-oriented trinitarian model teaches that the one divine substance or essence is a sort of fourth entity that logically precedes the divine persons and, therefore, that the one divine substance is the ultimate ontological category in trinitarian discourse. In chapter 2, I will critically engage the social trinitarian thought of both Balthasar and Volf as they critique these trinitarian models from a hierarchical and an egalitarian perspective, respectively. More constructively, I will argue for a mutual hierarchy critique of these other trinitarian models in such a way that both the uniqueness and the dignity of the divine persons will be accounted for more consistently than in Balthasar and Volf's trinitarian critiques.

Chapter 3 will look at the question "What is the place of the economic Trinity in a social model of the Trinity?" Here I will attempt to show that Balthasar's hierarchical conception of the relationships between the divine persons in the economy, and particularly on Holy Saturday as the chief redemptive period for Balthasar, inadequately accounts for the dignity of the divine persons. And I will show that Volf's manner of stressing equality among the divine persons, and particularly at the cross as the chief redemptive period for Volf, does not account adequately for the unique vocation of each divine person. More constructively, I will utilize a mutual hierarchy framework to look at the economic Trinity during the life of Jesus as evident in John's Gospel.[5] Here I will argue for the *differentiated kenotic vocations* of the divine persons to more adequately account for both the dignity and the uniqueness of the divine persons.[6]

Chapter 4 will look at the question "What is the place of the immanent Trinity in a social model of the Trinity?" Here I will attempt to show that Balthasar's hierarchical understanding of the immanent Trinity inadequately accounts for the dignity of the divine persons. I will also try to show that Volf's egalitarian understanding of the immanent Trinity emphasizes equality among the divine persons in such a way that the uniqueness of each divine person is not accounted for adequately. More constructively, I will utilize a mutual hierarchy framework to account for both dignity and uniqueness in the immanent Trinity and argue for the *mutual constitution* of the divine persons, where the divine persons use the hierarchy associated with their personal properties to constitute each other.

The next three chapters will attempt to identify some of the practical benefits of a mutual hierarchy social model of the Trinity. Chapter 5 will look at the question "What are some basic ways that a mutual hierarchy framework is helpful in ecclesiology?" Here a mutual hierarchy framework will be applied to three particular areas of ecclesiology: the relationship between a pastor and a congregation, trans-congregational relations, and relations between the church and the mission field. The main contours of the ecclesiological thought of Balthasar and Volf in these three areas will first be surveyed and evaluated, including some thoughts on how their ecclesiology and doctrine of the Trinity are related. Then the three ecclesiological areas will be considered from the perspective of a mutual hierarchy framework, including comparisons with Balthasar and Volf.

---

5. Unless otherwise noted, all Scripture references will be from the English Standard Version (ESV).

6. Here kenosis, which is often used as a christological term to describe the Son's self-limiting of his divine power in connection with his humiliation, will be applied to each divine person in a unique way as they serve each other and the world.

Chapters 6 and 7 will deal with hermeneutics and some further practical implications of a mutual hierarchy understanding of the Trinity. Chapter 6 will look at the question "Do the Scriptures have a more systematic way of teaching the doctrine of the Trinity?" Here a triadic macrostructure will be posited for the Gospel of Matthew where each third emphasizes Christ exercising a distinct king-prophet-priest category and a corresponding person of the Trinity. The chapter will then look at how the divine persons in the three thirds of Matthew work together in a dignified way. Thus, both the uniqueness and the dignity of the divine persons—needed in a mutual hierarchy framework—will be seen in conjunction with a triadic macrostructure in the Gospel of Matthew. The chapter will also briefly discuss how this mutual hierarchy reading of the Gospel of Matthew is potentially fruitful for such practical matters as sermon preparation and personal Christian devotion.

Finally, chapter 7 will look at the question "Is there a discipleship-centered reading of Matthew's Gospel that complements the christocentric (and trinitarian) reading from the previous chapter?" The chapter will associate each third of Matthew with a most-prominent discipleship form in conjunction with the king, prophet, and priest categories, respectively, from the previous chapter. Then it will look at how the three discipleship forms associated with the three thirds of Matthew, respectively, work together and foster each other's dignity in the Gospel. Thus, both the uniqueness and dignity needed in a mutual hierarchy framework will be seen in the discipleship forms in Matthew in conjunction with the doctrine of the Trinity. Finally, the chapter will also briefly discuss how this mutual hierarchy reading of the Gospel of Matthew is potentially fruitful for such practical matters as sermon preparation and mentoring disciples.

A discussion of a few of my assumptions will conclude this introduction. I assume that a mutual hierarchy framework is limited in that it serves merely as a tool that a theologian uses in formulating dogma. The productivity of a framework or model depends on its ability to answer certain types of questions. It is not meant to be a dogma but a model to articulate doctrine in response to some issues.[7] This is important because a mutual hierarchy framework as a tool to be used in formulating dogma cannot replace the biblical narrative itself. Rather, the framework should always be used in service to the narrative as a tool that points to the nar-

---

7. For some helpful commentary on the limitations of the framework of a social model of the Trinity in general, see Thompson, *Imitatio Trinitatis*, 149–56.

rative and to a better understanding of the narrative. The biblical narrative should continually inform how we understand a mutual hierarchy framework.

I also assume the distinction between the economic Trinity and the immanent Trinity. For the purposes of this dissertation, I understand the immanent Trinity as the Trinity considered apart from its relation to the world, especially prior to creation. The economic Trinity refers to the Trinity in its relation to creation, especially beginning with the creation of the world. I agree with most Social Trinitarians that the second half of Rahner's rule (i.e., "The economic Trinity is the immanent Trinity, and the immanent Trinity is the economic Trinity") must not be interpreted to mean that the immanent Trinity is somehow reducible to the economic Trinity.

Finally, I am certainly not interested in completely replacing the existing forms of a social model of the Trinity with an understanding of the Trinity completely unlike them. On the contrary, to a large extent the dissertation is meant to supplement and strengthen the field of Social Trinitarianism by pointing out some potential pitfalls or inconsistencies. The reader will note, for example, how I will often appropriate certain positive contributions from Balthasar, Volf, and other Social Trinitarians. The book seeks to increase awareness of various positive elements in Social Trinitarianism as it now stands. However, the book is also interested in reconciling or integrating what Social Trinitarianism tends to polarize, namely, the hierarchy and equality of the divine persons. The book thus seeks to put many of the current claims made by prominent Social Trinitarians on firmer doctrinal ground.

1

Identifying Themes and a Tension in Social Trinitarianism

THIS CHAPTER SEEKS TO identify themes and an inherent tension in social trinitarian systems. The chapter will first look at some chief themes that are characteristic of Social Trinitarianism and, in connection with these themes, identify a tension that is typically present in social trinitarian systems in three different areas. I will call this tension a *hierarchy-equality polarity*, a viewing of hierarchy and equality as opposites. The chapter will then show how Balthasar and Volf are helpful as representative figures for assessing Social Trinitarianism.

SOME KEY THEMES AND AREAS OF TENSION IN SOCIAL TRINITARIANISM

In what follows, I will lay out three chief themes that are characteristic of Social Trinitarianism. In the process, I will also identify a hierarchy-equality polarity or tension in connection with three areas associated with these themes.

Social Trinitarian Critiques of Other Trinitarian Models

A first important theme associated with Social Trinitarianism is that it critiques other trinitarian models in accordance with its stressing community as the ultimate ontological category in trinitarian discourse.

Thus, Leonardo Boff in *Trinity and Society* distinguishes between Social Trinitarianism, a Western-Augustinian understanding of the Trinity, and an Eastern-Cappadocian understanding of the Trinity.[1] Boff sees these as teaching community, substance, and person, respectively, as the ultimate ontological category in trinitarian discourse. In what follows, I will first provide examples of both person-oriented and unity (substance)-oriented trinitarian models which have been influential in the history of trinitarian discourse. I will then proceed to describe some of the general characteristics of social trinitarian critiques of these two trinitarian models.

A person-oriented trinitarian model teaches that the relative independence of the divine hypostases (in particular, the person of the Father as cause) is the ultimate ontological category in trinitarian discourse. A good example of a foundational description of this model may be seen in the work of Basil the Great, one of the Cappadocian Fathers associated with the church's fight against Arianism leading up to the second ecumenical council. Najeeb Awad in his article "Between Subordination and *Koinonia*: Toward a New Reading of the Cappadocian Theology" provides a helpful example of a place where Basil sets forth a person-oriented trinitarian model.[2] Awad argues that among the Cappadocian Fathers, "the idea that 'the origination of the Godhead is by virtue of the Father alone' is found at center stage primarily in Basil's writings."[3] Awad makes his case based primarily on portions of Basil's *On the Holy Spirit*:

> In Basil's *On the Holy Spirit*—especially chapter sixteen onwards—Basil explicates the eternal Trinity in terms of successively *linear* relationships between the Father, the Son and the Spirit. Whereas in the earlier chapters of this treatise, he states that causal prepositions (i.e. from, through) refer equally to the three persons, in the later chapters he rather insists that the Father *alone* remains the source and the center of the Godhead.[4]

Awad goes on to identify two significant features in Basil's presentation. First, Basil, although also concerned to protect the equal divinity of the divine persons against the *Pneumatomachoi*, nevertheless stresses the

---

1. Boff, *Trinity and Society*, 77–84.
2. Awad, "Between Subordination and *Koinonia*," 181–204.
3. Awad, "Between Subordination and *Koinonia*," 182, italics original. See also Pannenberg, *Systematic Theology*, 1:279–80.
4. Awad, "Between Subordination and *Koinonia*," 183, italics original.

linear ordering of the divine persons. Thus, for example, Awad notes that Basil in *On the Holy Spirit* emphasizes that only the Father is the "fountain and source of all gifts" whereas the Son is the sender of the gift and the Spirit is the messenger through whom the gift is sent.[5] Second, Basil in *On the Holy Spirit* tends to associate the word "God" with the Father alone. Awad summarizes as follows:

> This does not mean that for him [Basil] the Spirit and the Son are not expressive of God. It simply means that the Spirit and the Son are so as each is "God from God," whereas the Father alone is "God the Father." That the Spirit and the Son are "God from God" and not "God," as the Father is, is a conclusion that Basil derives from the language about the Son and the Spirit as conveyers, transmitters, of the divine gift (i.e., the Son is the sender, the Spirit is the messenger), and not, as is the Father, "the fountain and source of all gifts."[6]

According to Awad, Basil emphasizes the fact that the person of the Father is the source of the Godhead and in so doing overshadows other, more relational themes in his understanding of the Trinity.

A basic problem of a person-oriented view from the perspective of many Social Trinitarians is that it tends to teach a logical subordinationism in connection with the priority that it gives to the Father as the unoriginated cause of the divine life. Many Social Trinitarians, and especially egalitarian Social Trinitarians, warn of a danger of Arianism in connection with this alleged subordinationism in an Eastern-Cappadocian trinitarian understanding.[7] However, some hierarchical Social Trinitarians tend to cast the problem of a person-oriented trinitarian model

---

5. Awad, "Between Subordination and *Koinonia*," 186.

6. Awad, "Between Subordination and *Koinonia*," 186.

7. Boff, *Trinity and Society*, 4, says that the Greek fathers taught that the Father is the source and origin of all divinity who communicates his whole substance to the Son and to the Holy Spirit, causing unequal hierarchy or subordination, which position Boff goes so far to say is Arianism. The following also warn of Arianism here: Pannenberg, *Systematic Theology*, 1:322–23; Erickson, *God in Three Persons*, 298–310; Gruenler, *Trinity in the Gospel of John*, xviii.

Also relevant is that Social Trinitarians often tie a charge of "tritheism" to the issue of subordinationism and Arianism. See Boff, *Trinity and Society*, 61; Gruenler, *Trinity in the Gospel of John*, 5; Pannenberg, *Systematic Theology*, 1:274, 297; Plantinga, *Hodgeson-Welch Debate*, 224–32; and Thompson, *Imitatio Trinitatis*, 87–98. One interesting note by Plantinga is that accusations of tritheism today against Social Trinitarians do not really resemble tritheism accusations in the patristic period but rather accusations that came after the time of Augustine.

not so much as a problem of the Father's hierarchy over the other divine persons (although they typically see this as a related problem), but more as a problem of reconciling the "one" and the "many" in the doctrine of the Trinity so that there is an inadequate accounting for the distinctness of the many.[8] That is, hierarchical Social Trinitarians often do not see the problem chiefly in terms of hierarchy but rather in terms of the distinctness of the divine persons.

A substance (unity)-oriented trinitarian model teaches that the divine substance, logically speaking, precedes the divine persons and that this divine substance is the ultimate ontological category in trinitarian discourse. It is widely recognized that the fifth book of Augustine's *On the Trinity* is a foundational text for this substance view. In this place, Augustine looks at what he sees as the three main categories in the doctrine of the Trinity: substance, relation, and person. Augustine here emphasizes that the divine substance is completely unchangeable, admitting no analogy from the world of creation since in creation all things are accidents and as such may either lose their qualities or have their qualities diminished. But the divine substance admits no accidents whatsoever. However, not all things in God are spoken of in reference to substance. Rather, certain things are spoken of according to relation. Here Augustine looks at how such terms as Father, Son, begetter, and begotten are fully relational terms and in no way refer to themselves. Thus, for example, the term Father only makes sense in relation to the Son, and the term Father in no way refers to the divine substance or to the Father himself. And thus we already arrive at Augustine's third chief term: person. For Augustine, there are three divine persons who each equally possess the divine substance and are relations to one another. In sum, Augustine in this chapter sets up a hierarchy between his three terms where substance receives the most attention and emphasis, relation less so, and person still less.

Social Trinitarians tend to critique a substance (unity)-oriented trinitarian understanding to the extent that it teaches that the divine substance is a sort of fourth entity that is primary and logically precedes the divine persons.[9] For example, Moltmann critiques what he can simply

---

8. See, for example, Pannenberg, *Systematic Theology*, 1:283.

9. Karl Rahner is a key figure in the trinitarian renaissance of the twentieth century, who early on noted and explored some of the problems of a substance-oriented view. See Rahner, *The Trinity*, 15–20.

Social Trinitarians tend to critique a substance-oriented trinitarian model more

refer to as monotheism that has been present in the church throughout its history as follows: "The Christian church was therefore right to see monotheism as the severest inner danger."[10] Pannenberg critiques Augustine for, allegedly, insufficiently conceiving the relationship between the one and the many in the Trinity by blurring the distinctness of the divine persons within the undifferentiated unity of the divine essence due to Augustine's concern to guarantee the equality of the persons.[11] Some Social Trinitarians, such as Gunton, even warn of a *pre-personal monism* in connection with the priority of the divine substance in this substance-oriented view since the divine persons allegedly would be in danger of losing their freedom beneath the impersonal divine substance and being absorbed into it.[12]

As is probably already somewhat apparent, social trinitarian critiques of other trinitarian models are typically marked by a hierarchy-equality polarity. On the one hand, most Social Trinitarians have overall egalitarian trinitarian trajectories—albeit with certain hierarchical elements interspersed—and chiefly critique what they see as illegitimate hierarchy in the doctrine of the Trinity. Moltmann is a foundational figure here. Also relevant are the various egalitarian Social Trinitarians mentioned above who critique the person-oriented view for its alleged subordinationism.[13] On the other hand, a few Social Trinitarians have

---

vigorously than they do a person-oriented model. Oftentimes the feeling is mutual, as it is typically those holding to a substance-oriented model that most vigorously critique a social model. For examples of critiques of a social model from those holding to a substance view, see O'Donnell, "The Trinity as Divine Community," 5–34; Leftow, "Anti Social Trinitarianism," 203–49; Coakley, "'Persons' in the 'Social' Doctrine of the Trinity," 123–44; Norman, "Problems for the 'Social Trinity,'" 3–13; and Cross, "Two Models of the Trinity," 275–94. See also Brink, "Social Trinitarianism," 337–49, for a discussion of recent objections to Social Trinitarianism.

10. Moltmann, *Trinity and the Kingdom*, 131.

11. See Pannenberg, *Systematic Theology*, 1:282–85, 323–24.

12. See Gunton, *Promise of Trinitarian Theology*, 58–62, 71–73, and Gunton, *One, the Three, and the Many*, 210–13.

13. Kevin Giles, an evangelical egalitarian Social Trinitarian, also evidences this polarizing tendency in the first chapter of his book *Jesus and the Father* where he gives an overview of the debate among evangelicals on the issue of trinitarian hierarchy. According to Giles, for evangelicals the trinitarian hierarchy debate is inseparable from the anthropological and ecclesiological debates over whether women should be subordinate to men in the church and in the home, with those favoring hierarchy saying yes and those favoring equality saying no. However, as the title of his book makes clear, Giles so favors the egalitarian trajectory that he claims that the majority of evangelical scholars who hold to a hierarchical view of the Trinity "reinvent the Trinity."

overall hierarchical trinitarian trajectories—albeit with certain egalitarian elements interspersed—and chiefly critique what they see as illegitimate equality or homogenization in the doctrine of the Trinity. Pannenberg is a good example of this.[14] The first area of tension in Social Trinitarianism is thus that Social Trinitarians typically view hierarchy and equality as opposites and heavily prioritize either hierarchy or equality in their critiques of other trinitarian models.

Besides critiquing other trinitarian models proper, often Social Trinitarians will be quite critical of some of the practical problems they see as connected with these models. For example, Moltmann, in connection with his critique of forms of certain traditional trinitarian views, has a related criticism of "political and clerical monotheism" and provides as examples such things as "the European absolutism of the Enlightenment period" and in the church the "monarchical episcopate" and the "theology of the papacy."[15] Boff, perhaps following the lead of Moltmann, criticizes other trinitarian models for allegedly justifying a sort of inequality among different classes of people in society, including in the church.[16] The hierarchical social trinitarian Pannenberg stresses that conceptual incongruities in other trinitarian models between the oneness and the

---

14. Grenz, *Reason for Hope*, is sympathetic to Pannenberg's hierarchical Social Trinitarianism; likewise, Grenz seems supportive of Balthasar and his hierarchical Social Trinitarianism as he asks the question, "Does the future belong to Balthasar?" (*Rediscovering the Triune God*, 199). Horrell's understanding of the Trinity is hierarchical as he extensively critiques egalitarian Social Trinitarians for allegedly being weak on distinguishing among the divine persons. See Horrell, "Toward a Biblical Model of the Social Trinity," 416–17. In fact, Horrell's entire article is organized around the debate over hierarchy versus equality within Social Trinitarianism, with Horrell favoring hierarchy. See also Horrell, "The Eternal Son of God in the Social Trinity." Brink, "Social Trinitarianism," 338, lists as the first critique of Social Trinitarianism that its proponents often come to such different conclusions in connection with the tension between hierarchy and equality.

15. Moltmann, *Trinity and the Kingdom*, 191–202.

16. See Thompson, *Imitatio Trinitatis*, 141–43, for a summary of Boff on this issue. Plantinga says the following: "In the last two decades, certain Catholic and Protestant writers have presented such theories [utilizing social themes to reflect upon the Trinity] in the context of reflection on human suffering and human community in the face of it. By contrast with earlier Anglicans, these 'suffering and solidarity' theologians (e.g. Jan Lochman, Juan Luis Segundo, Geevarghese Mar Ostathios, and especially Jürgen Moltmann) offer ethically and even politically ambitious Trinity statements. They tend, for instance, to associate monotheism with oppression and to find in the Trinity vast implications not only for life in community but also—and particularly—for socialism" ("The Perfect Family," 26).

threeness of God have caused much turmoil in the church. The hierarchical social trinitarian Gunton is similar to Pannenberg in that for Gunton, the historical hindrance to the proper understanding of the Trinity was the particular understanding of the unknowability of God.[17] If the egalitarian Social Trinitarians Moltmann and Boff protest against certain oppressive understandings of God for justifying oppression in the church and society, the hierarchical Social Trinitarians Pannenberg and Gunton are concerned about certain mystifying and homogenizing understandings of God that lead to a certain agnosticism in the church that is also unappealing to those outside of the church.

Economic Trinity Issues

A second key theme and area of tension associated with Social Trinitarianism is its understanding of the economic Trinity. The tension here revolves around matters of interpretation associated with the place, in the biblical narrative, of the Son, who became incarnate and receives the bulk of attention in the Gospels, yet who is involved in relationships with the other divine persons.

Egalitarian Social Trinitarians tend to account for this emphasis on the Son in the biblical narrative vis-à-vis the Father and the Spirit by stressing things like mutual relations among the divine persons and the mutual indwelling of the divine persons. However, this somewhat confuses the vocations of the divine persons due to the posited similarity between these vocations. For example, an egalitarian Social Trinitarian like Erickson is typical here, as he says,

> If each person of the Trinity shares the consciousness of each of the others, thinks the other's thoughts, or at least is conscious of those thoughts, then there really are no such things as separate experiences.[18]

Hierarchical Social Trinitarians typically account for the place of the person of the Son vis-à-vis the other divine persons in the biblical narrative by stressing the Father's hierarchical sending of the Son. Pannenberg's understanding of the Trinity provides an example of this as

---

17. Gunton, *Promise of Trinitarian Theology*, 31–55.
18. Erickson, *God in Three Persons*, 224. Erickson often speaks of something like the divine persons "thinking each other's thoughts" (*God in Three Persons*, 225–26, 236–38).

he emphasizes the monarchy of the Father in the economy and stresses that "God" in the New Testament generally refers to the Father and that the Son is characterized by human obedience, an obedience where the Son allegedly will not allow himself to be called equal to God.[19] By the manner in which they stress hierarchy in the economy, Pannenberg and other hierarchical Social Trinitarians arguably tend to portray Jesus in the economy as isolated or oppressed.

Immanent Trinity Issues

Another key theme and area of tension in Social Trinitarianism is the place of the immanent Trinity. With regards to the area of tension, Moltmann distinguishes in his doctrine of the immanent Trinity between a "level of constitution" where the Father constitutes the Son and Spirit in a hierarchical fashion (i.e., begetting and spirating), and a "level of relation" where the divine persons relate to one another in a fully mutual and egalitarian way.[20] Stated otherwise, the tension here is over how to reconcile the fully egalitarian mutual relations that Moltmann emphasizes with the hierarchical level of constitution where the Father can appear "alone."[21] Cornelius Plantinga and Miroslav Volf are good examples of Social Trinitarians who have appropriated Moltmann's two-level view and whose trinitarian thought bears some significant resemblances to his in this context.[22]

Clearly distinguishable from Moltmann's two-level solution are other Social Trinitarians like Wolfhart Pannenberg, Leonardo Boff, Millard Erickson, Royce Gruenler, and Colin Gunton, who reject Moltmann's two-level solution and rather view the divine processions (i.e., begetting

---

19. Pannenberg, *Systematic Theology*, 1:319–27.

20. Moltmann, *Trinity and the Kingdom*, 175–76.

21. Pannenberg, *Systematic Theology*, 1:334, notes that there is a tension between Moltmann's call for the unity of the divine persons to be based on their reciprocal fellowship and Moltmann's deriving the Son and Spirit from the Father as the source of deity.

22. Balthasar also typically works with something like "two levels" in the immanent Trinity, although his two levels evidence a clearly hierarchical trajectory in contrast to the case with Moltmann. See further chapter 4.

Although Thomas Thompson is harder to classify, he also seems to hold to a two-level position. See, for example, Thompson, *Imitatio Trinitatis*, 132–33.

and spirating) as mutual relations.[23] Pannenberg is a foundational figure here. We noted above that Pannenberg stresses what he sees as the conceptual incongruities in other trinitarian models between the oneness and the threeness of God. Pannenberg's solution to this problem is to view the divine processions as mutual relations and in this way to stress the mutual constitution of the divine persons. However, within this group of Social Trinitarians who view the processions as mutual relations, there remains a trinitarian tension in connection with a hierarchy-equality polarity, as we will now see.

Similar to the tension in the two-level solution, the tension in the processions-as-mutual-relations view revolves around a hierarchy-equality polarity. For example, Erickson and Gruenler in connection with their egalitarian views on the Trinity stress the eternal mutual indwelling of and even the overlap of consciousness of the divine persons. Because these theologians tend to view hierarchy and equality as opposites and allow no hierarchy among the divine persons in the immanent Trinity, they insufficiently account for the distinctness of the persons in this mutual indwelling. Related to the fact that Gruenler and Erickson do not allow hierarchy in the immanent Trinity, there is thus a tension between their statements about the highly egalitarian overlap of consciousness of the divine persons, where the divine persons are not clearly distinct from one another, and their other statements asserting that the divine persons are distinct even though there is no hierarchy among them that would distinguish them.[24]

---

23. See Pannenberg, *Systematic Theology*, 1:325; Boff, *Trinity and Society*, 141–46; Erickson, *God in Three Persons*, 303–10; Gruenler, *Trinity in the Gospel of John*, x–xx; Gunton, *One, the Three, and the Many*, 214; and Gunton, *Promise of Trinitarian Theology*, 165–70.

24. Erickson allows that there is a "temporary subordination" of the divine persons in the economy, although this does "not indicate any intrinsic relationship between the three" in the immanent Trinity (*God in Three Persons*, 309, 331). See also ibid., 281, 331–39, for various statements that point to Erickson's overall egalitarian understanding of the immanent Trinity. Although Boff is not as egalitarian as Gruenler and Erickson, he also at times uses modalistic language. For example, Boff says, "At most we can say that in the Trinity there is one substantial consciousness (nature) which is really expressed by three divine, conscious beings (Persons)" (*Trinity and Society*, 89). See further ibid., 84, 89, 128, 145. This modalistic tendency in Boff seems to be connected to his tendency to stress the divine persons containing each other (ibid., 84) or being in one another (ibid., 144). Significantly, Boff also states that he even desires to "diminish differences" between the divine persons (ibid., 6).

Finally, a few words should be said about Moltmann and especially Pannenberg in connection with the ontological stability of the immanent Trinity. By ontological stability I am referring to the divine persons prior to creation not being dependent upon the world for their existence. Both Moltmann and especially Pannenberg hold to a problematic coupling of *ontological priority of the future* with *retroactive causality* that causes them to not sufficiently account for the ontological stability of the immanent Trinity. By "ontological priority of the future" I refer to the teaching that what the divine persons do in the future is most constitutive for their life together. And by "retroactive causality" I refer to the teaching that future occurrences among the divine persons actually cause past occurrences between them. For example, Pannenberg evidences this sort of position in the following quotation:

> But the eschatological consummation is only the locus of the decision that the trinitarian God is always the true God from eternity to eternity. The dependence of his existence on the eschatological consummation of the kingdom changes nothing in this regard. It is simply necessary to take into account the constitutive significance of this consummation for the eternity of God.[25]

This quotation shows that for Pannenberg the divine persons' decision about their identity or being comes at the eschaton and has retroactive force, even "from eternity to eternity." This has problematic effects when it comes to the proper distinction between God and creation. First, it shows that Pannenberg tends to have a rigid view of immutability since the Trinity is always the same, even if the decision for this comes only at the end. Similarly, second, it shows that Pannenberg makes the Trinity overly dependent upon the consummation of its work in the world for its existence, since Pannenberg's doctrine of the Trinity must of necessity always entail the divine persons' real relationships to creation, even from eternity. By saying "real relationships" here I am using the language of Aquinas (who said that God actually has no real relationships with the world) and refer to the divine persons being genuinely affected by creation. In the present instance from Pannenberg, it would seem that logically he would have to say that creation exists even from all eternity since the divine persons' work in creation is what chiefly constitutes their existence, even from all eternity. Although Pannenberg explicitly speaks

---

25. Pannenberg, *Systematic Theology*, 1:331.

against such charges, numerous critics of Pannenberg point out that such conclusions logically follow from Pannenberg's central notion of the ontological priority of the future coupled with retroactive causality.[26]

Moltmann also does not adequately account for the stability of the immanent Trinity. To begin it should be noted that Moltmann can make extreme statements in connection with the Trinity's suffering at the cross. For example, for Moltmann at the cross there is a "breakdown of the relationship that constitutes the very life of the Trinity"; "The Father loses his fatherhood"; "The innermost life of the Trinity is at stake"; "What happens on Golgotha reaches into the innermost depths of the Godhead, putting its impress on the trinitarian life in eternity"; and finally, "Yet on the cross the Father and the Son are at the same time so much one that they represent a single surrendering movement."[27] Here Moltmann's extreme language on the suffering of the Trinity at the cross is in danger of making the divine persons dependent upon the world (and especially the cross) for their eternal existence, or lack thereof.

Furthermore, Moltmann's views on the economic Trinity influence what he says about the immanent Trinity in such a way that the latter is in danger of being dissolved into the former. Thus Moltmann says,

> The cross is at the centre of the Trinity. This is brought out by the tradition, when it takes up the Book of Revelation's image of "the Lamb who was slain from the foundation of the world" (Rev. 5:12). Before the world was, the sacrifice was already in God. No Trinity is conceivable without the Lamb, without the sacrifice of love, without the crucified Son. For he is the slaughtered Lamb glorified in eternity.[28]

Here we see how closely Moltmann eternally ties the cross from the economic Trinity with the constitution of the immanent Trinity. The flip side of this is the way that Moltmann describes the creation of the world:

> Christian panentheism, on the other hand, started from the divine essence: Creation is a fruit of God's longing for "his Other" and for that Other's free response to the divine love. That is why the idea of the world is inherent in the nature of God himself from eternity. For it is impossible to conceive of a God who is

---

26. See, for example, Grenz, *Reason for Hope*, 93–102.
27. Moltmann, *Trinity and the Kingdom*, 80–82.
28. Moltmann, *Trinity and the Kingdom*, 83.

not a creative God. A non-creative God would be imperfect compared with the God who is eternally creative.[29]

Moltmann again does not account adequately for the immanent Trinity having a prior existence to the world that is not dependent upon the world as the divine essence seems dependent upon creation.

It is true that Moltmann does not show as much ontological dependence between the Trinity and creation in his thinking as Pannenberg does. For Pannenberg is much more concerned to say that the divine persons constitute themselves at the eschaton, whereas Moltmann rather seems to focus on the economy and on God from eternity being *affected* by creation and by the cross.[30] Nevertheless, by this more limited talk of the retroactive causality of the world on the immanent Trinity, Moltmann does not account adequately for the stability of the immanent Trinity. Moltmann, like Pannenberg, gives a certain ontological priority to the future since it is here that God is able to be in a relationship with his "other" and says that this future retroactively causes the divine persons from eternity. To this extent, Moltmann, like Pannenberg, does not characterize the larger field of Social Trinitarianism.

BALTHASAR AND VOLF AS REPRESENTATIVE FIGURES FOR ASSESSING SOCIAL TRINITARIANISM

This section will now look at Balthasar and Volf as representative figures for Social Trinitarianism. First, some of Balthasar's trinitarian work will be examined. The same procedure will be repeated for Volf. Based on this analysis, I will summarize how both Balthasar and Volf represent some of the major themes and inherent areas of tension associated with the hierarchy-equality polarity in Social Trinitarianism. Finally, through a comparison of Balthasar and Volf in the context of the areas of tension in Social Trinitarianism, I will argue that, especially because of Balthasar's preference for hierarchy and Volf's preference for equality, they are complementary figures for assessing Social Trinitarianism.

---

29. Moltmann, *Trinity and the Kingdom*, 106, italics original.

30. On Moltmann having less of an ontological dependence between the Trinity and creation than Pannenberg, see especially Olson, "Trinity and Eschatology," 213–27.

The Social Trinitarian Trajectories of Balthasar and Volf

Among Balthasar's vast corpus, he is probably best known for his theological trilogy that consists of the seven-volume *The Glory of the Lord: A Theological Aesthetics*, the five-volume *Theo-Drama: Theological Dramatic Theory*, and the three-volume *Theo-Logic: Theological Logical Theory*.[31] This trilogy will now be briefly considered for its theological and especially trinitarian value.

In *The Glory of the Lord*, Balthasar expends much effort to appreciate the less propositional side of Scripture, as the subtitle of the work clearly shows that it is a theological aesthetics. One notable instance where this aesthetical concern shines through is when Balthasar considers the history of metaphysical thought beginning with the Homeric myths. John O'Donnell summarizes well Balthasar's thought here:

> In the period of myth meaning was found through the action of the gods; their intervention in human affairs explained the "why" of human events. The shift from myth to logos, which is witnessed especially in the rise of Greek philosophy, is the search for the meaning of human life through reason. Plato and Aristotle in differing ways affirmed that reality has a rational structure. This rational structure, which for them had a divine origin, is the meaning of logos.
>
> This shift from myth to logos for Balthasar marks the rise of the Western philosophical tradition. Neo-Platonism taught that worldly realities must be left behind in one's flight toward the One, and it portrayed Christ as opposed to myth. For Balthasar, on the other hand, Christ integrates the world of myth into himself. Myth, more than logos, serves the positive function of showing that the infinite can become involved in the finite.[32]

This quotation points both to the Christocentrism of Balthasar, also evident in his exchanges with Barth, as well as to the fact that Balthasar sees Christ and the other divine persons in terms of beauty, a beauty that is not merely static but that is also capable of action.

---

31. See, for example, Grenz, *Rediscovering the Triune God*, 182, where Grenz mentions that interest in Balthasar has increased greatly in recent years with the translation of the trilogy and the subsequent wider recognition of his theological skill. The trilogy was originally published in German as *Herrlichkeit: Eine Theologische Ästhetik*; *Theodramatik*; and *Theologik*.

32. O'Donnell, *Hans Urs von Balthasar*, 33.

Theo-Drama continues the line of thought found in *The Glory of the Lord*, only now focusing on the good action of the divine persons in the economy of salvation. Here Balthasar stresses what he sees as the drama in the economy that occurs among the divine persons themselves and between the divine persons and human beings culminating in the paschal events, which drama is grounded in and hence made possible by an eternal drama between the divine persons in the immanent Trinity.[33]

Finally, *Theo-Logic* is especially associated with the Holy Spirit and demonstrates the unity of *The Glory of the Lord* and *Theo-Drama*. Aidan Nichols summarizes this as follows:

> A theological logic is concerned with salvation's intelligible structure—not its attractive radiance, which belongs to theological aesthetics, nor its power to resolve life's conflicts in favor of the good, the subject matter of theological dramatics. In this perspective, Balthasar [in *Theo-Logic*] speaks of the Spirit as "expounding" a twofold movement—from Father to Son in the incarnation and from Son to Father in the Resurrection of the Crucified."[34]

Theo-Logic continues the themes of the earlier works, only now from the perspective of a more logical analysis of these phenomena. Balthasar's trilogy thus clearly evidences a trinitarian structure and focus, which trilogy makes room for visible beauty or glory, the dramatic interpretation of goodness, as well as the more propositional and logical analysis of these phenomena.

Besides these general features of each part of the trilogy, crucial for the current work is that there is a sort of development and intensification of Balthasar's trinitarian discussion as one proceeds through the trilogy. Cyril O'Regan well notes this:

> The symbol of the Trinity is not thematized in any full-blown way in *The Glory of the Lord*. Throughout Balthasar's great trilogy, the symbol of the Trinity becomes more and more important. In the second part of his trilogy, his *Theo-Drama*, Balthasar begins the move from a rich constructive Christology

---

33. For the trinitarian value of Balthasar's *Theo-Drama* see, for example, Mansini, "Balthasar and the Theodramatic Enrichment of the Trinity," 499–519.

34. Nichols, "Theologic," 169. For more background on *Theo-Logic* see also Nichols, *Say It Is Pentecost*.

to its trinitarian supposition, a move completed in *Theologik*, the third part of the trilogy.³⁵

Balthasar thus became more consciously trinitarian as he proceeded through the trilogy. In *Theo-Logic* one finds Balthasar's most developed trinitarian views.

The second volume of the *Theo-Logic* in particular is helpful for illustrating Balthasar's trinitarian views as they pertain to the life and work of Jesus.³⁶ Here it is helpful to quote Balthasar from about halfway through that volume where he discusses his method chapter by chapter:

> Our first step was to grope upward toward the mystery of God from trinitarian analogies in the world (I–II)—all the while tacitly presupposing, of course, a knowledge of the Trinity in God. We then attempted, as far as was humanly possible, to circle about this mystery itself (III). From this point on, however, we will follow (in IV and V) the path that descends from the Trinity to the world.³⁷

From this we can see that the second volume of *Theo-Logic* is a highly trinitarian work; one can see Balthasar critiquing from his hierarchical perspective various theologians whom he sees as being overly egalitarian. Here Balthasar often argues that certain trinitarian errors can lead to significant theological problems in general and can cause a significant threat to the church (usually the Roman Catholic Church). In addition, reflecting Balthasar's Johannine emphasis in the trilogy in general, this volume shows how Balthasar bases his hierarchical doctrine of the Trinity especially upon the Father hierarchically sending the Son into the world as he sees it present in the Johannine narrative. Here the pinnacle of the mission of the Son is his descent into hell on Holy Saturday, which is the key redemptive event in Balthasar's theology. Finally, in this volume we see the nature of Balthasar's hierarchical understanding of the immanent Trinity. The second volume of *Theo-Logic* gives a nice overall view of Balthasar's hierarchical social model of the Trinity, which volume we will deal with later on in this work.

35. O'Regan, "Von Balthasar and Thick Retrieval," 234. O'Regan also says that Balthasar does not deal that extensively with the Trinity in *The Glory of the Lord* ("Von Balthasar's Valorization and Critique," 152).

36. Volume one of *Theo-Logic* is a slightly edited republication of Balthasar's much earlier work *Wahrheit*. Volume three of *Theo-Logic* is a thoroughly trinitarian work but focuses more on how the divine persons work in the post-Easter church.

37. Balthasar, *Theo-Logic*, 2:169.

We move now to Volf, who is probably best known for his views on work in *Work in the Spirit: Toward a Theology of Work*, for his views on ecclesiology in *After Our Likeness: The Church as the Image of the Trinity*,[38] and for his views on social injustice in *Exclusion and Embrace: A Theological Exploration of Identity, Otherness, and Reconciliation*. In each of these works, Volf roots his respective views in his egalitarian understanding of the Trinity.[39]

Volf's most extensive trinitarian teaching appears in *After Our Likeness*.[40] Volf begins this book with an extended analysis of the trinitarian teaching and corresponding ecclesiological views of both John Zizioulas and Joseph Ratzinger. Here Volf argues that in each case, certain hierarchical trinitarian errors lead to what he sees as significant hierarchical problems in ecclesiology. In the second, constructive part of the book, Volf returns to the trinitarian views of these two theologians in the chapter "Trinity and Church," where Volf critically dialogues with them as he lays out his own constructive, egalitarian trinitarian and ecclesiological views.[41] Here as elsewhere Volf is a trinitarian theologian whose understanding of the Trinity informs his theology, in this case his ecclesiology. This "Trinity and Church" chapter of Volf's book draws heavily on John's Gospel, which Volf sees as especially stressing the egalitarian relations and perichoresis of the divine persons in the economy. These two concepts are key for understanding how Volf accounts for the place of Son vis-à-vis the Father and Spirit in the biblical narrative, as Volf argues that the Father and the Spirit work together closely with the Son in an egalitarian manner. Volf in this chapter also appropriates Moltmann's two-level understanding of the immanent Trinity and places great stress on the egalitarian relations of the divine persons. Here Volf also gives reasons for rejecting the processions-as-mutual-relations view associated with Pan-

---

38. *After Our Likeness* was translated from the original German *Trinität und Gemeinschaft: Eine Oekumenische Ekklesiologie*.

39. Besides these three major works of Volf, the following are also notable trinitarian works of Volf: "Being as God Is: Trinity and Generosity"; "Community Formation as an Image of the Triune God: A Congregational Model of Church Order and Life"; "The Spirit and the Church"; "The Trinity and Gender Identity"; "The Trinity Is Our Social Program: The Doctrine of the Trinity and the Shape of Social Engagement"; "Trinity, Unity, Primacy: On the Trinitarian Nature of Unity and Its Implications for the Question of Primacy."

40. See Volf, *After Our Likeness*, 24–25, for Volf's discussion of the structure of this work.

41. Volf, *After Our Likeness*, 191–220.

nenberg. Finally, in *After Our Likeness* Volf is also helpful for critiquing such notions as retroactive causality and the ontological priority of the future that appear in Moltmann and Pannenberg. Although Volf says that he has an eschatological perspective in his understanding of the Trinity in some ways similar to Moltmann and Pannenberg,[42] Volf also clearly differs from them in this context and explicitly critiques such things as retroactive causality that he finds present in Zizioulas and Pannenberg.[43]

Besides *After Our Likeness*, Volf's book *Exclusion and Embrace* is also significant for its trinitarian teaching. Volf notes that *After Our Likeness* deals with mainly the inner, formal nature of the church and not its mission per se; *Exclusion and Embrace* is a "necessary companion" to *After Our Likeness* and is grounded in the same view of the Trinity as *After Our Likeness*, although *Exclusion and Embrace* differs by pursuing the question of the relationship between churches and the societies they inhabit and the way one ought to "live in a world suffused with deception, injustice, and violence."[44] In harmony with this context of living in an evil world, *Exclusion and Embrace* has much material on the self-giving of the divine persons as they work together in a generally egalitarian manner at the cross. Thus Volf writes,

> Without wanting to disregard (let alone discard) the theme of divine solidarity with victims, I will pick up and develop here the theme of divine self-donation for the enemies and their reception into the eternal communion of God. Moltmann himself has drawn the social implications of his theology of the cross and of the Trinity mainly from the theme of divine solidarity: as God suffers with victims, protects them, and gives them rights of which they have been deprived, he argued, so should we. In contrast, I want to spell out the social significance of the theme of divine self-giving: as God does not abandon the godless to their evil but gives the divine self for them in order to receive them into divine communion through atonement, so also should we—whoever our enemies and whoever we may be.[45]

---

42. Volf, *After Our Likeness*, 128.

43. See Volf, *After Our Likeness*, 90, 102, 202, 216. For more background on Volf's views on eschatology see especially Volf's works "After Moltmann"; "Being as God Is"; and "Eschaton, Creation, and Social Ethics."

44. Volf, *After Our Likeness*, 7.

45. Volf, *Exclusion and Embrace*, 23. For a fuller description of the structure and method of the book see ibid., 28–31.

On the topic of the egalitarian divine self-giving at the cross, *Exclusion and Embrace* complements *After Our Likeness*, which does not have much discussion of this issue.

Balthasar and Volf in the Context of the Themes and Areas of Tension of Social Trinitarianism

Based on this analysis of resources, we will now see that studying the trinitarian thought of Balthasar and Volf together shows that, especially due to the difference between the overall hierarchical trinitarian trajectory of Balthasar and the overall egalitarian trinitarian trajectory of Volf, they are complementary figures for assessing the strengths and weaknesses of Social Trinitarianism. First, both spend significant time from their own significantly different perspectives critiquing other trinitarian models, with Balthasar opposing what he sees as overly egalitarian trinitarian trajectories and Volf opposing what he sees as overly hierarchical trinitarian trajectories. Second, especially due to their respective understandings of the need for the stability of the immanent Trinity, both Balthasar and Volf are more representative of the wider field of Social Trinitarianism than Pannenberg and Moltmann; that is, both Balthasar and Volf reject the positions of Pannenberg and Moltmann on the ontological priority of the future coupled with retroactive causality as described above. Third, both Balthasar and Volf show the basis of their own trinitarian views in the biblical economy. Here we note that both use the Gospel of John as a basis for their understanding of the Trinity, and both discuss significant matters of biblical interpretation in Social Trinitarianism such as the significance of the vocation of the Son in his life relative to the Father and the Spirit for understanding the Trinity. In this regard, both give a framework for showing how the hierarchy and equality evident between the divine persons in the economy should influence our understanding of hierarchy and equality in the immanent Trinity. And finally, Balthasar and Volf both heavily emphasize the immanent Trinity and clearly discuss hierarchy and equality in connection with this. Because Balthasar and Volf share a common social trinitarian trajectory yet understand it so differently with respect to the question of hierarchy, studying them together will prove complementary and better represent the field of Social Trinitarianism than only dealing with one of them.

CHAPTER CONCLUSION

In this chapter we have seen that Social Trinitarians have certain key themes in common. For example, Social Trinitarians posit community as the ultimate ontological category in trinitarian discourse. Social Trinitarians also tend to argue that certain trinitarian models that they critique, namely substance (unity)-oriented and person-oriented trinitarian models, lead to harmful effects on the church and society. For example, egalitarian Social Trinitarians often warn that other trinitarian models are too hierarchical and that this hierarchy is connected with a view of church or society that has leaders exercising an oppressive hierarchy over the various people they lead. Again, Social Trinitarians emphasize that a stable doctrine of the immanent Trinity is necessary in theology because it helps prevent dissolving God into the world, which would call into question God's power and ability to save human beings. However, Moltmann and especially Pannenberg are notable exceptions here in that they both tend to emphasize the ontological priority of the future and retroactive causality in their understanding of the Trinity so that the divine persons seem to be dependent on the world for their constitution or existence.

In this chapter I have also argued that one key tension, a hierarchy-equality polarity, in Social Trinitarianism leads to a certain reading of (1) classic substance (unity)-oriented and person-oriented trinitarian models, (2) the economic Trinity, and (3) the immanent Trinity. First, Social Trinitarians tend to define hierarchy and equality as opposites and choose either hierarchy or equality in the doctrine of the Trinity, depending on which Social Trinitarian is under consideration, and critique other trinitarian models accordingly. Second, Social Trinitarians advocate either equality or hierarchy to the neglect of the other in the economic Trinity. And finally, Social Trinitarians similarly polarize equality and hierarchy as they emphasize either an egalitarian or a hierarchical understanding of the immanent Trinity.

Finally, this chapter argued that Balthasar and Volf are representative figures in Social Trinitarianism. Through a general analysis of certain key primary works I showed that each represents the key themes mentioned above. Similarly, I showed in a general way that they also illustrate the three areas of tensions in the field of Social Trinitarianism. Finally, I argued that because Balthasar and Volf share a common social trinitarian trajectory yet understand it so differently with respect to the question of hierarchy, studying them together will prove complementary and better represent the field of Social Trinitarianism than if only one or the other was studied.

2

A Mutual Hierarchy Critique of Traditional Trinitarian Models

THE QUESTION THIS CHAPTER will be trying to answer is "How does a social model of the Trinity critique person-oriented and unity (substance)-oriented trinitarian models?" We will approach this question by taking a look at how Balthasar and Volf in their critiques of these other models tend to conceive of hierarchy and equality as opposites and correspondingly give preference to either hierarchy or equality. The chapter will first present the basic contours of Balthasar's critique of person-oriented and unity (substance)-oriented trinitarian models by critically utilizing relevant secondary works on Balthasar's trinitarian critiques as well as highlighting some key features of Balthasar's critique as evident in portions of the second volume of *Theo-Logic*. Next the chapter will present the basic contours of Volf's critique of these other trinitarian models by utilizing his critiques in *After Our Likeness*. After this, the positions of Balthasar and Volf will be compared and evaluated for whether they account adequately for the sociality of the divine persons. To recall, sociality here refers to how consistently the divine persons are understood as existing together as a community, where such a community requires both the uniqueness and dignity of each divine person. I will then argue for a mutual hierarchy framework for critiquing the person-oriented and unity (substance)-oriented trinitarian models. The chapter concludes with a comparison of my mutual hierarchy critique of other models with the corresponding critiques by Balthasar and Volf.

BALTHASAR'S CRITIQUE OF OTHER TRINITARIAN MODELS

Balthasar tends to critique other trinitarian models in the context of his larger, yet related, criticism of what he sees as the recurring appearance in the history of dogma of a "gnostic" worldview that threatens the church. In harmony with this basic theological concern of Balthasar, my method in this section will be to look at Balthasar's trinitarian critique utilizing the helpful works of Kevin Mongrain and Cyril O'Regan. Then I will look at the second volume of *Theo-Logic* in order to supplement the thought of Mongrain and O'Regan, especially by showing that Balthasar's critique of other trinitarian models extends to notable mainstream Roman Catholic figures, such as Augustine, as well as the Eastern-Cappadocian tradition, things not clearly evident in Mongrain and O'Regan's presentations.

Balthasar's Trinitarian Critique in the Secondary Literature

Kevin Mongrain in the introduction to his book *The Systematic Thought of Hans Urs Von Balthasar* frames the work of Balthasar around the figure of Irenaeus and the economic Trinity (the Trinity considered in relation to the world).[1] Important in the present context is that Balthasar, according to Mongrain, sees himself as especially battling modern, more anthropocentric forms of Gnosticism just as Irenaeus battled the original, more cosmological forms of Gnosticism. Here two "epic" forms of Gnosticism are discernable for Balthasar, one that sees God collapsed into the world in a monistic fashion and one that sees God as dwelling in philosophical sublimity above the world, absorbing the world in a monistic fashion.[2] According to Mongrain, for Balthasar the latter view characterizes gnostic thought during the period of the early church and the former view characterizes especially some gnostic thought of the last two centuries or so. According to Mongrain, about the only time for Balthasar that Gnosticism emerged *within* Christianity between these two periods was in the figure of Joachim of Fiore and his teaching of three successive historical moments in God's dealing with the world. As for the modern form of

---

1. Mongrain, *Systematic Thought*, 16.

2. Mongrain, *Systematic Thought*, 44, quoting *Theo-Drama*, 2:9. Mongrain, *Systematic Thought*, 6, 59–60, 97, argues that Balthasar uses Irenaeus's conception of the economic Trinity to support the notion of the unity within distinction of the divine community in contrast to a monistic Gnosticism.

Gnosticism, according to Mongrain, Balthasar associates it heavily with Hegel, who held to a three-part process of divine self-development in the world in a way somewhat reminiscent of Joachim. Mongrain asserts that for Balthasar "in Hegel's epic theology of history all finite reality is ultimately 'absorbed in identity,' and all personal reality is in the end overcome by 'the impersonality of destiny,'" which ultimately results in "a monistic equation of the divine and human."[3]

In order to show some of the limitations of Mongrain's presentation of Balthasar as well as supplement it, the thought of Cyril O'Regan from the article "Balthasar and Gnostic Genealogy" will now be adduced. O'Regan, like Mongrain, sees Balthasar mainly opposing a modern, monistic form of Gnosticism, especially as focused in "German Idealism and its theological fallout in the nineteenth and twentieth centuries."[4] Nevertheless, O'Regan's presentation shows some advancements over that of Mongrain. One chief difference between Mongrain and O'Regan's presentations is that O'Regan better captures the fact that Balthasar's critique of Gnosticism is most fundamentally grounded in the doctrine of the immanent Trinity (the Trinity considered apart from relating to the world). For example, O'Regan says the following:

> As German Idealism, and particularly Hegel, brings the Trinity back into theological circulation, after its having been made an adiaphora by Enlightenment and Romantic thinkers alike, the battle is now fought on the grounds of whether the more traditional view as sketched in Irenaeus—and as fully elaborated in

---

3. Mongrain, *Systematic Thought*, 140–41. Mongrain, *Systematic Thought*, 160–77, also argues that Balthasar tends to "grade" various modern theologians or theologies that Balthasar finds troubling for their insufficient resistance to the pull of Gnosticism. Here Mongrain looks at four recent theologians or theological movements that he asserts that Balthasar grades from most resistant to least resistant to Gnosticism in the following order: Rahner, Barth, liberation theology, and Moltmann. Mongrain shows that Balthasar typically sees each of these theologians or movements as being in danger of a monism capable of denying the distinctions between the divine persons and dissolving the divine persons into the world.

4. O'Regan sees Balthasar as a sort of successor to the nineteenth century Tübigen school as seen especially in Franz Anton Staudenmaier and to a lesser extent Johan Adam Möhler as they develop "genealogies" for the re-emergence of Gnosticism in modernity. Balthasar is also influenced by Ferdinand Christian Baur, who is associated both with the privileging of the term Gnosticism for labeling modern speculative discourse and with relating multiple genealogical terms to Gnosticism ("Balthasar and Gnostic Genealogy," 610–21).

Augustine, Anselm, Aquinas, and Bonaventure (especially the latter)—is the authentic one.[5]

Although O'Regan is not explicit here as to what the difference between Irenaeus and the medieval fathers mentioned is, the context points to the clearer place of the immanent Trinity in the latter.[6] For example, O'Regan goes on to argue that Hegel wrongly grounded the kenotic vocations of the divine persons in the eternal divine substance rather than, as in Balthasar, in the relations of the divine persons in the immanent Trinity. Balthasar thus emphasizes the immanent Trinity as he contrasts his position with Hegel, who Balthasar says makes God dependent on creation for his constitution in a form of monism that does not adequately distinguish between God and the world.[7]

In a related way, O'Regan also accounts for how Balthasar's critique of Gnosticism is wider than in Mongrain's presentation of Balthasar, as O'Regan argues that Balthasar frequently relates the worldviews of Neoplatonism and apocalypticism to Gnosticism.[8] Whereas for Balthasar the designation "Gnostic" unambiguously marks invalidity in a theologian or a theology, according to O'Regan "Neoplatonic" and "apocalyptic" "usually function critically," but not always.[9] Elsewhere O'Regan notes that for Balthasar, "Neoplatonic" often refers to a tendency in theology to deny distinctions between things in favor of the transcendent "One."[10] "Apocalyptic," on the other hand, for Balthasar refers to a worldview that

---

5. O'Regan, "Balthasar and Gnostic Genealogy," 626–27.

6. O'Regan distinguishes Balthasar's emphasis on the immanent Trinity from Irenaeus's trinitarian theology as follows, "[F]rom a post-Nicene perspective Irenaeus is relatively indeterminate, or underdetermined, with respect to the relations that hold between Father, Son, and Spirit. He satisfies himself by expostulating on the relations as they are disclosed in the economy. And what he does say by way of addressing the issue at a relatively more structural level, namely, what is summed up in his image of the Son and the Spirit as the two hands of the Father, is from the post-Nicene vantage point determinate in the wrong way because it is subordinationist in its implications. At the very least, Irenaeus's articulation of the Trinity is just one of many possible articulations and by no means the most sophisticated at that. Thus, it requires supplementation. In the theological tradition this supplementation comes in many forms, for example, in the form of the Cappadocians, Augustine, Aquinas, Bonaventure, Barth, Rahner, and Balthasar" (*Gnostic Return in Modernity*, 163).

7. O'Regan, "Balthasar and Gnostic Genealogy," 628–29.

8. O'Regan, "Balthasar and Gnostic Genealogy," 616.

9. O'Regan, "Balthasar and Gnostic Genealogy," 617.

10. See O'Regan, "Von Balthasar and Thick Retrieval," 227–60.

sees God immanent in creation, in danger of being dissolved into creation, as it focuses on such things as historical progress and the inbreaking of God's eschatological kingdom.[11] Thus for Balthasar, Neoplatonism matches up with what Mongrain refers to as the older form of Gnosticism, and apocalypticism matches up with what Mongrain refers to as the newer, more dangerous form of Gnosticism. Because O'Regan recognizes the explicit connection of Neoplatonism and apocalypticism with Gnosticism in Balthasar's theology, O'Regan sees better than Mongrain that Balthasar often critiques various prominent figures in church history due to certain allegedly Gnostic elements within their thought. For example, according to O'Regan, early in his career Balthasar worries about the Gnostic danger of a Neoplatonic monism in Pseudo-Dionysius and Gregory of Nyssa, and later in his career he has a similar worry about Eckhart and Nicholas of Cusa.[12] O'Regan's presentation thus advances on that of Mongrain in that it better captures both the extent of Balthasar's critique of Gnosticism and the fact that Balthasar's critique is fundamentally grounded in the doctrine of the immanent Trinity.

A Sampling of Balthasar's Trinitarian Critique of Gnosticism in Volume Two of *Theo-Logic*

In the present section I will supplement the critique of Gnosticism by Balthasar as evident in Mongrain and O'Regan by utilizing the second volume of *Theo-Logic*. I will look especially at how Balthasar critiques certain mainstream trinitarian theologians and traditions in church history since Mongrain and O'Regan do not much mention this sort of critique by Balthasar and since it is highly relevant. First, I will look at the section "Negative Theology" in order to analyze Balthasar's critique of theologians who, according to Balthasar, in their particular manner of arguing "from below" have certain of the older gnostic elements in their theology. Second, I will utilize the "Kata-Logical Aspects" chapter in order to analyze Balthasar's critique of certain theologians who, according to Balthasar, in their particular manner of arguing "from above" (only in the end to be in danger of arguing from below, according to Balthasar) have especially some of the newer gnostic elements in their theology.

---

11. For more on the meaning of apocalypticism for Balthasar, see Lösel, "Unapocalyptic Theology," 201–25.

12. O'Regan, "Balthasar and Gnostic Genealogy," 622.

Balthasar has a significant critique of the medieval Roman Catholic Church in the "Negative Theology" section. For example, after having closely associated Neoplatonism and Gnosticism,[13] Balthasar makes the following statement:

> It both makes sense from the nature of the case and is a historically proven fact that Neoplatonism and Christian theology were able to travel a good part of the way together. On the other hand, their paths diverged from their very origin. The contrast between the biblical and nonbiblical "concepts" of God already suggests this, and Christian thought came to realize it at the latest by the time of the Council of Nicea. Now, this divergence has left open two possible outcomes: Christians have either fundamentally reinterpreted the theoretical and practical methods of Neoplatonism or else have ignored, or, at least, insufficiently corrected, the divergence itself—a move that has taken a bitter toll in the history of Christian theological theory and mystical praxis.
>
> Let us begin with what is most fundamental, with the axiom, enunciated both by Bonaventure and by Thomas, that (derived, worldly) otherness vis-a-vis God presupposes an (original, trinitarian) otherness in God, an otherness that, as such, is supreme positivity. We can immediately infer from this basic axiom that anyone who reckons the world's otherness as purely negative in comparison with the sheer divine One will ipso facto take a path radically divergent from that of Christianity.[14]

In one sense, this quotation seems to be in harmony with O'Regan's work, for we note that Bonaventure and Thomas appear as champions of the immanent Trinity opposed to a sort of Gnostic (a)Trinitarianism that denies distinctions. Here we can also make the point, not clearly brought out by Mongrain and O'Regan, that key to Balthasar's critique of Gnosticism is that Gnosticism is *egalitarian*, which is the basis for Gnosticism to deny distinctions in the world. Finally, Balthasar's strong language about the presence of Neoplatonism within the church already suggests a much greater presence of the threat of Gnosticism within the Roman Catholic Church itself than what either O'Regan or especially Mongrain suggests.

---

13. In his introductory comments in the "Negative Theology" section, Balthasar states, "negative (philosophical) theology . . . is the strongest bastion against Christianity" (*Theo-Logic*, 2:95).

14. Balthasar, *Theo-Logic*, 2:107.

Balthasar continues by further warning about the dangers of Neoplatonism. Balthasar again finds a harmful sort of Neoplatonic influence pervasive in church history:

> Even prescinding entirely from the "heavenly ladder spirituality" of Byzantium (of which John Climacus is merely one exponent), this spiritualizing doctrine of perfection wrought the greatest havoc throughout the Middle Ages and on into the modern era (a John of the Cross cannot be excepted on this point). Contrarily to Christianity's basic incarnational thrust, a gradual unbodying became the model, not only for asceticism, but especially for mystical theory. This tendency continued, with few exceptions, all the way up to the time of Ignatius of Loyola's Exercises, which, however, were unable to break the Neoplatonic trend effectively enough. It would be good to think back on Augustine, who, while vigorously denouncing the Neoplatonists' lack of Christ's descending humility in the *Confessions*, sets forth in his treatise on mysticism a decidedly ascending model—from bodily to imaginative to purely spiritual visions—which remained authoritative for the whole period that followed. . . . An extreme outgrowth of this tendency is Eckhart's mystical teaching. For Eckhart, the creature as a whole does not have its truth in itself but in God's idea of it, so that, as a whole, it has to un-be or un-do itself as image in order, by losing itself, to find itself in God.[15]

In this quotation Augustine is associated with Eckhart and a Neoplatonic negative theology that focuses on God's transcendence.[16] We also note here that Balthasar associates this Neoplatonism with a monism where the world has an egalitarian relationship with God and in connection with this is in danger of being absorbed into him.[17]

The "Negative Theology" section also contains some critique of theologians that Balthasar more associates with the Eastern, or "Byzantine" church, which critique in turn harmonizes with Balthasar's corresponding critique elsewhere. For example, in the preceding paragraph, the quotation from Balthasar alluded to the Byzantine church as it critiqued the "heavenly ladder spirituality of Byzantium" that "wrought the

---

15. Balthasar, *Theo-Logic*, 2:110–11.

16. For more on Balthasar's views on Eckhart, see O'Regan, "Balthasar and Eckhart," 1–37.

17. Balthasar, *Theo-Logic*, 2:111, associates Neoplatonism with both Gnosticism and Buddhism. Balthasar, *Theo-Logic*, 2:120, associates it with Hegel.

greatest havoc throughout the Middle Ages and on into the modern era." The Eastern figure that Balthasar seems to most associate with a harmful form of Neoplatonism is Pseudo-Dionysius, whom Balthasar identifies as "Proculus's disciple," where Pseudo-Dionysius "definitively elaborated" the "formidable apparatus of negative theology."[18] Balthasar's critical comments about theologians and theology that Balthasar classifies as Eastern remind one of Balthasar's comments in the section "The Father's Two Hands" in the third volume of *Theo-Logic*; here Balthasar asserts that some in the East, such as Photius, began seeing the Spirit as from the Father alone due to "a residue of Hellenistic philosophy according to which the absolutely One is the truly Divine, whereas what is 'caused' by him . . . is subordinate."[19] Similar to in our present section, here Balthasar associates the Eastern tradition as represented by Photius with a harmful Neoplatonism where the Father in an egalitarian manner is identified as the transcendent One with whom all things are identified and ultimately are in danger of being absorbed into. Thus Balthasar senses a sort of hyper-personal monism danger in the Eastern tradition in connection with the older, Neoplatonic form of Gnosticism.[20]

As far as the "Kata-Logical Aspects" chapter is concerned, it too gives examples of Balthasar critiquing theologians for how well they resist Gnosticism, albeit here he critiques theologians who he says believe are working from above (although Balthasar believes that some of them are in danger of actually working from below). In this "Kata-Logical Aspects" chapter Balthasar shifts to warning about the newer, more dangerous form of Gnosticism associated with an apocalyptic worldview where God is immanent in the world.

---

18. Balthasar, *Theo-Logic*, 2:104. For other statements in the present section that associate Pseudo-Dionysius with negative theology and Neoplatonism as negative entities, see ibid., 104, 109–10. For much more on Balthasar's critique of Pseudo-Dionysius, see O'Regan, "Von Balthasar and Thick Retrieval," 227–60.

19. Balthasar, *Theo-Logic*, 3:215.

20. Hyper-personal monism is a view that heavily emphasizes the person of the Father in such a way that the other divine persons and all things are negated by being absorbed into him.

In the chapter "Logos and Logic in God" of volume two of *Theo-Logic* that will be discussed in the fourth chapter, Balthasar also associates Augustine and after him Anselm with a tendency to consider the divine essence as a sort of transcendent "fourth entity" in the Trinity that threatens to absorb the divine persons (*Theo-Logic*, 2:128–29).

In the "Kata-Logical Aspects" chapter, Joachim of Fiore and Nicholas of Cusa appear as the chief medieval culprits paving the way for the newer Gnosticism that felt itself to "be inspired from above," albeit falsely.[21] Balthasar states,

> No one will dispute Joachim's zeal for the cause of Christendom and of revelation in general. Yet, in spite of this zeal, he unsuspectingly opened the door to all those who have since sought a Church of the Spirit to supersede the Church of Christ, whether politically (Cola di Rienzo, Michelet, Marx), morally (the Rosicrucians), or speculatively (from Lessing to Schelling and Hegel). Of significance for theo-logic is Joachim's reduction of the Logos to Jesus's *Pneuma*, of Christ's in-spiration of his own Spirit into the Church to a precursor of the eschatological truth. The result: the Cross and Resurrection no longer play any decisive role in salvation. Although Dante places Joachim next to Bonaventure in his *Paradiso*, just as he puts Siger of Brabant next to Thomas Aquinas, both Thomas and Bonaventure distanced themselves from him.[22]

Here Joachim "opened the door" for the newer, apocalyptic form of Gnosticism that is in danger of "reducing" all things into the "Spirit" immanent in the world. The quotation also portrays Thomas and Bonaventure, whom Balthasar views as champions of an orthodox view of the immanent Trinity, distancing themselves from this egalitarian Gnosticism that denies trinitarian distinctions.[23]

It is highly significant that Balthasar also has some significant critiques in this chapter of mainstream figures from the medieval Roman Catholic Church, such as Augustine. For example, the opening sentences of the chapter warn that Augustine, like the transitional figure Joachim, could claim to be arguing from above, while actually more resembling the modern, more dangerous form of Gnosticism:

> The descent [by doing theology "from above"] must by planned out with a great deal of caution, lest it start—and stop—with anything secondary. Under no circumstances may it begin ("existentially"), like the Augustinian *"imago Trinitatis in mente"* [image of the Trinity in the mind], with the individual subject,

---

21. Balthasar, *Theo-Logic*, 2:205.

22. Balthasar, *Theo-Logic*, 2:208.

23. Balthasar, *Theo-Logic*, 2:214, notes Nicholas of Cusa' tendency to remove "every threeness from God."

for there is no such thing as an individual without a social context.[24]

A few pages later Balthasar again warns about Augustine's teaching on the soul as the chief image of the Trinity:

> The essence of man unfolds for the child only in a communion of love—yet another index of the insufficiency of Augustine's location of the *imago Trinitatis* in the individual soul's "self-love." To be sure, Augustine also considered certain social approaches ("amans et quod amatur et amor" [the lover, the object of love, and love]; notice, too, that God is always implicitly loved in "amor"). In the end, however, he thought it necessary to confine himself to self-love in order to protect the unity of God's essence.[25]

Here it is significant that Balthasar suggests that Augustine's overly stressing God's immanence in the world was connected to his stressing God's unity, which again shows that for Balthasar Augustine was in danger of in an egalitarian manner not sufficiently distinguishing among the divine persons and in this way teaching a sort of pre-personal monism.

A final notable critique of Augustine in this chapter comes within Balthasar's critique of the transitional figure Nicholas of Cusa. In analyzing how Nicholas "handles the *imago Trinitatis* that has been at the center of the present chapter," Balthasar groups Pseudo-Dionysius, Nicholas, and Augustine closely together:

> The overall structure of his [Nicholas'] *imago*-doctrine is shaped by his philosophy, which implies that his doctrine of the immanent Trinity—influenced most powerfully by Dionysius—stands under the sign of negative theology. God's unity in its triune fullness is beyond number. The triply self-positing one (to which the Bonaventurian *imago* is reduced) remains a mere phantom, even though Cusanus musters all the *imagines* provided by the tradition in order to enliven it. Nevertheless, the Trinity, as an item of faith, remains the background for the numerous *imagines Trinitatis* that present themselves in the creaturely world. However numerously and subtly Cusanus differentiates these intraworldly images (his first effort to find such an image in the ontological structure of the world—*materia-forma-connexio* [matter—form—connection] is unconvincing),

24. Balthasar, *Theo-Logic*, 2:173.
25. Balthasar, *Theo-Logic*, 2:179.

the Augustinian image, refashioned and further developed in diverse ways, stands at the center. Nevertheless, Cusanus characteristically enlarges the Augustinian image in two ways. The mind that comes to know its ternary structure can do so only in a double movement toward the divine archetype and toward the world the mind recapitulates; only thus is the mind a *viva imago* [living image]. Now, this duality has two consequences, one negative and the other positive. Cusanus, like Augustine, "hardly ever" consciously asks whether the distinctions made in God are only attributions or notional distinctions, especially because the Areopagite's negations dominate his doctrine of God.[26]

Here Balthasar associates Augustine's unity-oriented trinitarian understanding with theologians whose trinitarian understanding Balthasar has explicitly found very problematic, many of whom paved the way to the modern, more dangerous form of Gnosticism. We may conclude that Balthasar sees Augustine as mainly one who was, like other church Fathers, influenced by Neoplatonism, which for Balthasar was associated with a less dangerous form of Gnosticism that was in danger of absorbing worldly realties into God in heaven. However, Balthasar also associates Augustine with the transition to the modern, apocalyptic Gnosticism in danger of dissolving God into the world. In both cases Balthasar portrays Augustine as being in danger of in an egalitarian manner insufficiently distinguishing among the divine persons and ultimately blurring the distinction between God and the world in a sort of pre-personal monism.[27]

Conclusion

Kevin Mongrain rightly portrays Balthasar as seeing himself as an Irenaean opponent of especially a more anthropocentric form of Gnosticism from the last two centuries whereas Irenaeus himself opposed a more cosmological form. Cyril O'Regan's work critically complements Mongrain's both by showing that Balthasar, in distinction from Irenaeus, foundationally utilizes the distinctness of the divine persons in the immanent Trinity for opposing what he sees as gnostic thoughtforms that

---

26. Balthasar, *Theo-Logic*, 2:216–17.

27. Pre-personal monism is a view that heavily emphasizes the divine substance, whether conceived of as transcendent over the world or as immanent within the world, in such a way that the divine persons and all things are negated by being absorbed into it.

deny distinctions. O'Regan also broadens the scope of Balthasar's critique by noting that Balthasar in speaking of Neoplatonism and apocalypticism is often also addressing Gnosticism. My sampling of the second volume of *Theo-Logic* critically expanded upon this work of Mongrain and O'Regan. For example, it showed at one point that Balthasar saw a gnostic danger of a sort of hyper-personal monism in the Eastern-Cappadocian tradition with its person-oriented understanding of the Trinity where the Father in an egalitarian manner would absorb all things into himself. Balthasar could associate Augustine with this older form of Gnosticism as well as the more "Western," older form of Gnosticism where the divine substance and its transcendence were so emphasized that there was the danger of the divine substance in an egalitarian manner absorbing all things into itself in a sort of pre-personal monism. Finally, Balthasar could also associate Augustine with what he views as the modern, more dangerous form of Gnosticism that emphasizes God's immanence in the world in such a way that God is in danger of being absorbed into it in an egalitarian manner in a sort of pre-personal monism. Thus Balthasar has an extensive trinitarian critique of Gnosticism in church history, including even in mainstream theologians revered by the Roman Catholic Church like Augustine, a critique that warns of an egalitarianism that could lead to monism.

VOLF'S CRITIQUE OF OTHER TRINITARIAN MODELS

The core of Volf's critique of a person-oriented and a substance (unity)-oriented understanding of the Trinity are present in his book *After Our Likeness*. "We are the people!" are the words of protest that begin the introduction to this book.[28] Volf notes that these words came as a part of the 1989 "Eastern European velvet revolution" against the "patronization by the Communist Party and by its appointed government." However, rather than being a book dealing with political revolution, Volf intends his book to inspire a similar protest in the church using the slogan "We are the church!" Volf in his book places himself chiefly against what he considers the overly hierarchical trinitarian ecclesiology of Roman Catholicism and Eastern Orthodoxy.[29] Thus Volf has "tried to develop a nonhierarchical but truly communal ecclesiology based on a nonhierarchical doctrine of

28. Volf, *After Our Likeness*, 9.
29. Volf, *After Our Likeness*, xi.

the Trinity."[30] The current chapter is concerned especially with Volf's understanding of the Trinity. In this regard, we note that part of the reason that Volf chooses Joseph Ratzinger and John Zizioulas to study is because he believes they are representative of the substance (unity)-oriented and the person-oriented understandings of the Trinity, respectively.[31] In what follows I will consider Volf's basic critique in *After Our Likeness* of the understanding of the Trinity by Ratzinger and Zizioulas separately.

Volf's Critique of the Understanding of the Trinity by Ratzinger

The section "Trinitarian and Ecclesial Communion" in the first chapter "Ratzinger: Communion and the Whole" of *After Our Likeness* addresses Ratzinger's understanding of the Trinity. Volf here divides his presentation into two parts, one critiquing Ratzinger's understanding of divine personhood and the other critiquing his understanding of divine unity, and these will also structure our presentation.

Volf in the Trinitarian and Ecclesial Communion section says that Ratzinger basically follows Aquinas in saying that a divine person is a relation [*persona est relatio*]. For example, for Ratzinger, in the immanent Trinity "the Father is not the one begetting, but rather the 'act of begetting.'"[32] Similarly, Volf characterizes the economy for Ratzinger:

> The Son "really loses his own identity in the role of ambassador"; he is the activity of being sent. Ratzinger tries to anchor this view of trinitarian personhood in the New Testament witness to Jesus Christ. According to his interpretation of Phil. 2:5-11, Jesus Christ is a person who has "emptied" himself, and, "surrendering existence-for-himself, entered into the pure movement of the 'for.'" Divestment is "*pure* movement," a process of "consisting *completely*" in being sent. This movement does not take place *on* the person of Christ; rather, Christ's personhood itself consists in divestment. To arrive at this understanding of personhood, however, Ratzinger must withdraw the subject from this activity of self-divestment and then condense the activity itself into a person. As in Nietzsche's anthropology, so also here: the agent is nothing; the activity is everything. Nor does Ratzinger shy away from expressly drawing this conclusion;

---

30. Volf, *After Our Likeness*, 4.
31. Volf, *After Our Likeness*, 200.
32. Volf, *After Our Likeness*, 67.

there is no "I" remaining behind the deeds and actions of the divine persons; their actions *are* their "I."[33]

According to Volf, for Ratzinger each divine person *is* his relationality rather than *having* relations.[34]

As Volf in the "Trinitarian and Ecclesial Communion" section begins to evaluate this understanding of divine personhood in Ratzinger, the sort of tension Volf sees present in Ratzinger becomes evident. Volf states,

> Robert Krieg has rightly pointed out that the notion of person as relation evades clear understanding. Quite apart from Ratzinger having to reinterpret radically the biblical story of the Son—the *Son* does not divest *himself*, but rather is the activity of divestment—he still has difficulty conceiving Christ's being as pure relation, something already evident in the inconsistency of his formulations. Next to his references to total relationality, one also finds statements such as "if there is nothing in which he [the Son] is just he, no kind of fenced-off private ground, then he coincides with the Father, is 'one' with him." Ratzinger's conclusion does not follow. That there is nothing wherein the Son is just himself means that the Son is determined in everything *also* by the Father, and this in its own turn means that the Son is determined *also* by himself. If this is the case, then neither *is* he *pure* relation, but rather is determined in every aspect of his being *by* the relation to his Father. Moreover, Ratzinger's understanding of the trinitarian persons as pure relations does not reconcile with his assumed biblical basis of trinitarian personhood in the "phenomenon of God who is *in* dialogue," unless one were to seek behind this divine dialogue something more profound or more real. Pure relations can neither speak nor hear.[35]

Here Volf characterizes Ratzinger's position that a person is a relation as being inconsistent or even incoherent. However, we also note that Volf suggests that the reason for this is that Ratzinger seeks "behind" the divine persons "something more profound or more real."[36] Already Volf is

---

33. Volf, *After Our Likeness*, 67, italics original.

34. Volf similarly adds that for Ratzinger "'being from' and 'being toward' constitute the fundamental structure of communality" (*After Our Likeness*, 39).

35. Volf, *After Our Likeness*, 69, italics original.

36. Volf in a footnote explicitly accuses Ratzinger of subordinating the divine persons to some other unreal thing: "Ratzinger has a tendency to search for something

hinting that Ratzinger conceives of the divine substance as impersonal, separable from the divine persons, and in fact "over" the divine persons.

Volf in his "Relational Personhood" discussion in the Trinity and Church chapter again alludes to the position of Ratzinger on trinitarian personhood, further filling out the contours of his critique of the notion of divine personhood in Ratzinger. For Volf, defining the divine persons as pure relations has two consequences:

> The persons become so transparent that it is difficult to distinguish them from the one, sustaining divine substance. The consequence is not only that the one substance gains the upper hand over the three persons, but also that the three persons actually become redundant. If behind the actions of the divine persons there is no "I" of these persons, then the three persons are superfluous in the economy of salvation, and "the Triune God's relationship to us is . . . unitary," as Catherine LaCugna correctly maintains with regard to Augustine's doctrine of the Trinity. Second, the persons seem to dissolve into relations; the Father becomes fatherhood; the Son, sonship; and the Spirit, procession. Understood in this way, these persons are not only superfluous but also incapable of action.[37]

For Volf, Ratzinger's defining the divine persons as pure relations means that the divine substance is over the persons. Resulting from this hierarchy of the divine substance over the divine persons is both that the persons become homogenized and that they become impersonal.[38] For Volf, this ultimately means that "although this is admittedly not Ratzinger's intention," "human persons together with the divine persons dissolve into the one substance of God."[39] Volf thus associates seeing the divine persons as relations with a sort of pre-personal monism where all things divest themselves in favor of a hierarchical divine substance over them and are in danger of being absorbed by it.[40] This charge of pre-personal

---

more profound or real behind the historical, and to view concrete reality merely as a sign for spiritual, transcendent content. Hence the earthly Jesus is portrayed less as a concrete human being than as 'merely an *exemplum* of human beings.' . . . This is a result of Ratzinger's Platonizing 'commitment to the primacy of the invisible as that which is genuinely real'" (*After Our Likeness*, 49).

37. Volf, *After Our Likeness*, 205.

38. See also Volf, *After Our Likeness*, 187, 205, 209, where Volf further clarifies the divine persons being impersonal in Ratzinger.

39. Volf, *After Our Likeness*, 206.

40. Volf in the context of a discussion of Ratzinger speaks of a "spirituality of

monism due to hierarchy will also be central in what follows on divine unity.

As should already be somewhat apparent, integrally related to Volf's critique of divine personhood is his critique of divine unity. As we saw above that Volf explicitly rejected Ratzinger's notion that a person is a relation, in his "Trinitarian and Ecclesial Communion" discussion he also associates Ratzinger with a certain inadequate understanding of unity:

> Because all persons are total relationality [for Ratzinger], their unity cannot come about by way of their specific personal selfhood. For this reason, trinitarian unity is also not a differentiated unity of persons standing in these relations, but rather a unity in which the Father, Son, and Holy Spirit "coincide" and in this way are "*pure* unity." From this perspective, it is consistent when Ratzinger locates the unity of the triune God not at the level of persons, but rather together with the whole tradition of Western trinitarian thought at the level of substance. The result, however, is that the one substance gains the upper hand over the three relations. Ratzinger does maintain that the relations represent a form of being equiprimal with that of substance. Reference to this equiprimacy "of the element of the one" and "of that of the triad" suggests a reciprocity in the relation between the two. Yet he expressly asserts that this equiprimacy of substance and persons can obtain only under the presuppositions of an "all-embracing dominance of oneness" of substance.[41]

Thus, related to Volf's critique of divine personhood is a strong critique of Ratzinger's understanding of divine unity. For Volf, Ratzinger teaches a unity of the divine substance that threatens to overwhelm the divine persons. Volf here chiefly opposes the hierarchy of the divine substance over the divine persons, a hierarchy so extreme that Volf calls it an "all-embracing dominance of oneness."

Because for Volf this dominance of the unity of the divine substance over the divine persons is so pervasive in Ratzinger, Volf claims in the "Trinitarian and Ecclesial Communion" section that the divine substance becomes the actual agent in the Trinity. Volf says,

> If persons are *pure* relations, if *no* person possesses anything of its own (and according to Ratzinger, the Father apparently

divestment consisting in perpetual renunciation of what is one's own" (*After Our Likeness*, 60).

41. Volf, *After Our Likeness*, 70, italics original.

constitutes no exception), then they can hardly be distinguished from one another and from the divine substance sustaining them. Although Ratzinger criticizes Augustine's doctrine of the Trinity insofar as in it "the persons of God are enclosed completely in God's interior, and that externally God becomes a pure I," nonetheless, if all persons are total relationality with regard to one another, then the agent in the deity can only be the one substance, both externally and internally.[42]

Volf thus asserts that Ratzinger makes the divine substance hierarchical over the divine persons the true agent in both the economic Trinity and in the immanent Trinity. For Volf this leads to pre-personal monism. This may be further seen in Volf's following discussion about the relation between ecclesiology and the doctrine of the Trinity in Ratzinger:

> It is more consistent with Ratzinger's own (sketchy) trinitarian thinking *to conceive ecclesial structures by way of the one substance of God*. The one, externally acting divine substance corresponds to the one church that, together with Christ, constitutes one subject and in that way becomes capable of action. A *monistic structure* for the church emerges from this.[43]

Volf asserts that there is the danger of a monistic structure of the church and by extension the danger of a pre-personal monism where the hierarchical divine substance not only absorbs the divine persons but also all things.

Volf's Critique of the Understanding of the Trinity in Zizioulas

In the section "Trinitarian Personhood" in the first chapter, "Zizioulas: Communion, One, and Many," of *After Our Likeness*, Volf has his central discussion of Zizioulas's person-oriented understanding of the Trinity. Volf begins by pointing out that for Zizioulas especially the Cappadocian Fathers laid the groundwork for an ontology of a divine person by effecting a "'revolution' within monistic Greek philosophical thinking by identifying 'hypostasis' (ὑπόστασισ, *substantia*) with 'person' (πρόσωπον, *persona*)." For Zizioulas, this has two consequences:

> (a) The person is no longer an adjunct to a being, a category we *add* to a concrete entity once we have first verified its ontological

---

42. Volf, *After Our Likeness*, 70–71, italics original.
43. Volf, *After Our Likeness*, 71, italics original.

hypostasis. *It is itself the hypostasis of the being.* (b) Entities no longer trace their being to being itself—that is, being is not an absolute category in itself—but to the person, to precisely that which *constitutes* being, that is, enables entities to be entities.[44]

Volf goes on in this section to evaluate these two consequences, the first dealing with Zizioulas's "negative point of departure" where the Eastern tradition attempted to move beyond "the monistic ontology of Greek philosophy,"[45] and the second dealing with Zizioulas's understanding of the monarchy of the Father and his relation to the other two divine persons. These two points will also structure our presentation.

With regard to the first point about Zizioulas seeing the Eastern tradition attempting to move beyond monistic Greek philosophy, Volf in the "Trinitarian Personhood" section quotes a famous dictum of Cyril of Alexandria and summarizes Zizioulas's warnings about it. Volf says that for Zizioulas,

> If one understands the trinitarian postulate μία οὐσια τρία πρόσωπα ("one substance, three persons") to mean that God at first (in the ontological sense) *is* the one God, and only then exists as three persons, then "the ontological principle" of the deity is lodged at the level of substance, and one still remains entangled in monistic ontology.[46]

According to Volf, Zizioulas chiefly opposes a substance-oriented understanding of the Trinity for leading to a pre-personal monism where the divine substance threatens to absorb the divine persons into itself. Volf says that in opposition to this, Zizioulas rather postulates that "God the Father perpetually confirms—constitutes!—his own existence in the free personal activity of the divine life."[47] Here the person of the Father constitutes the divine essence rather than vice versa. It is significant here that Volf agrees with Zizioulas when Zizioulas sees a trinitarian understanding that emphasizes the divine substance as superordinate to the divine persons as tending toward a pre-personal monism. Similarly, Volf agrees with Zizioulas's stressing of the personal nature of the divine persons. However, we will now see that Volf finds the *manner* in which Zizioulas stresses divine personhood highly problematic.

44. Volf, *After Our Likeness*, 76, italics original.
45. Volf, *After Our Likeness*, 80.
46. Volf, *After Our Likeness*, 76, italics original.
47. Volf, *After Our Likeness*, 77.

According to Volf in the "Trinitarian Personhood" section, for Zizioulas the second consequence of the Cappadocian revolution is the priority given to the person of the Father as the one who constitutes being. Already in his first paragraph of discussion on this topic, Volf hints at his opposition to Zizioulas when he quotes Zizioulas as saying, "the concept of hierarchy inheres in the idea of person."[48] It is precisely this sort of hierarchy that Volf opposes in Zizioulas's trinitarian understanding. This can be seen as Volf further describes Zizioulas's constructive position:

> On the one hand, the Father never exists alone, but rather only in communion with the Son and Spirit; the other two persons are the presupposition of his identity, indeed, of his very existence. On the other hand, the Son and the Spirit exist only through the Father, who is their cause, and in "a kind of subordination" to him. The communion is always *constituted and internally structured by an asymmetrical-reciprocal relationship between the one and the many*. The reciprocity consists in the many being unable to live as communion without the one, and in the one being unable to exist without the many. The asymmetry, however, consists in the many being constituted by the one, whereas the one is only conditioned on the many; although he cannot exist without them, they are not his cause, but rather he theirs.[49]

Volf summarizes this position of Zizioulas by saying that Zizioulas teaches a "constituting versus conditioned-by" framework in his doctrine of the Trinity. The Father constitutes the Son and Spirit but is not also constituted by them but only conditioned by them, and Volf sees this as a very hierarchical position. Furthermore, Volf asserts that this hierarchical, asymmetric constituting versus conditioned-by framework affects basically every aspect of Zizioulas's theology in general. In short, Volf is concerned about especially the hierarchy present in Zizioulas's trinitarian understanding.

Volf goes on to critique this hierarchical trinitarian understanding of Zizioulas. Volf says,

> [For Zizioulas it is impossible to say that] *all* the persons can exhibit mutually reciprocal causality, for then it would be impossible [according to Zizioulas] to distinguish them from one another (unless one were to identify the immanent and economical Trinity). The monarchy of the Father is the presupposition

---

48. Volf, *After Our Likeness*, 78.
49. Volf, *After Our Likeness*, 78, italics original.

of the distinction between the persons. What remains obscure [according to Volf], however, is why the monarchy of the Father should be necessary for preserving the unity of God, who is, after all, love, or why the only alternative for securing the unity of God is by way of recourse to "the ultimacy of substance in ontology." This remains merely a postulate for Zizioulas that does not correspond to the attempt at providing a personal grounding for the unity of God, for it presupposes that the unity of God cannot be conceived without numerical oneness and accordingly without something apersonal.[50]

Volf here rejects the "either-or" decision that he says Zizioulas forces: either the person of the Father or the divine substance is the ultimate category in the Trinity. We should also note here that Volf asserts that Zizioulas's stressing the person of the Father should actually be seen as his stressing "numerical oneness"; for Volf this means that Zizioulas arguably is similar to those whom Zizioulas opposes, such as Ratzinger, and Zizioulas is guilty of making "something apersonal," namely this oneness, ultimate in his trinitarian understanding. Volf thus here critiques Zizioulas by saying that the hierarchy connected with his making the person of the Father the ultimate ontological principle in trinitarian discourse ironically makes the Father himself impersonal and hence, similar to Zizioulas's pre-personal monism critique of the substance position of Ratzinger, makes Zizioulas's position be in danger of a closely-related hyper-personal monism that would make the Son and Spirit be absorbed into the Father.

Volf in the section "Christ: Person and Community" in his chapter on Zizioulas shows that the flip side of Zizioulas's alleged depersonalization of the Father is the depersonalization of the Son and Spirit due to their subordination to the Father. Here Volf says that Zizioulas teaches a "deindividualization of Christ" in his filial relationship with the Father.[51] This deindividualization of the Son is reminiscent of the sort of de-centered self that Volf saw present in Ratzinger for each divine person under the divine substance, only Volf says that for Zizioulas the Son is subordinated to the hierarchical Father rather than the divine substance. Volf asserts that Zizioulas's hyper-personal monism where the Father is oppressively hierarchical over the Son not only depersonalizes the Father but also depersonalizes the Son.

50. Volf, *After Our Likeness*, 79, italics original.
51. Volf, *After Our Likeness*, 85.

Returning to the "Trinitarian Personhood" section, Volf advances another criticism of Zizioulas in connection with the hierarchy of the Father in the "constituting versus conditioned-by" framework. Volf says,

> Another question is whether the notion [in Zizioulas] that the Father confirms his relational being through the begetting of the Son and the emergence of the Spirit does not already contain the logical priority of person over communion. A human being who begets is constituted as such only through the actual process of begetting; in this case, however, being as begetter is added to being as person; a person who has begotten becomes one who begets. God the Father, however, is identical with the one begetting and thus also with himself as God. This is why God cannot become Father only through begetting, but rather must already have been Father and thus person even before this begetting—before, that is, in the ontological, not the temporal sense. The begetting can then only *confirm* his being as Father. The Father is not constituted relationally; rather, his fatherhood is necessarily expressed and confirmed relationally.[52]

Here Volf stresses that Zizioulas's stress on the term "constituting" in his "constituting versus conditioned-by" framework causes a tension. For Volf, if the Father is not constituted by the Son and the Spirit, and the person of the Father is the ultimate ontological category in trinitarian discourse, then Zizioulas most stresses that the Father is alone and hence Zizioulas causes a tension between person and community. Ultimately, according to Volf, for Zizioulas the Father did not logically actually need the Son in order to be the Father. Hence in the tension between person and community, person tends to overwhelm community and make even any conditioning of the Father by the Son and Spirit quite difficult. Again Volf sees Zizioulas's position as in danger of a hyper-personal monism due to the sort of hierarchy the Father exercises over the Son and Spirit.[53]

Conclusion

Volf's critique of the substance (unity)-oriented and person-oriented models of the Trinity comes about through his critique of Ratzinger and Zizioulas, respectively. According to Volf, Ratzinger has an unstable

---

52. Volf, *After Our Likeness*, 79, italics original.

53. See also Volf, *After Our Likeness*, 203, where Volf criticizes the Eastern and the Western traditions together in connection with divine unity.

concept of divine personhood where persons are defined in terms of relations in the one divine substance and not as relatively independent ontological realities. The root of this problem is that Ratzinger has an inadequate understanding of divine unity where the divine persons are constituted by their relations to the one divine substance above them and therefore are logically subordinated to the one divine substance. For Volf, the ontological priority given to an impersonal divine substance vis-à-vis the persons ultimately leads to a pre-personal monism where the divine substance absorbs the persons.

As for Zizioulas, Volf argues that Zizioulas works with a hierarchical "constituting versus conditioned-by" framework to describe the relationship of the Father with the Son and Spirit. Zizioulas argues that the Father constitutes the Son and Spirit but is not also constituted by them but is merely conditioned by them. Here Volf states that Zizioulas so stresses the hierarchy of the Father over the Son and Spirit in constituting them that he is in danger of making the Father appear more as a substance than as a person. In the process, Zizioulas allegedly also depersonalizes the Son and the Spirit, both of whom are subordinated to the Father in the system. Reminiscent of the case with Ratzinger, Zizioulas is in danger of a sort of monism, although in the case of Zizioulas it is a hyper-personal monism where the person of the Father in logically preceding the Son and Spirit becomes impersonal, which for Volf logically leads to the danger of the Father absorbing the Son and the Spirit. Because of the hierarchies he sees present in both Ratzinger and in Zizioulas, Volf thus warns of pre-personal and hyper-personal monism, respectively.

A BRIEF COMPARISON OF AND EVALUATION OF BALTHASAR AND VOLF

Various similarities and differences are evident in the trinitarian critiques by Balthasar and Volf. Both Balthasar and Volf critique other models of the Trinity along the lines of a hierarchy-equality polarity, that is, seeing hierarchy and equality as opposites, although Balthasar generally opposes what he sees as egalitarian conceptions of the Trinity while Volf generally opposes what he sees as hierarchical conceptions. Balthasar warns against a substance-oriented trinitarian model, which he sees as an egalitarian, gnostic conception of the Godhead that would homogenize the divine persons in a sort of pre-personal monism. But Volf warns that a substance-oriented trinitarian model subordinates the divine persons to an impersonal divine substance and thus leads to pre-personal monism. Balthasar also warns against a person-oriented trinitarian model as ultimately being in an egalitarian danger of so stressing the One, the Father, that it absorbs the Son and the Spirit into this One and in this way homogenizes the divine persons in a hyper-personal monism. But Volf warns that a person-oriented trinitarian model subordinates the Son and the Spirit to the Father and in the process depersonalizes the solitary Father as well as the subordinated Son and Spirit, again ultimately leading to a hyper-personal monism.

We are now in a position to evaluate how well Balthasar and Volf capture the sociality of the divine persons in their respective trinitarian critiques. Again we recall that sociality in my proposal requires both the uniqueness and the dignity of each divine person. Balthasar's critiques are helpful to the extent that he exposes that certain egalitarian trinitarian conceptions detract from the uniqueness of the divine persons and hence their sociality. But Balthasar is less helpful to the extent that he is one-sided in rejecting the equality of the divine persons, which causes him to not account adequately for the dignity of the divine persons in his critiques.[54] As for Volf, his critiques of the tradition are helpful to the extent that he exposes that certain hierarchical trinitarian conceptions do not adequately account for the dignity of the divine persons and hence their sociality. But Volf is less helpful to the extent that he is one-sided in rejecting hierarchy among the divine persons, which causes Volf to not account adequately in his critiques for the uniqueness of the divine persons and hence their sociality. Finally, the critiques by both Balthasar and Volf tend to be amplified in intensity because the critiques are one-sided, either against equality (Balthasar) or hierarchy (Volf).

A MUTUAL HIERARCHY CRITIQUE OF OTHER TRINITARIAN MODELS

In the introduction to this book I stated that a mutual hierarchy framework aims to uphold both the uniqueness and the dignity of the divine persons. That each divine person has a positive uniqueness in his relations with the other divine persons entails each person having a hierarchy

---

54. Some have even seen Balthasar's thought resembling some of the allegedly gnostic positions he opposes. See Mongrain, *Systematic Thought*, 211, 214, 227–28.

over the others; however, this hierarchy is of such a dignified kind that it does not detract from but rather fosters the dignity of the other divine persons and hence the mutuality among the divine persons. In the current section, we will see how a mutual hierarchy framework can critique other trinitarian models for how well they simultaneously account for both the uniqueness and dignity of each divine person, which uniqueness and dignity are necessary for the full sociality of the divine persons. My method will be to first briefly critique the substance (unity)-oriented model of Augustine utilizing a mutual hierarchy framework.[55] I will then utilize a mutual hierarchy framework to critique the person-oriented model of Zizioulas.[56]

A Mutual Hierarchy Critique of Augustine

In order to establish the general contours of Augustine's understanding of the Trinity, we will first enlist the aid of Cornelius Plantinga's article "The Fourth Gospel as Trinitarian Source Then and Now," which has a concise discussion of Augustine's understanding of the Trinity.[57] Plantinga critiques Augustine mainly in connection with Augustine's derivation of the Trinity from the biblical narrative in *On the Trinity*: "In *On the Trinity* one finds a powerful and subtle statement of the doctrine of the Trinity that self-consciously derives trinitarian principles largely, though not wholly, from Scripture."[58] Plantinga's presentation of Augustine's trinitarian understanding revolves around Augustine's understanding of what Plantinga refers to as three sorts of passages in the Gospel of John: mutual relations passages, sending passages, and unity passages.[59] We will now

55. We have seen that Balthasar often explicitly critiqued Augustine; Volf sometimes mentions him in connection with his critique of Ratzinger.

56. In the previous section, Volf also critiqued Zizioulas as a representative of a person-oriented trinitarian model.

57. Plantinga, "Fourth Gospel," 303–21.

58. Plantinga, "Fourth Gospel," 308. For more on Augustine's biblical understanding of the Trinity and its relation to Neoplatonism see Dunham, *Trinity and Creation in Augustine*, 25–29, and Photius, *St. Photius*, 17–56.

59. See also Plantinga, *Hodgson-Welch Debate*, 291–93, where Plantinga describes the structure of *On the Trinity* in terms of these three sorts of passages. According to Plantinga, books 1–4 treat especially sending, books 5–7 treat especially unity, and book 15 treats especially social themes. Books 8–14 involve all three and witness a progression from more social analogies of the Trinity to more psychological analogies. See also chapter 1 of the book where I discussed book five of Augustine's *On the*

look at each of these three kinds of passages. According to Plantinga, for Augustine in the Gospel of John mutual relations passages refer to those places where some or all of the divine persons mutually know, love, or glorify one another; sending passages refer to those places that speak of the sending of the Son or the Spirit; and unity passages refer especially to those places where the Father and the Son are said to be in one another, especially in John 10:38 and John 17:21.

According to Plantinga, the Johannine sending passages are in many respects the least important for Augustine among the three sorts of passages. Here Augustine interprets the vast majority of the Johannine sending passages in a way that prevents any subordination among the divine persons.[60] However, Augustine does teach that a few sending passages allow hierarchy between the divine persons in the economy; it is these few sending passages that Augustine uses as a textual basis for the divine processions (i.e., generation and spiration) in the immanent Trinity.[61] However, although Augustine allows that these passages involve hierarchy in the economy, he does not allow that they point to any hierarchy in the immanent Trinity. Based on all of this, Plantinga notes that the majority of sending passages, since they are fully egalitarian for Augustine, allow an accurate revelation of what Augustine sees as the fully egalitarian relations in the immanent Trinity; but the few sending passages that Augustine says allow for a temporary hierarchy among the divine persons in the economy do not accurately reveal the mutual relations of the divine persons in the immanent Trinity.[62] Based on this different hermeneutic for understanding different sending texts, Plantinga concludes that there is "methodological strain" in Augustine's derivation of the doctrine of the Trinity from the Scriptures.[63]

Trinity where Augustine utilizes three chief systematic terms for the Trinity: substance, relation, and person.

60. Plantinga, "Fourth Gospel," 318.

61. Here Plantinga cites *On the Trinity* 1.4.7 as an example, where Augustine references John 14:26 and John 15:26 to connect the *filioque* to the sending of the Spirit by both the Father and the Son.

62. Plantinga, "Fourth Gospel," 318.

63. Plantinga, "Fourth Gospel," 317. Closely associated with this methodological strain is that Augustine employs a "double rule" where a passage is classified as either treating of Jesus according to his equality with God according to his divine status (his *forma dei*) or according to his inequality with God according to his human status (his *forma servi*) (ibid., 306). See further Plantinga, *Hodgson-Welch Debate*, 291.

According to the presentation of Plantinga, more important for Augustine than the sending passages in John are the many more passages that he sees referring to the egalitarian mutual relations of the divine persons. For example, in the context of a discussion of Augustine's use of certain social analogies of the Trinity, Plantinga says,

> Augustine draws heavily on those places in the Fourth Gospel in which Father, Son, and Spirit/Paraclete appear as distinct divine centers of love, will, knowledge, and purposeful action—indeed, as *mutually* knowing, loving, glorifying entities. The divine persons share a unity (not an identity) of will akin to that of humans, and a "society of love."[64]

Augustine thus connects the mutuality of the divine persons seen in various passages in John's Gospel with the equality of the divine persons.[65] These passages speaking of equality and mutuality between the divine persons are thus superordinate to the few sending passages that speak of the temporary subordination of the Son in the economy.

According to the presentation of Plantinga, the most important passages for Augustine are the passages that speak of mutual indwelling or unity. Plantinga says,

> In Augustine's overall thought, the oneness statements of John 10 and 17 (which, however mysterious, include oneness of work) plus Augustine's remorseless philosophical tendency to unify and simplify the divine life—these things lead him to a general indivisibility-of-work principle that, in ranging speculatively far beyond any ordinary sense of Scripture, sometimes reaches heroic proportions. Accordingly, he has the whole Trinity (including the Son) working the conception in and birth from Mary. In fact, not content with the anti-subordination claim that "the Son and Spirit are not less because sent," Augustine uses a fancy paralogism, loosely based on the Fourth Gospel, to argue that the Son actually sends himself.[66]

---

64. Plantinga, "Fourth Gospel," 311, italics original.

65. Plantinga, "Fourth Gospel," 305, discusses the derivation of the doctrine of the Trinity from the biblical narrative in the fourth century in general. In this context, Plantinga suggests the following six central trinitarian phenomena in John's Gospel: "common will, work, word, and knowledge, plus reciprocal love (excluding the Spirit) and glorifying." In a footnote, Plantinga offers the following verses as examples: "Will: 4:34; work: 5:19–22; 15:26; word: 3:34; 16:14; knowledge: 10:14–15; love: 3:35; glory: 16:14; 17:22."

66. Plantinga, "Fourth Gospel," 316–17.

Here Plantinga makes it clear that Augustine emphasizes the few unity passages of John 10 and 17 over the sending passages of John for a specifically "anti-subordination," or egalitarian, purpose, which purpose Plantinga earlier said was to preserve the equal deity of the divine persons. The context of Plantinga's statement here also indicates that Augustine emphasized these few unity passages over the mutuality passages as well.[67] According to Plantinga, Augustine thus most emphasizes the unity passages, the mutuality passages less, and the sending passages least in his attempt to preserve the equal deity of the divine persons.

The critique by Plantinga that is of most interest to the present section on a mutual hierarchy trinitarian critique is that Plantinga asserts that there is methodological strain in Augustine over how Augustine can see a certain economic hierarchy among the divine persons utilizing a few sending passages but then deny any hierarchy in the processions in the immanent Trinity based on those same sending passages as well as the other sending passages. My mutual hierarchy proposal agrees with Plantinga on this point. However, my proposal is more interested in the more comprehensive point that Augustine sees hierarchy and equality as opposites and tends to encourage one to choose equality over hierarchy. This arguably is a large part of what drives Augustine to interpret the biblical narrative in the way that he does. Hence when Augustine interprets most of the Johannine sending passages in an egalitarian manner in books 1 through 4 of *On the Trinity* he does this in order to combat an Arian interpretation of these verses.[68] Augustine thus combats an Arian hierarchical reading of John with an egalitarian reading, and thus brings together the majority of the sending passages with the mutuality passages and makes them all fully egalitarian. The few sending passages where Augustine allows for a temporary, economic subordination among the divine persons are exceptions to the rule and are allowed in order to try to safeguard the uniqueness of each divine person in the economy.

---

67. See also Plantinga, *Hodgson-Welch Debate*, 294–95, 306–8, where Plantinga further discusses this preeminence of unity and its association with equality in Augustine's trinitarian understanding.

68. For example, Augustine mentions various Johannine verses in connection with the theme that "The Son and Holy Spirit are not therefore less because sent," such as John 1:10–11, 1:14, 14:26, 16:7, and 16:28; Augustine here begins his discussion by opposing what he associates with an Arian interpretation of these verses: "But being proved wrong so far, men betake themselves to saying, that he who sends is greater than the Son, because the Son continually speaks of Himself as being sent by the Father" (*On the Trinity*, 2.5).

Finally, we saw from Plantinga's presentation that Augustine associates the divine unity passages with egalitarianism among the divine persons. My proposal asserts that Augustine's grading of biblical passages has the effect of making the divine persons as equal to one another as possible, only allowing a temporary economic hierarchy among the persons for the purpose of distinguishing the divine persons. In so doing, Augustine arguably distorts much of the Johannine narrative. For Augustine interprets many Johannine passages as egalitarian that clearly involve hierarchy among the divine persons, especially the various Johannine sending passages. Similarly, Augustine gives disproportionate space to the few Johannine unity passages and denies that such passages can involve any hierarchy among the divine persons. The net effect of all of this is an overwhelming stress on the equality of the divine persons, where equality is understood in such a way that leaves little room (in the economy) to no room (in the immanent Trinity) for hierarchy among the divine persons. While Augustine accounts for the dignity of the divine persons, he detracts from the uniqueness of the divine persons and hence from their sociality, which requires this uniqueness.

A Mutual Hierarchy Critique of Zizioulas

Next we will critique the trinitarian understanding of Zizioulas. First, we will briefly recount Volf's basic characterization of Zizioulas's understanding of the Trinity. Next, supplementing the presentation of Volf, we will briefly examine some of the key biblical evidence Zizioulas uses to support his notion of the person of the Father as the ultimate ontological category in his doctrine of the Trinity. Finally, we will critique Zizioulas's views utilizing a mutual hierarchy framework.

Above, we saw that Volf characterizes Zizioulas as emphasizing the priority of the person of the Father in the Trinity as the personal cause of the divine communion. As summarized by Volf, Zizioulas works with a hierarchical and asymmetrical "constituting versus conditioned-by" framework where the Father constitutes the Son and the Spirit but is only conditioned by them in return. According to Volf, a key reason that Zizioulas formulates his doctrine in this way is because he sees a pre-personal monistic danger in a substance-oriented trinitarian model.

Although I agree with Volf's basic presentation of Zizioulas's understanding of the Trinity, I believe that it would be helpful to supplement

Volf by looking more at Zizioulas's stated biblical basis for his constructive trinitarian views.[69] To support his position, Zizioulas tends to use four major types of interrelated biblical arguments. The first, and probably chief, argument is that the designation "God" in the New Testament almost always refers to the Father. For example, in the opening chapter of *Being as Communion*, after Zizioulas emphasizes the person of the Father as the ultimate ontological category in theology, he cites 1 John 4:7-17 for support of this and says that "God" in these verses refers to the Father: "the word 'God' is identified with Him who 'sent His only-begotten Son.'"[70] This quotation already brings us to Zizioulas's second and third biblical arguments, from the Johannine μονογενής (which Zizioulas translates as "only-begotten") texts and from various sending texts, respectively.[71] Concerning the Johannine μονογενής texts, Zizioulas further says,

> The word "only-begotten" [μονογενής] in the Johannine writings means not only the unique mode of generation of the Son by the Father, but also "Him who is beloved in a unique manner" . . . It is precisely this identification of ontology with love in God that signifies that eternity and immortality do not belong to His [the Son's] "nature" but to the personal relationship which is initiated by the Father.[72]

Keeping in mind our previous quotation about "God" referring to the Father in 1 John 4:7-17, the present one suggests that, for Zizioulas, the Johannine writings in general point to the priority of the Father in connection with the begetting passages and the closely-related sending passages.[73] A final biblical argument Zizioulas utilizes is from the bap-

---

69. See also chapter 1 where I gave an example of Basil's statement of a person-oriented trinitarian model.

70. Zizioulas, *Being as Communion*, 46. Zizioulas here also looks at the phrase "God is love" from 1 John 4:16 and concludes that "God" here refers to the Father. For more background on Zizioulas emphasizing that the term God refers to the Father in the New Testament, see especially Zizioulas, *Communion and Otherness*, 113-18, 137, 152-54.

71. The Johannine μονογενής texts are the following: John 1:14, 18; 3:16, 18; and 1 John 4:9. For a listing by Zizioulas of some of the sending texts that support the priority of the person of the Father, see especially Zizioulas, *Communion and Otherness*, 139. Here Zizioulas also argues for the priority of the Father based on John 14:28 where it says, "the Father is greater than I;" for more on John 14:28 see also ibid., 129-30, 143.

72. Zizioulas, *Being as Communion*, 49.

73. Pannenberg, *Systematic Theology*, 1:305, asserts that in the early church the East distinguished yet closely associated the Father's generating the Son and spirating

tismal formula of Matthew 28:19. For example, Zizioulas asserts that the predecessor creeds to the Apostles' Creed connect the term God with the Father in the phrase "God the Father almighty" and asserts that the origin of this is Matthew 28:19 and the ecclesial experience of baptism.[74] These four arguments are prominent in Zizioulas's biblical basis for the priority of the Father in the Trinity.

Having briefly looked at Zizioulas's biblical basis for his trinitarian views, we are now in a position to evaluate Zizioulas's trinitarian understanding utilizing a mutual hierarchy framework. A mutual hierarchy framework suggests that it is not that Zizioulas has hierarchy in his understanding of the Trinity that is problematic; rather it is the sort of hierarchy he sees as he pits hierarchy against equality and chooses hierarchy over equality. Zizioulas fears that if the divine persons would together constitute the divine substance, there would be a monistic danger that the impersonal divine substance would take precedence over the persons. Accordingly, Zizioulas is more interested in protecting the person of the Father than he is in preserving the mutuality between the divine persons; here he tends to stress the hierarchy of the Father. Similarly, to support his view, Zizioulas stresses what he sees as hierarchical passages from Scripture, especially ones that can speak of the Father logically preceding the other divine persons, and these passages color how Zizioulas sees the Father exercising hierarchy over the other divine persons in other passages that speak about relations between the divine persons.[75] Because of the way that Zizioulas understands hierarchy, Zizioulas does not account

---

the Spirit in relation to the Father's sending of them in the economy.

74. Zizioulas, *Communion and Otherness*, 113. See also Zizioulas, ibid., 150. Zizioulas, *Being as Communion*, 48–49, also connects Jesus's baptism to the priority of the Father in the generation of the Son.

75. For Zizioulas, after the priority of the Father, next in importance is the relation of the divine persons to one another, while least important is the substantial unity of the divine persons. For Zizioulas, hierarchical passages are the pivotal passages, whereas Augustine subordinated their importance to the mutuality and especially oneness passages. See also Zizioulas, *Being as Communion*, 83–87, where Zizioulas critiques the trinitarian understanding of Athanasius.

That John's Gospel may be understood in such different ways may also be seen today through a comparison of Köstenberger, *Father, Son, and Spirit*, which evidences a clearly hierarchical doctrine of the Trinity, and Gruenler, *The Trinity in the Gospel of John*, which evidences a clearly egalitarian doctrine of the Trinity. It is noteworthy that Köstenberger relies largely on the sending passages in John for his position while Gruenler focuses on passages he sees as pointing to the mutuality between the divine persons.

adequately for the dignity of the Son and Spirit, since for Zizioulas the Father with his divine nature to a certain extent logically may be thought of without the Son and Spirit; ultimately, while Zizioulas accounts for the uniqueness of each divine person, he does not account adequately for the dignity of the Father himself who can be thought of in an asocial way.[76]

Conclusion

In this section we have seen that a mutual hierarchy framework allows one to critique other trinitarian models with respect to *both* the uniqueness and dignity of each divine person. Utilizing a mutual hierarchy framework, I critiqued Augustine for tending to define equality and hierarchy as opposites and then largely choosing equality over hierarchy, and for his manner of emphasizing certain biblical passages in John's Gospel. Not only did this create a tension in Augustine's theology, it also caused him to not adequately account for the uniqueness of each divine person. Similarly, I critiqued Zizioulas for similarly tending to define equality and hierarchy as opposites, although in the case of Zizioulas he chooses hierarchy over equality and does it more by way of not mentioning much the equality of the divine persons. In this way Zizioulas did not adequately account for the dignity of the divine persons. Thus my mutual hierarchy proposal could effectively critique traditional trinitarian proposals in terms of uniqueness and dignity, categories necessary for the full sociality of the divine persons. Finally, my critique was nuanced and balanced by also acknowledging that Augustine accounted for the dignity of the divine persons and Zizioulas accounted for the uniqueness of each divine person.

---

76. There seems to be ambiguity in the title of Volf's book *Being as Communion*. Seemingly the more natural reading would be that the divine persons may only be thought of together and because of this all beings must have a communal structure. But Zizioulas more likely means by the title that for any entity other than the Father, that person or thing may only have true being by being in communion *with the Father*. This includes the Son and Spirit, who only have being by being in communion with the Father. Although at first glance this distinction may seem subtle, it actually entails two completely different ultimate ontological categories in theology: the person of the Father versus the divine persons in communion.

CHAPTER CONCLUSION

Both Balthasar and Volf critique other trinitarian models along the lines of a hierarchy-equality polarity, seeing hierarchy and equality as opposites, although Balthasar generally opposes what he sees as egalitarian conceptions of the Trinity while Volf generally opposes what he sees as hierarchical conceptions. Here Balthasar critiques both a substance (unity)-oriented trinitarian model and a person-oriented trinitarian model for being egalitarian, which for Balthasar leads the former to be in danger of a pre-personal monism and the latter to be in danger of a hyper-personal monism. But Volf critiques both a substance (unity)-oriented trinitarian model and a person-oriented trinitarian model for being hierarchical, which for Volf leads the former to be in danger of a pre-personal monism and the latter to be in danger of a hyper-personal monism. Balthasar and Volf thus both come to the same conclusions about monism, but Balthasar in connection with critiquing equality and Volf in connection with critiquing hierarchy. Finally, Balthasar's proposal is really only effective at critiquing other trinitarian models in terms of the uniqueness of the divine persons, while Volf's proposal is really only effective at critiquing in terms of the dignity of the divine persons, and that lack of nuance and balance tends to amplify the severity of the critique.

My mutual hierarchy proposal critiqued other trinitarian models not simply for being egalitarian or hierarchical but rather for making hierarchy and equality opposites. Thus it critiqued Augustine as an example of a substance (unity)-oriented model for making equality and hierarchy opposites and then choosing equality. Here it critiqued Augustine for not adequately accounting for the uniqueness of the divine persons even while acknowledging that Augustine accounted for the dignity of the divine persons. My proposal then critiqued Zizioulas as an example of a person-oriented model for making equality and hierarchy opposites and then choosing hierarchy. Here it critiqued Zizioulas for not adequately accounting for the dignity of the divine persons even while acknowledging that Zizioulas accounted for the uniqueness of the divine persons. In this way, it was capable of effectively critiquing trinitarian models both with respect to uniqueness and dignity (which are both necessary for full sociality in the Trinity) while Balthasar could only do the former and Volf the latter. Finally, because my proposal could better identify positives in other trinitarian models, it did not have to logically lead to so quickly identifying differing trinitarian models as monistic, whereas this weighty charge of monism is what Balthasar and Volf's less-nuanced trinitarian critiques seemed to logically lead to.

3

A Mutual Hierarchy Approach to the Economic Trinity

THE QUESTION THIS CHAPTER will be trying to answer is "What is the place of the economic Trinity in a social model of the Trinity?" I will show that Balthasar and Volf evidence a hierarchy-equality polarity in their understandings of the economic trinitarian trajectory of the life of Jesus in connection with their strong preferences for hierarchy and equality, respectively, which cause them to not adequately account for the dignity and uniqueness, respectively, among the divine persons. I will also argue that a mutual hierarchy framework for reading the trinitarian trajectory of the life of Jesus in the Gospel of John entails the *differentiated kenotic vocations* of the divine persons. Differentiated kenotic vocations here refers to each divine person having a unique vocation involving authority over the other divine persons even while each divine person in exercising this vocation limits his power to foster dignity in the trinitarian work. Through thus accounting for both the uniqueness and dignity of the divine persons, the chapter will argue for a more consistently social understanding of the economic Trinity.

The chapter will first present the basic contours of Balthasar's hierarchical understanding of the economic Trinity during the life of Jesus. Next the chapter will present the basic contours of Volf's egalitarian understanding. After this, the positions of Balthasar and Volf will be compared and evaluated. Finally, I will show how a mutual hierarchy framework that posits the differentiated kenotic vocations of the divine persons offers a way of reading the story of Jesus in the Gospel of John that accounts more adequately for the sociality of the divine persons by more consistently maintaining both their uniqueness and dignity.

BALTHASAR'S HIERARCHICAL UNDERSTANDING OF THE ECONOMIC TRINITY

Balthasar's hierarchical understanding of the economic Trinity is oriented toward Holy Saturday and the descent of Jesus into hell that he sees occurring there. For Balthasar, it is this descent that is the chief redemptive period of the economic Trinity. Assuming this hermeneutical priority, my method in this section will be to first briefly present a couple of key conclusions from Alyssa Pitstick's book *Light in Darkness: Hans Urs von Balthasar and the Catholic Doctrine of Christ's Descent into Hell*. I will then look at Balthasar's understanding of the economic Trinity in his "Hell and Trinity" discussion in the chapter "The Word Was Made Flesh" of the second volume of *Theo-Logic* in order to critically supplement the work of Pitstick.

Balthasar's Understanding of the Son's Descent into Hell on Holy Saturday as Presented by Pitstick

Pitstick's main concern in her book is to compare Balthasar's view of the descent into hell with certain traditional views to determine whether Balthasar's view is sufficiently "Catholic." Her conclusions on this topic will not concern us here but rather her presentation of some of Balthasar's central views. A key theme that recurs in Pitstick's work is that there is a tension in Balthasar's understanding of the economic Trinity between two sets of opposing statements in Balthasar where the Son can *fully* give himself away to the world out of obedience to the Father and yet still retain his own stable personal being. For example, Pitstick identifies mission as an overarching category in Balthasar's understanding of the vocation of the Son in his life, death, and resurrection. Balthasar in speaking about this sometimes says that Jesus *is* his mission in the sense of fully giving himself away for the world as the obedient son of the Father.[1] For

---

1. Pitstick, *Light in Darkness*, 145. For much more background on Balthasar's view that the Son is his mission, see especially the section "Jesus's Consciousness of Mission" in *Theo-Drama*, 3:149–259. Balthasar bases his mission Christology chiefly on

Pitstick there is a tension here over how Jesus can have his own stable personal being if he completely gives himself away to the Father in his mission. In order to illustrate Balthasar's trinitarian theology, Pitstick uses the analogy of a container filled with a substance. The Son in coming into this world in humiliation takes his divine attributes, which are the contents of his container, out of his container and deposits these divine attributes into the container that is the person of the Father. The container that is the person of the Son is then filled with new contents—his human nature with human attributes—that is, until the Son also deposits his human attributes with the Father on Holy Saturday.² In connection with this kenotic activity of the Son, Pitstick concludes, "Thus contradictions (Balthasar prefers the word *paradoxes*) will arise frequently in the course of God's involvement with man."³ Thus Pitstick argues that there are unconvincing contradictions in Balthasar's thought over how Jesus can remain the Son of God and a true human being in the midst of highly kenotic activity involving the full removal of his divine and human attributes, and these contradictions amplify the closer Jesus gets to the descent into hell.⁴

Balthasar's Understanding of Holy Saturday as Evident in the Second Volume of *Theo-Logic*

In the present section I will critically supplement the presentation by Pitstick on the Son's descent into hell on Holy Saturday by sampling Balthasar's discussion in a section entitled "Hell and Trinity" in the second volume of *Theo-Logic*.⁵ Doing so will confirm that Pitstick's presentation of the relationship between the divine persons in Balthasar's

---

the Gospel of John.

2. Pitstick, *Light in Darkness*, 154–55.

3. Pitstick, *Light in Darkness*, 150, italics original.

4. See also Pitstick's chapter, "Christ's Descent in Light of the Trinity: The Spirit, Bond of Love, Bridge of Separation," where she sees a related tension in Balthasar's thought in connection with the Holy Spirit, namely, how the Son can simultaneously spirate the Spirit with the Father and yet so deposit his divine attributes in his humiliation that he seems incapable of spirating the Spirit. Pitstick, *Light in Darkness*, 231, says that Balthasar resorts to apophaticism to explain the basis for the "trinitarian inversion" (the Spirit appearing over the Son in the economy).

5. Balthasar's discussion in "Hell and Trinity" is influenced very liberally by the thought of his friend Adrienne von Speyr.

understanding of Holy Saturday is generally accurate. However, it will also critically supplement Pitstick's presentation by clearly demarcating and explaining certain mediating concepts that Balthasar employs in addition to Balthasar's two sets of statements in tension with one another.

In the "Hell and Trinity" section, Balthasar argues that Holy Saturday "signals the beginning of an indescribable paradox."[6] The nature of this paradox in Balthasar's thought is evident in the following:

> He [The Son] is the dead "sin-bearer" of all sins. As such, he passes through what, looked at objectively, is his victory, the sin separated from man on the Cross, which God eternally damns as the second—man-created—chaos. However, because he is dead, he cannot know it subjectively as what he has made it to be. He can only "take cognizance" of it as the fearsome agglomeration of all sins that no longer has the slightest connection with the Father who is the good Creator. This involves an absolute overtaxing of knowledge.[7]

The tension in Balthasar's thought in connection with Holy Saturday may be seen here as Balthasar speaks of the Son having consciousness as he is able to "take cognizance" in hell and simultaneously not having consciousness through an "absolute overtaxing of knowledge." In the midst of this paradoxical tension is a mediating concept where the unconscious Son in hell somehow does in fact exercise consciousness. This mediating concept seems to try to make somewhat more palatable the paradox itself as it connects the two sets of statements in tension with one another. In the process it tends to make more palatable the extreme hierarchy of the unconscious Son's existence by somehow connecting it to the second set of statements where the Son is conscious; at the same time, it seems to amplify the conscious suffering of the Son by connecting it with the first set of statements where the unconscious Son is severed from the Father.

The tension in Balthasar's thought between two paradoxical sets of statements involving the Son on Holy Saturday may be seen further as Balthasar continues. Balthasar writes,

> [For the Son on Holy Saturday] there is only the purely objective stock-taking of the abomination that is the sin of the world. This is a downright "mechanical" inspection, inasmuch as the

---

6. Balthasar, *Theo-Logic*, 2:348.

7. Balthasar, *Theo-Logic*, 2:348. Balthasar here also quotes from von Speyr, *Kreuz und Hölle*.

> onlooker (who, after all, is dead) does not know who he is and whether he is in the first place. In a sort of "automatism" without "interiority," which is therefore "without pain," he is a pure "remains," and it is as such that he takes note of what is there. The I becomes purely neuter, an "it that does" and a "that that is done," but neither of the two can be cleanly identified.... To endure this is sheer horror, which generates an unnamable dread (of which Adrienne speaks again and again). This dread makes it plain that the one who is reconnoitering is not the horror itself: "The horror is in sin and in the sinner and is borne by the Lord without his being it himself.... In the horror he recognizes what separates him from the horror and yet connects him with the it and the that, namely, the form of the darkness of his mission in the darkness of the Father."[8]

On the one hand, Balthasar here indicates that on Holy Saturday the dead Son was "objectively" lacking "interiority." On the other hand, Balthasar indicates that the Son on Holy Saturday subjectively "recognizes" and "endures" the horror of sin and is aware of the Father who has given him his mission.[9] And here again Balthasar utilizes the mediating concept that the Son is somehow able to do the impossible, such as when Balthasar says in the same sentence that the Son lacks interiority and yet "takes note of what is there." This mediating concept both tries to make more palatable the horror of the Son somehow having no conscious existence by connecting it with the Son's consciousness, and amplifies the conscious suffering of the Son by connecting it with his more intense existence as fully severed from the Father. In this way the mediating statement seems to maximize the potential for hierarchy between the Father and the Son, as well as, in this case, to maximize the horror of the situation.

For Balthasar, the tension between two paradoxical sets of statements involving the Son on Holy Saturday is also connected to time. Balthasar writes,

> To have to seek God, the lost Father, here [in hell on Holy Saturday] is sheer futility, absolute contradiction, especially since all time, every past or future, has completely disappeared. "Hell is timeless": von Speyr hammers home this principle over and over again in many variations. The Cross itself was atemporal, because all the sins of past and future were gathered in the Son

---

8. Balthasar, *Theo-Logic*, 2:350–51. Balthasar here also quotes from von Speyer, *Kreuz und Hölle*.

9. Balthasar, *Theo-Logic*, 2:350.

who had been "made sin." Hell is atemporal in another way, because it is definitive and affords no prospect of escape on any side. Thus, "hell is the extreme opposite to heaven, where all time is fulfilled in God's eternity." The absolute solitude of hell also makes this apparent. Since its "substance" is the sin of the world, become (or becoming) anonymous, there is no community in hell; one simply goes "missing" there without a trace. Everything that looks like love is now deposited; nor is there any hope. Consequently, one can at most guess at the footsteps of the Lord who has passed through hell, but because there is no path in hell, there is no following him, either, and his footsteps cannot really be located.[10]

On the one hand, Balthasar indicates that the Son in hell is in a sort of atemporal limbo and is without consciousness since he is "missing." On the other hand, Balthasar says that the Son in hell is still aware of and searches for the Father. Balthasar also employs a mediating statement here as he says that even though it was impossible for the atemporal Son to find the Father, somehow the Son did in fact find the Father since the Son successfully "passed through hell." Again this mediating statement has the effect of further amplifying the horror the Son experiences, for it helps rationalize that somehow the Son can experience in a moment an eternity of suffering.

Finally, as Balthasar continues, it becomes more evident how the Father himself is related to the tension on Holy Saturday. Balthasar writes,

> And now the Father, so to say, "draws back" in order to admit the incarnate Son into this ultimate darkness, which the Father discloses to him, as the Redeemer of sinners, only here, at the end of the way of redemption.[11]

Here we see the same tension as above between two opposing statement, only now from the perspective of the Father. The Father "draws back" from the Son, indicating absence from the Son, yet the Father "discloses" things to the Son, indicating communication with the Son. Here it is important to note that for Balthasar it is only the Son who suffers in hell. It is true that Balthasar in a footnote can also quote von Speyr that "hell is a 'Cross' for the Father," thus teaching that there is a certain kenosis

---

10. Balthasar, *Theo-Logic*, 2:348–49. Balthasar here also quotes from von Speyer, *Kreuz und Hölle*.

11. Balthasar, *Theo-Logic*, 2:352–53. Balthasar here also quotes from von Speyer, *Kreuz und Hölle*.

and suffering of the Father on Holy Saturday.[12] Nevertheless, the present quotation shows that for Balthasar, the Father is largely transcendent and neutral relative to the Son. Whereas for Balthasar, the Son simultaneously experiences impossible conscious and unconscious suffering, the Father merely simultaneously draws back and discloses things. Here the mediating concept that the isolated Father does actually disclose things tends to further amplify the hierarchy of the Father over the Son by providing some way for the isolated Father to have minimal contact with his Son even while he remains removed from the scene in heaven.[13]

Conclusion

Alyssa Pitstick repeatedly notes that Balthasar has a tension in his understanding of the economic Trinity that is most pronounced in his discussion of Holy Saturday. This tension centers around two sets of opposing statements about the Son on Holy Saturday where Balthasar says both that the dead Son somehow loses consciousness as he fully gives away both his divine and human attributes to the Father and that the Son still somehow retains a conscious existence. My reading of Balthasar's discussion in the "Hell and Trinity" section critically supplemented Pitstick's work by reflecting on mediating statements in Balthasar that seek to bridge between his two sets of opposing statements. The main thrust of these mediating statements is that the dead Son does the impossible. One effect of these mediating statements is to provide some rationale for how the unconscious Son can be completely separated from the Father through connecting this kind of statement to other statements where the Son is consciously relating with the Father. A second effect of the mediating statements is to further amplify the conscious suffering of the Son by connecting this sort of statement to others where the Son is completely severed from the Father in hell. Finally, these things are connected to a hierarchy-equality polarity in Balthasar's thought as Balthasar tends

---

12. Balthasar, *Theo-Logic*, 2:352.

13. Pitstick, *Light in Darkness*, 190–202 records many of Balthasar's more extreme statements about the hierarchy of the Father over the Son on Holy Saturday. Pitstick, *Light in Darkness*, 157, concludes that the tension over how Jesus can have his own stable being if he completely gives his divine attributes away to the Father is so dangerous that Balthasar could be in danger of causing "the undoing of the Trinity." Pitstick, *Light in Darkness*, 217–18, also adds that Balthasar has little to say about the Holy Spirit on Holy Saturday in comparison with the Father and the Son.

to maximize the hierarchy of the Father over the Son, and in this case maximize the suffering of the Son in hell, with little mention of equality.

VOLF'S EGALITARIAN UNDERSTANDING OF THE ECONOMIC TRINITY

Volf's understanding of the economic Trinity is generally egalitarian, although he also allows for a certain limited hierarchy among the divine persons that is in tension with this. Volf's economic Trinitarianism is oriented toward the cross, which for Volf is the chief redemptive period in history. My method in this section will be first to look briefly at the general contours of Volf's egalitarian understanding of the economic Trinity as evident in the "Trinity and Church" chapter of *After Our Likeness*. Then I will look more specifically at what Volf says about the economic Trinity in the context of the cross, using his work *Exclusion and Embrace*.

Egalitarian Relations vs. Hierarchical Sending in Volf's Understanding of the Economic Trinity

Volf's basis for his understanding of the economic Trinity in the Trinity and Church chapter of *After Our Likeness* is predominantly an egalitarian reading of the trinitarian aspects or trajectory of the Johannine narrative. For example, Volf writes,

> Within salvation history they [the divine persons] do appear as persons standing in reciprocal relationships to one another. With regard to the immanent Trinity, salvation history thus allows us to infer the fundamental equality of the divine persons in their mutual determination and their mutual interpenetration; even if the Father is the source of the deity and accordingly sends the Son and the Spirit, he also gives everything to the Son and glorifies him, just as the Son also glorifies the Father and gives the reign over to the Father (see Matt 28:18; John 13:31–32; 16:14; 17:1; 1 Cor 15:24). Moreover, within a community of perfect love between persons who share all the divine attributes, a notion of hierarchy and subordination is inconceivable. Within *relations* between the divine persons, the Father is for that reason not the one over against the others, nor "the First," but rather the *one among the others*.[14]

14. Volf, *After Our Likeness*, 217, italics original.

For Volf, the *relations* among the divine persons in the economy are fully egalitarian, which can be seen in the Johannine concept of mutual glorification. In tension with this is that Volf also states that the Father hierarchically sends the Son and the Spirit into the world. Here it is striking that the present quotation is the only explicit occurrence in *After Our Likeness* of the Father's hierarchical sending of the Son in Volf's constructive argumentation. In Volf's presentation of the economic Trinity, there is a tension between the hierarchical sending of the Son by the Father and the fully egalitarian relations of the divine persons, with the latter receiving the much greater emphasis.[15]

In connection with the tension between the egalitarian relations and the hierarchical sending among the divine persons in Volf's economic trinitarian understanding, he utilizes perichoresis as a mediating concept. For example, Volf writes,

> Perichoresis refers to the reciprocal *interiority* of the trinitarian persons. In every divine person as a subject, the other persons also indwell; all mutually permeate one another, though in so doing they do not cease to be distinct persons. In fact, the distinctions between them are precisely the presupposition of that interiority, since persons who have dissolved into one another cannot exist in one another. Perichoresis is "co-inherence in one another without any coalescence or commixture." This is why both statements can be made: "Father and Son are in one another," and "Christians are in *them*" ("in us"—plural!; John 17:21). Being in one another does not abolish trinitarian plurality; yet despite the abiding distinction between the persons, their subjectivities do overlap.[16]

This statement at least partially has the economy in view since it cites John 17:21 where Christians are in the Father and Son. It shows that in the economy Volf mostly associates the mediating concept of perichoresis (mutual indwelling) with the fully egalitarian relations of the divine persons.[17] Here the fully egalitarian relations of the divine persons

---

15. Chapter 4 will show that Volf's understanding of the immanent Trinity explicitly distinguishes between a hierarchical level of constitution and an egalitarian level of relation; these correspond in the economic Trinity to hierarchical sending and the egalitarian relations among the divine persons, respectively. See also Volf, "The Spirit and the Church," 385, 397, for more background on Volf's understanding of the hierarchy of the Father over the Son in the economic Trinity.

16. Volf, *After Our Likeness*, 209, italics original.

17. See also Volf, "Spirit and the Church," 396–98, where Volf stresses the

are so intense that the divine persons permeate one another and their subjectivities "overlap," a concept that raises the question of whether Volf adequately accounts for the distinctness of the divine persons. Here perichoresis is related to the fully egalitarian relations of the divine persons but clearly distinguished from these relations. Volf here also vaguely relates perichoresis to hierarchical sending among the divine persons. For although Volf alludes to hierarchical sending in his statement that the distinctions between the divine persons are presuppositions for their existence in mutual interiority, elsewhere Volf associates the distinctions among the divine persons with hierarchy among them.[18] Perichoresis is thus ambiguous for Volf and reflects a tension in his economic trinitarian understanding, for he associates perichoresis primarily with the fully egalitarian relations of the divine persons, but also vaguely associates it with hierarchical sending.[19] Based on his heavy emphasis in the economic Trinity upon the equality of the divine persons especially in their mutual relations but also in their perichoresis, Volf "resolves" his hierarchy-equality polarity or tension by giving logical priority in his economic Trinitarianism to the egalitarian pole of the system.

Egalitarian Relations vs. Hierarchical Sending in Volf's Understanding of the Cross

Volf's understanding of the economic Trinity finds its climax in his treatment of the cross, which for him is the chief redemptive period in history. Similar to what we have seen thus far, Volf's presentation stresses the equality of the divine persons at the cross, but also at a few points allows for a certain hierarchy of the Father over the Son and Spirit. In what

---

perichoresis, equality, and love of the divine persons as those aspects of the Trinity that are especially relevant for the church in its imaging of the Trinity.

18. The quotation in the previous paragraph clearly connected the Father being the source of deity in the immanent Trinity and the Father's sending of the Son in the economic Trinity. In the next chapter I will show that in Volf's understanding of the imminent Trinity, the Father being the source of deity is associated with hierarchy and distinctness among the divine persons.

19. Volf probably uses John 17 more than any other portion of the Bible to describe the Trinity. This is significant since John 17 is the main place in John's Gospel, and probably the New Testament in general, that describes the mutual indwelling (perichoresis) of the divine persons. It is also significant that John 17 also speaks much about mutual glorification.

follows I will sample Volf's views on the economic Trinity in the context of the cross utilizing his discussion in *Exclusion and Embrace*.

At a few points *Exclusion and Embrace* contains statements that clearly point to a certain hierarchy of the Father over the Son at the cross. Probably most notable among these is the following from Volf's introductory chapter:

> At its core, however, the scandal of the cross in a world of violence is not the danger associated with self-donation. Jesus's greatest agony was not that he suffered. Suffering can be endured, even embraced, if it brings desired fruit, as the experience of giving birth illustrates. What turned the pain of suffering into agony was the *abandonment*; Jesus was abandoned by the people who trusted in him and by the God in whom he trusted. "My God, my God, why have you forsaken me?" (Mark 15:34). My God, my God, why did my radical obedience to your way lead to the pain and disgrace of the cross? The ultimate scandal of the cross is the all too frequent failure of self-donation to bear positive fruit: you give yourself for the other—and violence does not stop but destroys you; you sacrifice your life—and stabilize the power of the perpetrator. Though self-donation often issues in the joy of reciprocity, it must reckon with the pain of failure and violence. When violence strikes, the very act of self-donation becomes a cry before the dark face of God. This dark face confronting the act of self-donation is a scandal.[20]

Here Jesus at the cross had to trust the Father with a "radical obedience," which points to a certain humiliation of Jesus and a hierarchy of the Father over him in connection with the Father sending him. However, even here the equality of the Father and the Son is dominant since the repeated mentioning of "self-donation" hints at the fact that for Volf, the Father, similar to the Son, experiences abandonment by human beings at the cross, a point that will become clearer as we continue.

Even if *Exclusion and Embrace* in its teachings on the cross contains a few statements that point to a certain hierarchy of the Father over Jesus, its emphasis is clearly upon the egalitarian relations of the divine persons. This may be seen in Volf's purpose statements in the introductory chapter. Volf says,

> Here are the contours of my attempt to spell out the promise of the cross in this volume. I present them here following the *inner*

---

20. Volf, *Exclusion and Embrace*, 26, italics original.

logic of my argument rather than tracing the path of its presentation. Chapter III develops the basic argument, best summarized in the Apostle Paul's injunction to the Romans: "Welcome one another, therefore, just as Christ has welcomed you" (15:7). To describe the process of "welcoming," I employed the metaphor of "embrace." The metaphor seems well suited to bring together the three interrelated themes that are central to my proposal: (1) the mutuality of self-giving love in the Trinity (the doctrine of God), (2) the outstretched arms of Christ on the cross for the "godless" (the doctrine of Christ), (3) the open arms of the "father" receiving the "prodigal" (the doctrine of salvation).[21]

Note that it is difficult to distinguish the self-giving of the Son in point (2) from that of the Father in point (3), a fact only exacerbated by the mutuality (and hence equality, in Volf's theology) of the divine persons in point (1). Point (2) may presuppose some hierarchy of the Father over the Son at the cross, but Volf does not mention it. Rather, Volf in the pages preceding discusses at length some of Moltmann's egalitarian views on the cross. For example, Volf cites approvingly Moltmann's discussion of the "passion of God" in *The Trinity and the Kingdom* where Moltmann associates all of human history with the suffering of "God" in general.[22] As we will see, Volf similarly places any hierarchy of the Father over the Son at the cross within a larger framework that stresses the fully egalitarian relations of the divine persons as they together give themselves to the world throughout human history, which culminates at the cross.

Besides this more material statement of Volf's purpose in *Exclusion and Embrace*, his second, more formal, purpose statement is also telling with regard to the relationship between hierarchy and equality in Volf's understanding of the economic Trinity in the context of the cross. Volf writes,

---

21. Volf, *Exclusion and Embrace*, 29, italics original.

22. See Volf, *Exclusion and Embrace*, 22–25. Volf in a discussion called "Space for the Other: Cross, Trinity, Eucharist" also cites Moltmann to support placing the hierarchy of the Father over the Son within a larger, egalitarian framework: "If the fate of the Crucified and his demand to walk in his footsteps disturb us, then we will also be disturbed by the *God* of the Crucified. For the very nature of the triune God is reflected on the cross of Christ. Inversely, the cross of Christ is etched in the heart of the Triune God; Christ's passion is God's passion (Moltmann 1981, 21ff.). As Rowan Williams puts it, 'the inconceivable self-emptying of God in the events of Good Friday and Holy Saturday is no arbitrary expression of the nature of God: this is what the life of the Trinity is, translated into the world' (Williams 1979, 177)" (*Exclusion and Embrace*, 127, italics original).

> The second comment concerns an aspect of my *method*, in particular the use of the biblical texts in relation to the theological theme of "the self-donation and reception of the other." Most chapters contain extended interpretation of some key biblical texts. . . . As I have argued following Luke Johnson, at the center of the New Testament lies the narrative of the death and resurrection of Jesus Christ understood as an act of obedience toward God and an expression of self-giving love for his followers as well as the model for the followers to imitate. This narrative, in turn, is intelligible only as a part of the larger narrative of God's dealing with humanity recorded in the whole of Christian Scripture.[23]

Volf here speaks of Christ's "obedience toward God," which involves a certain hierarchy of the Father over the Son. But this hierarchical relationship is subordinated to the "larger narrative of God's dealing with humanity recorded in the whole of Christian Scripture," which emphasizes the egalitarian relations of the divine persons as they work together throughout history. Again the egalitarian relations and the hierarchy among the divine persons at the cross are in unresolved tension with each other, as Volf subordinates the latter to the former.

The tension in Volf between the egalitarian relations of the divine persons and the hierarchical sending of the Son and the Spirit by the Father is also prominent in the chapter "Deception and Truth" in *Exclusion and Embrace*. Here Volf extensively uses the Johannine passion narrative for his trinitarian discussion. For example, Volf says that Jesus witnesses to a different sort of power than Pilate has as he witnesses to the truth of his Father:

> A witness, unseduced by the lure of power, strives not to bring anything of her own to her speech; not seeking her "own glory" (7:18), she strives to point precisely to what is *not* her own. There is no better summary of Jesus's mission as a witness than his statement, "My teaching is not mine but his who sent me" (7:16; cf. 12:49; 14:24).[24]

Volf refers to a certain hierarchy of the Father over Jesus by mentioning the words "mission" and "sent," words that are connected to each other and the latter of which we have seen that Volf explicitly describes as hierarchical. Nevertheless, Volf's main point is connected to glorification,

---

23. Volf, *Exclusion and Embrace*, 30, italics original.
24. Volf, *Exclusion and Embrace*, 267–68, italics original.

where we recall that Volf associates mutual glorification with the fully egalitarian mutual relations of the divine persons. That Volf has such mutual glorification in mind is further shown as Volf continues,

> A man dressed in a purple robe with a crown of thorns on his head, a man stripped naked hanging on the cross, represents the victory of truth and life, not their defeat. Should we be surprised that John considers crucifixion an act of *glorification* (13:31–32)!?[25]

Although Volf allows for a hierarchy of the sending Father over the sent Son at the cross, his larger framework is that the divine persons mutually glorify each other in an egalitarian way as they give themselves in a nonviolent manner to the world at the cross.[26] Again Volf's conception of the cross allows for some hierarchy, but this hierarchy is in tension with the fully egalitarian relations of the divine persons where these relations provide the larger framework for Volf's thought.[27]

Finally, Volf also discusses the mediating concept of perichoresis in the context of the cross. For example, after citing some statements by Moltmann to the effect that the divine persons are eternally in one another through love, Volf says the following:

> When the Trinity turns toward the world, the Son and the Spirit become, in Irenaeus' beautiful image, the two arms of God by which humanity was made and taken into God's embrace.... That same love that sustains nonself-enclosed identities in the Trinity seeks to make space "in God" for humanity. Humanity is, however, not just the other of God, but the beloved other who has become an enemy. When God sets out to embrace

---

25. Volf, *Exclusion and Embrace*, 268, italics original.

26. See also the final chapter of *Exclusion and Embrace*, "Violence and Peace," where Volf associates hierarchy at the cross with Satan, which tends to further stigmatize hierarchy. For more background on nonviolence and eschatology in Volf, see especially Coker, "Peace and the Apocalypse," 261–68. Coker shows that Volf interprets the book of Revelation as teaching that God defers violence until the eschaton, and even here it is only a violence against those who did violence in the world. Coker contrasts Volf's position with the corresponding position of Stanley Hauerwas, who according to Coker argues that there is no divine violence even at the eschaton.

27. Volf's article "The Trinity is Our Social Program" was published at about the same time as *Exclusion and Embrace* and shares many of its basic themes, such as the triune God's self-donation at the cross and mutual glorification. On the topic of glorification, Volf has likely been influenced by Moltmann, who extensively discusses egalitarian mutual glorification in his writings. See Thompson, *Imitatio Trinitatis*, 84–85.

the enemy, the result is the cross. On the cross the dancing circle of self-giving and mutually indwelling divine persons opens up for the enemy; in the agony of the passion the movement stops for a brief moment and a fissure appears so that sinful humanity can join in (see John 17:21). We, the others—we, the enemies—are embraced by the divine persons who love us with the same love with which they love each other and therefore make space for us within their own eternal embrace.[28]

Although Volf here alludes to a certain hierarchy among the divine persons by mentioning Irenaeus's comment about the two arms of God, his main emphasis again is on the "dancing circle of self-giving and mutually indwelling divine persons," where the terms "dancing circle" and "self-giving" refer to the fully egalitarian relations of the divine persons. Here the perichoresis (mutual indwelling) of the divine persons is associated with these egalitarian relations and seems to be very egalitarian. Thus Volf stresses the egalitarian relations of the divine persons at the cross, although he also allows for hierarchy. Bridging between Volf's sets of statements in tension with one another is Volf's mediating concept of perichoresis, which Volf tends to make quite egalitarian. Finally, the effect of this bridging is to further tilt the scales toward equality among the divine persons.

Conclusion

In this section I have shown that Volf exhibits a tension between hierarchy and equality in his understanding of the economic Trinity. Utilizing *After Our Likeness* I laid out the basic shape of this tension as Volf pits the hierarchical sending of the Son and the Spirit by the Father against the fully egalitarian relations among the divine persons and largely chooses the latter over the former. *After Our Likeness* also showed that Volf used perichoresis as a mediating concept between the hierarchical sending category and the egalitarian mutual relations of the divine persons, especially associating it with the latter. With this basic structure in place, I further evaluated the nature of the tension in Volf's trinitarian understanding as it pertains to the cross as evident in *Exclusion and Embrace*. Here Volf sometimes speaks of a certain hierarchy of the Father over the Son at the cross in connection with Christ's obedience to the Father and the Father's

---

28. Volf, *Exclusion and Embrace*, 128–29.

abandonment of the Son. However, Volf places such hierarchy into the larger, egalitarian framework of the fully egalitarian mutual relations of the divine persons at the cross and especially in history generally. In considering the cross, Volf also employs perichoresis as a mediating concept that he closely associates with the egalitarian relations of the divine persons. We thus saw how Volf "resolves" his hierarchy-equality polarity or tension by giving logical priority in his economic Trinitarianism to the egalitarian pole of the system.

A BRIEF COMPARISON OF AND EVALUATION OF BALTHASAR AND VOLF

Various similarities and differences are evident in the understandings of the economic Trinity by Balthasar and Volf. Both Balthasar and Volf distinguish between two sets of contradictory statements about the divine persons as they work together during the life of Jesus. In the case of Balthasar, the conflict between his two sets of statements is most easily seen in his views on Holy Saturday, which he views as most redemptively significant, as the Son simultaneously is capable of relating with the Father and not capable. On both counts, Balthasar stresses the hierarchy of the Father over the Son and places comparatively little emphasis on their equality. In the case of Volf, the conflict is most easily seen in his views on what he views as the chief redemptive period, the cross, as the divine persons have fully egalitarian mutual relations with each other even while simultaneously the Father has unilateral hierarchy over the suffering Son he has sent into the world. If for Balthasar both sets of opposing statements were hierarchical, in Volf one set is fully egalitarian and the other fully hierarchical, with Volf greatly emphasizing the former over the latter.

Both Balthasar and Volf also utilize concepts to try to mediate between their two sets of opposing statements. However, these mediating statements function differently in the two theologians. In Balthasar, the mediating statements are hierarchical and connect one set of hierarchical statements where the Son lacks consciousness in some way with another set of hierarchical statements where the Son is consciously obedient to the Father. The hierarchical mediating statements thus tend to reinforce the hierarchy present in both sets of statements. But Volf's mediating category of perichoresis seeks to mediate between statements on either side of the hierarchy-equality polarity. Here Volf overwhelmingly associates perichoresis with the fully egalitarian relations of the divine persons and makes much less of a connection with hierarchical sending. Whereas in Balthasar hierarchical mediating statements tend to amplify the hierarchy in his two sets of opposing statements, in Volf largely egalitarian perichoresis tends to reinforce the egalitarian relations of the divine persons and minimize hierarchy.

Finally, both Balthasar and Volf do not adequately account for the sociality of the divine persons, for a maximally social understanding of the Trinity, by not adequately accounting for both the uniqueness and dignity of the divine persons necessary for this sociality. In Balthasar's two sets of opposing statements, the one set where the Son is unconscious ends up dividing the Father and the Son, leaving the Father to work majestically and powerfully from heaven and the Son to suffer inexplicably below. Such a situation involves an oppressive relationship between the Father and the Son, which does not account adequately for the dignity of either the Father or the Son. In Balthasar's other set of statements, the hierarchy is not as severe but this hierarchy remains unilateral, with the Father always over the Son and never vice versa, and because of Balthasar's mediating statements this other set of opposing statements end up having their hierarchy amplified by the first set of statements. Here again there is an undignified oppressive relationship between the Father and the Son.[29]

As for Volf's two opposing sets of statements, the fully egalitarian relations that Volf stresses have no value for distinguishing the uniqueness of each divine person in Volf's system. Volf's other set of statements is fully hierarchical and serves to help distinguish among the divine persons. But Volf minimizes the importance of these statements by not speaking as much about them and often indirectly minimizing them by

29. Consider the description of Balthasar's theology by Lösel: "Balthasar's concept of trinitarian, christological, and hence also Christian love begs a number of questions from biblical and/or theological perspectives. Certainly the model of self-surrender and filial obedience might be one possible biblical interpretation of christological and Christian existence—even if, as I would argue, it can hardly disguise its hermeneutical roots in Balthasar's Ignatian tradition. It can therefore function also as an interpretative key for understanding the immanent Trinity. Yet I question whether this model should be seen as the only one or even as the normative interpretative key to understanding divine and human love" ("A Plain Account of Christian Salvation," 168). Mongrain says something similar: "all roads in von Balthasar's theology lead back to the monotheistic axiom that ethical activity is the quintessential incarnational activity" (*Systematic Theology*, 126).

stigmatizing hierarchy. Volf's mediating category of perichoresis ends up exacerbating this situation both because it does not actually explain the hierarchy-equality polarity between the two sets of statements and because perichoresis ends up being highly egalitarian, which further minimizes the importance of Volf's hierarchical statements that would help distinguish among the divine persons. Whereas Balthasar does not account adequately for the dignity of the divine persons in the economy, Volf does not account adequately for the uniqueness of each divine person. In this way, neither theologian accounts adequately for the sociality of the divine persons, which requires both the uniqueness and dignity of the divine persons.

A MUTUAL HIERARCHY APPROACH TO THE ECONOMIC TRINITY

In this section, I will argue for a mutual hierarchy approach to the economic Trinity. In doing so, I will argue for the differentiated kenotic vocations of the divine persons. Here the word *hierarchy* from the mutual hierarchy framework in the context of the economic Trinity points to the fact that each divine person has a *unique*, or *differentiated*, vocation in relation to the other divine persons that involves *hierarchical* power over the others. Furthermore, the word *mutual* from the mutual hierarchy framework in the context of the economic Trinity points to the fact that each divine person limits the use of his power, or is *kenotic*, relative to the other divine persons in order to foster *dignity* in the trinitarian work. In what follows, I will offer a reading of John's Gospel utilizing this mutual hierarchy framework. I will first sample John's Gospel for how each divine person has a unique hierarchical vocation over the others. And then I will sample it for ways that each divine person exercises his vocation in a kenotic way. In proceeding thus I hope to show that such a reading of the trinitarian trajectory of the life of Jesus in John identifies both the uniqueness and dignity of the divine persons needed for a more fully social conception of the Trinity.

Mutual Hierarchy as a Framework for Understanding the Differentiated, Hierarchical Vocations of the Divine Persons

Earlier in the chapter we saw that both Balthasar and Volf can posit that there is a hierarchical ordering among the divine persons in connection with the Johannine notion of sending. In this section we will first briefly look at some of the Johannine passages connected to sending and illustrate the ordering of the divine persons with two diagrams. Following this, we will argue that even though there is an ordering of the divine persons in John, the greater reality is that each divine person in his vocation is hierarchical over the others in the midst of this ordering.

There are numerous passages in John that speak of a divine person or two divine persons sending the other(s). The Father is never sent by anyone, and the Holy Spirit is never said to send anyone. By far the Father is most often said to send the other divine persons. For example, Jesus repeatedly says that the Father has sent him into the world (e.g., John 3:16–17). John 14:26 speaks of the Father sending the Holy Spirit in Jesus's name. Here the Father is the only divine person explicitly said to send the Holy Spirit, which seems to indicate his leadership in this sending, but Jesus is also somehow involved (14:16). In John 15:26 and 16:7, Jesus tells his disciples that he will send the Holy Spirit from the Father. Here Jesus is the only divine person explicitly said to send the Holy Spirit, but that the Father is also implied as sending the Spirit as well is suggested by the texts also saying that the Holy Spirit proceeds from the Father (15:26) and saying that Jesus is going away, implicitly to the Father (16:7). This short discussion of the relationships between the divine persons in connection with sending one another makes it clear that there is a certain Father-Son-Spirit ordering of the Trinity in John's Gospel. The discussion also shows that the vocations of the divine persons may be clearly distinguished from one another on the basis of sending as the Father is never sent, the Spirit never sends, and the Son both sends and is sent.[30]

---

30. Here we recall Irenaeus's image of the Son and the Spirit as the two hands of the Father working in the world. Consider also Pannenberg: "The Father acts in the world only through the Son and Spirit. He himself remains transcendent. This fact comes to expression in the 'sendings' of the Son and Spirit into the world" (*Systematic Theology*, 1:328).

Two diagrams can help illustrate and further this discussion. The first diagram is borrowed from Balthasar:[31]

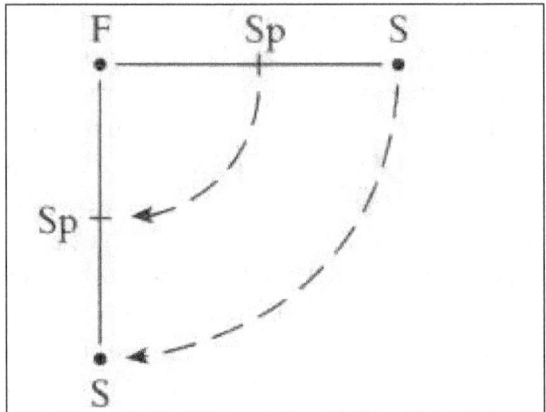

Diagram 1. The Sending of the Son

The vertical line in this diagram helps illustrate that the Father from heaven sends the Son down into the world. It also suggests some involvement by the Holy Spirit, a fact that will be discussed further shortly. The second diagram is related to the first but is my own construction and deals with the Father and the Son's sending of the Holy Spirit:

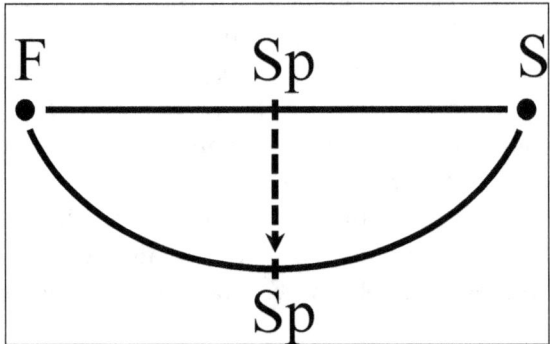

Diagram 2. The Sending of the Spirit

This diagram helps illustrate that the Father and the Son send the Holy Spirit into the world. These two diagrams also help illustrate that the

---

31. This diagram comes from Balthasar, *Theo-Drama*, 3:191. Used with permission. The immanent Trinity in both this diagram and Diagram 2 is represented by the horizontal line and will be discussed further in the next chapter.

vocations of the divine persons involve hierarchy. In the first diagram the Father is "above" the Son as he sends him "down" into the world, which shows that he uses his power to send the Son. The Son's being lower than the Father in the first diagram helps illustrate his being ordered behind the Father in the Trinity, while the Son's position above the Holy Spirit in the second diagram helps illustrate his being ordered before the Holy Spirit in the Trinity. The diagrams thus help illustrate not only the Father-Son-Spirit ordering of the divine persons in connection with the category of sending, they also help illustrate that the vocation of a divine person involves having a hierarchy over and exercising a power over the other divine persons.

Having discussed a certain ordering among the divine persons in John in connection with the category of sending, the remainder of this section will now show that the greater reality in John is that each divine person is hierarchical over the others in connection with his unique vocation. We'll begin with the Father. In John, the Father's sending of the Son and the Spirit into the world flows from the Father's vocation as creator (John 1:1–3). In John, the Father as creator is transcendent and invisible in heaven and thus does not work directly in the world. It is for these reasons that the Father sends the Son and Spirit to work in the world on his behalf.[32] Jesus, in connection with his mission received from the Father, often speaks of following the command of his Father (10:18; 12:49–50; 14:31; 15:10). Similarly, Jesus speaks of a servant not being greater than his master who sends him (13:16; 15:20), and in this context even speaks of the Father being greater than himself (14:28).[33] As the creator who sends the Son and Spirit, the Father is also able to empower and provide stability to the missions of the Son and the Spirit, for in his transcendence the Father is not in direct danger in the way, for example, that especially the Son is at the cross. For example, a key way that the Father glorifies the Son (17:1) is by so supporting the Son that the Son may complete his glorious passion. Finally, the Father as creator is also the goal of all things he has created (14:2; 20:17). In these various aspects of the Father's vocation as creator, the Father is unique and exercises a hierarchy over the Son and the Spirit.

---

32. Capdevila i Montaner, "El Padre en el Cuarto Evangelio," 103–7, uses verses like John 1:18 and John 6:46 in order to argue for the transcendence and invisibility of the Father in John's Gospel.

33. See also John 10:29.

Moving now to the Son, the Son in his vocation in John is the redeemer of the world. Or more in the language of John, the Son's glory is his cross and resurrection undertaken for the sake of the world, as can be seen in the many places John discusses Jesus's glory (e.g., John 7:39; 12:16; 12:23-24; 14:13).[34] The hierarchy of this glorious Son over the Spirit is often explicit in John. We already saw this somewhat above when we mentioned that the Son helps send the Holy Spirit into the world. In 7:39, Jesus says that the Spirit had not yet been given to the world, presumably in fullness, because Jesus had not yet been glorified, where such giving is reminiscent of sending and entails a hierarchy of Jesus over the Spirit.[35] Similarly, in 12:16 Jesus's glorification is what enables disciples to understand things about Jesus they didn't understand before, presumably through the power of the Holy Spirit (16:13). And in 12:23-24 Jesus's glorification is what produces great fruit, which anticipates the disciples bearing fruit in 15:1-17, which requires the aid of the Holy Spirit. These fruits of Jesus's vocation as redeemer are connected to Jesus's sending of the Holy Spirit, which entails a hierarchy over the Holy Spirit.

The Son, in his vocation in John as the glorious redeemer, also exercises a hierarchy over the Father, although this is less obvious than the Son's being hierarchical over the Spirit. This hierarchy of the Son over the Father may be seen in the fact that the Father is *dependent* upon the Son. For example, in John 17:1 Jesus prays, "Father, the hour has come; glorify your Son that the Son may also glorify you." In the previous paragraph, we noted that the Father glorifies the Son by enabling the Son to carry out his glorious work. But the term "glory" in John is actually more associated with the Son than the Father. In the present instance, the Father is dependent upon the Son's glorious work in order that the Father may be glorified in the world.[36] In other words, the Father is dependent upon the

---

34. On Jesus's glorification being connected to the cross in John, see Gieschen, "The Death of Jesus in the Gospel of John," 93-95, which makes a connection between Jesus's glory and his "hour."

35. Porsch, *El Espiritu Santo*, 27, argues that Jesus's reference in John 7:39, that the Spirit had not yet been given because Jesus had not yet been glorified, is a turning point in John's Gospel. Porsch argues that this verse shows that all of John's Gospel has an internal orientation toward the glorification of Jesus on the cross and the giving of the Spirit there.

36. Pannenberg, *Systematic Theology*, 1:348, similarly argues that the Father is dependent on the Son and the Spirit for the coming of his kingdom and for his glorification. Capdevila i Montaner, "El Padre en el Cuarto Evangelio," 112, suggests that John 17:5 shows that the Father is dependent upon the success of Jesus, his mission, and his

Son so that he himself may be revealed, honored, and his will effected in the world.[37] Jesus in his vocation as glorious redeemer in John exercises a hierarchy over the Father who is dependent upon Jesus's work for the success of his own work.

Moving now to the Holy Spirit, the Spirit's vocation in John is to be the sanctifier of human beings.[38] This vocation of the Spirit can be seen in John 20:21–23 where the resurrected Christ sends out the disciples, gives them the Holy Spirit, and commissions them to forgive sins. Here it should be noted that atonement and the forgiveness of sins were key methods for sanctifying people, making them holy and setting them apart for God, in the book of Leviticus from the Old Testament. Jesus himself through his glorious passion provided atonement for people, but the disciples in the power of the Holy Spirit would apply that atonement through forgiving sins in the world and thus sanctifying people. This sanctifying work of the Holy Spirit in John also seems connected to the theme of light. For example, in John 9, Jesus in the power of the Spirit acts as the light of the world as he heals a man born blind and calls his opponents away from spiritual blindness. Jesus's bringing light to people seems to have been associated with the Holy Spirit, for John the Baptist was also able to act as a light in the world (1:6–8; 5:35) and visibly point others to the atonement (e.g., 1:29–34). Seeing the Holy Spirit as the sanctifier in John also agrees with the "paraclete," or "helper," passages in John that associate the Holy Spirit with such things as sight, teaching all things, reminding disciples about Jesus, bearing witness, and convicting the world (14:16, 14:26, 15:26, 16:7).

The Spirit in his vocation in John as the sanctifier also exercises a hierarchy over the Father, although this may be less obvious than in the case of the Father and Son exercising hierarchy over the Spirit in connection with sending him. This hierarchy of the Spirit over the Father may be seen in the fact that the Father is dependent upon the Spirit. For example, in John 4:23, Jesus says that the time has come when true worshippers are

---

return to the Father in order for the Father to be glorified in the world.

37. Poston, *Motif of Glory*, 131, notes three aspects of glory in John. First, it is an eternal attribute of both the Son and the Father. Second, Jesus's mission, and especially his cross and resurrection, are glorious and reveal the glory of the Father. And third, Jesus is able to share his glory with his followers, which in turn enables them to glorify both him and the Father.

38. I use the term sanctifier here in a wide sense where the Holy Spirit works faith, love, and hope in disciples.

worshipping the Father in Spirit and truth and that the Father is seeking such people. Here the Father in heaven is dependent upon the Spirit on earth to bring people to faith and teach them to worship him. In this context, the Spirit exercises a hierarchical vocation over the Father. Similarly, in John 6:63-65, Jesus says that the Spirit gives life and that no one can come to Jesus unless it is granted by the Father. Here again the Father is dependent upon the Spirit to bring the life of faith to people so that they can come to Jesus. In this way, the Spirit in connection with his vocation as the sanctifier is hierarchical over the Father.

The Spirit in his vocation in John as the sanctifier also exercises a hierarchy over the Son, although again this may be less obvious than in the case of the Father and Son exercising hierarchy over the Spirit in connection with sending him. For example, there are indications in John that the Spirit plays some role in the sending of the Son by the Father. Thus in John 10:36, Jesus alludes to the Father consecrating the Son, presumably with the Holy Spirit, and sending him into the world.[39] Similarly, John 1:32-33 connects the Spirit to the Father at Jesus's baptism as the Spirit descends from the Father to the Son.[40] Besides his role in the incarnation, the Spirit, amidst the people of God at Jesus's time, also dynamically mediates the Father's will to Jesus during his life, so that Jesus is thus dependent upon the Spirit. Here Jesus sees what the Father is doing in his life largely through seeing the external works of the Spirit of the Father. In other words, Jesus witnesses the works of the Holy Spirit, traces them to their source in the Father, and internalizes them. For example, in John 4:31-35, Jesus is able to see the will of the Father by looking at the Spirit's work in the affairs around him (the harvest), whereas the disciples were not able to see this.[41] Finally, in John it is especially because Jesus is de-

---

39. See also Sánchez, *Receiver, Bearer, and Giver of God's Spirit*, 4-12, 34-39, for further discussion of the Son being anointed with the Spirit in preparation for the incarnation.

40. This interpretation of the Baptism of Jesus that associates the Spirit with the Father is in harmony with the Synoptic Gospels, which say that the Spirit descended from the Father to Jesus at Jesus's baptism. Considering that in John sending language is closely related to the motif of descending and ascending, this suggests that John connects Jesus's baptism with the Father *sending* the Spirit to Jesus. Further supporting a link between the descending of the Spirit upon Jesus at his baptism and the sending of the Spirit to Jesus at his baptism is that in John 1:33, John the Baptist speaks rather mysteriously about the "one" who sent him to baptize Jesus. John 1:6 clears this up when it identifies John as the man "sent by God." Thus the Father sent John the Baptist (along with the Spirit) to Jesus at his baptism.

41. On Jesus seeing and hearing, or having seen and having heard the Father, see

pendent on the Spirit's sanctifying work in the church that the Spirit exercises a certain hierarchy over the Son in his life. For example, at various points in the "Farewell Discourse," the Spirit is called the "Spirit of truth," so that Jesus seems dependent upon him for propagating the truth of his redemptive work. Thus the "Spirit of truth," who will be with the disciples after Jesus's departure at his resurrection (14:17), will bear witness about the truth (15:26) and will lead the disciples into all truth (16:13). As the Spirit of truth, the Spirit will witness to the truth of the Son, who refers to himself as the way, the truth, and the life (14:6).[42] Finally, there also seem to be connotations of the hierarchy of the Spirit over the Son in John 14:12, which speaks of the disciples doing greater works than Jesus.[43]

Mutual Hierarchy as a Framework for Understanding the Kenotic Vocations of the Divine Persons

Having briefly illustrated the differentiated vocations of the divine persons where each divine person has a hierarchy over the others in connection with his own unique vocation, we will now see how a mutual hierarchy framework also posits a *kenosis* of each divine person in the exercise of this hierarchy. In other words, each divine person in a unique way limits the use of his divine power in his vocation.[44] We have already

---

also John 3:32; 5:30; 6:46; 8:26; 8:38; 8:40; 8:47; 12:29; and 15:15. It is possible that when Jesus speaks in the past tense of having seen or heard the Father he could be speaking from his memory of his interaction with the Father prior to the incarnation. While not denying this, at least the present tense hearing and seeing of the Father are mediated by the Holy Spirit, and probably the past tense hearing and seeing of the Father reflect the Spirit's earlier working in Jesus's life.

42. In John, this witnessing to the Father and the Son by the Spirit happens largely through his working through the disciples. For example, in John 17, the main triad is the Father, the Son, and the disciples, with the Spirit nowhere explicitly mentioned but rather assumed to be with the disciples. This allusive, or quiet, nature of the Spirit will be considered in the next section in connection with the kenosis of the Spirit.

43. For Jesus as the receiver, bearer, and giver of the Holy Spirit in the biblical narrative, see Sánchez, *Receiver, Bearer, and Giver of God's Spirit*, 33–52.

44. Sometimes, critics of this sort of view that includes attributing kenosis to the Father seek to label it as the early church heresy of patripassionism. However, this is a serious misunderstanding of patripassionism since this heresy was rather of the modalist variety and said that it was the Father who was crucified on the cross. See Ngien, *Suffering of God*, 9–10. Ibid., 145–53, convincingly argues that Luther rejected the modalist form of patripassianism but accepted a form of theopaschitism that more clearly distinguishes between the divine persons since the two natures of Christ cannot

seen a couple of proposals earlier in the chapter that posited some sort of kenotic vocations by the divine persons. For example, Volf in speaking about the self-donation of the divine persons at the cross was also asserting a certain kenosis, or limiting of power, of the divine persons.[45] Balthasar also identified kenosis in the relationship between the Father and the Son on Holy Saturday, although in his thought the Son seemed to limit his power much more than the Father.[46] Also relevant here is the discussion in the previous section of the divine persons depending upon one another.[47] However, this discussion did not yet clearly say that each divine person necessarily exercises his vocational authority in a kenotic way. To take a crude human analogy, three human beings could in various ways depend upon one another in their vocations and yet still not much care for one another or even know one another, let alone use and limit their power in order to deliberately serve one another. Even worse, each of the three could exercise their power in order to oppress the others in the context of the particular things the others are dependent upon them for. Thus it is necessary to argue that each divine person deliberately and consistently exercises his authority in his vocation in a kenotic way in order to serve the other divine persons. Here positing a kenosis

---

be separated and the three divine persons cannot be separated. For more helpful discussion from a Lutheran perspective see Scaer, "Homo Factus Est," 111–26. For more background on discussion in the twentieth century about divine kenosis, see Bauckham, "Only the Suffering God Can Help," 6–12.

45. For more on how Volf's doctoral advisor, Moltmann, emphasizes the kenosis of the divine persons relative to the world and how Moltmann closely associates this kenosis with the suffering of the world, see Goetz, "Karl Barth, Juergen Moltmann and the Theopaschite Revolution," 17–28; and Linahan, "Experiencing God in Brokenness," 165–84.

46. Moltmann, "God's Kenosis," 140–41, summarizing trinitarian kenosis in Balthasar's thought, argues that Balthasar emphasizes kenosis among the divine persons more than kenosis toward creation. Sachs, "Holy Spirit and Christian Form," 391, says, "Balthasar's understanding of God as 'ever-greater' is at the same time grounded in a fundamentally kenotic conception of God's own being and reflects something of the inner-trinitarian surrender or 'obedience' of the Son to the Father that Balthasar understands as the foundation of Jesus's obedience in the economy." It is also worthy of note that Balthasar does not ascribe either kenosis or super-kenosis to the Spirit in either the economic Trinity or the immanent Trinity, respectively. See also Ward, "Kenosis," 15–68.

47. Pannenberg only sees the term kenosis as applicable to the Son; nevertheless, Pannenberg does hold that the other divine persons can suffer and that all of the divine persons mutually depend upon one another. See Pannenberg, "God's Love and the Kenosis of the Son," 244–50.

in each of the divine persons helps safeguard their dignity during Jesus's life. In what follows, I will describe individually the kenosis of the Son, the Father, and the Spirit in their vocations, as evident in John's Gospel.

In the previous section, we saw that Jesus in John's Gospel exercises a certain hierarchy over the Father and the Spirit in connection with his vocation as the glorious redeemer. Now we must focus on how Jesus in this vocation exercises his authority in a kenotic way. This kenosis of the Son should be looked at in two ways, in relation to creation and in relation to the other divine persons. In relation to creation, the Son limits the use of his divine power in order to voluntarily undertake ministry and go to the cross, and in both of these tasks he suffers in order to redeem mankind.[48] An example of this sort of kenotic exercise of authority may be seen in John 13:12–17 where Jesus acknowledges that he is the lord, master, and teacher of the disciples, but shows the disciples that his authority is best illustrated in the humble act of serving them and washing their feet. Here the Son is dignified in that he uses his authority in order to serve others. This serving of the disciples culminates in the cross. Thus Jesus in 10:17–18 says that he has the power to lay down his own life and the power to take it up again. These verses show that the Son is capable of limiting his divine power at the cross for the sake of human redemption. Similarly, in 15:13 Jesus says that the greatest love a human being can have is to lay down his life for his friends. Here Jesus was preparing to limit his power by laying down his life at the cross out of love for the disciples. We see an example of how these things plays out at the cross in 19:26–27 where Jesus serves Mary and John even in the midst of his agony. In fact, throughout John's Gospel there are references to Jesus taking the initiative to redeem people through suffering and the non-use of brute power: he is the Lamb of God who takes away the sin of the world (1:29, 36), the shepherd who lays down his life for the sheep (10:11), and the king who rules on a cross (19:19). Thus Jesus exercises his authority as the glorious redeemer in a kenotic way as he subjects himself to the power of sin and evil on earth in order to redeem humanity.

Besides being kenotic relative to creation, in an integrally related way the Son is kenotic relative to the Father and the Spirit by limiting the use of his divine power. As Jesus limits his power on earth in his humiliation, he allows and invites the Father and the Spirit to lead and help him.

---

48. Here we can also make the point that the divine Son, in being capable of and willing for such kenosis, is actually *more* powerful and dignified than if the Son were not capable of thus helping the world.

For example, in John 10:17–18, Jesus not only says that he has the power to lay down his life and take it up again, but he also says that he has been commanded by the Father to do so. In the previous section we also said that in 12:23–24 Jesus's glorification is what produces great fruit, which anticipates the disciples bearing fruit. Now it can also be said that the glory of Jesus's cross not only enables the work of the Spirit in the church, it also allows itself to be dependent upon the Spirit's work in the church in order to be made known and glorified (16:14). Thus the Son is dignified in that he does not try to perform his mission in isolation from the Father and the Spirit, but rather works with, trusts, and follows the Father and the Spirit in his redemptive mission.[49] And by so permitting the Father and the Spirit to help him, Jesus also fosters their dignity as they too are allowed their roles in humanity's salvation.

In the previous section we also saw that in John, the Father exercises a certain hierarchy over the Son and Spirit in connection with his vocation as creator. Now we will see that the Father in this vocation exercises his authority in a kenotic way. One way this occurs is in connection with his sending of the Son and Spirit. As the Father sends them, he not only makes them dependent upon himself, he also limits his power and allows himself to be dependent upon them and affected by their kenosis. A human analogy can help illustrate this kenosis of the Father. Consider a father, a son, and a worker working on a farm. If the son is sent off to war in a foreign country and the worker is sent back and forth to the son as a messenger, the father is affected by the danger of the son and the worker even if the father himself is not in direct danger. Something similar is evident in the Gospel of John. For example, John 5:21–23 says that the Father has entrusted all judgment to the Son, where such entrusting entails a certain self-limiting by the Father. But in so entrusting judgment to the Son, the Father also exposes himself to grief when the Son is not honored in the world (5:23).[50] Similarly, in John 17 we see Jesus praying to the Father as Jesus prepares for his redemptive suffering at the cross, for he knows that the Father sympathizes with him, hears his prayer, and will help him, for the Father similarly cared for him when Jesus prayed

---

49. Thompson and Plantinga, "Trinity and Kenosis," 165–89, argue in a helpful way that a kenotic Christology, in order to be successful, requires a social understanding of the Trinity.

50. See Gruenler, *Trinity in the Gospel of John*, 37–40, which says with respect to 5:21–23 that it is because the Father so trusts the Son's judgment that he sends him on such an important mission.

to the Father after Lazarus's death (11:38-42). This loving involvement of the Father in Jesus's life shows that the Father is affected by what happens to Jesus in his life.[51] Similarly, since the Father is also affected by the work and the sufferings of disciples (e.g., 17:14-15), he is also affected by the struggles of the Spirit who works among them. In John, the Father is kenotic relative to the Son and the Spirit both as he empowers and supports their missions and as he is affected by their struggles. Through such kenosis the Father is portrayed as dignified and as fostering the dignity of the other divine persons.[52]

Furthermore, the Father is also kenotic relative to creation itself during the life of Jesus in a way that is integrally related to his kenosis relative to the Son and the Spirit. However, in contrast to what was seen with the kenosis of the Son, the Father is kenotic relative to creation in an indirect way. For example, in John 3:16, God the Father sacrificially gives his Son to the world, pledging to endure the suffering of the Son, for the very reason that God loves the world and is affected by its plight. Similarly, in the context of 16:13 speaking of the Spirit guiding disciples into all truth and 16:26 speaking of disciples requesting things from the Father, 16:27 connects these things to the love of the Father for disciples who will be sorrowful for a time at Jesus's glorification at the cross (16:20).[53] Even though the Father is transcendent in heaven as the creator, he is intimately involved with creation and serves it in connection with his sending and interacting with his Son and Spirit. Thus the Father is dignified in that he utilizes his authority in order to serve others rather than seclude himself from creation.

---

51. See also the following numerous verses in John that demonstrate the Father's loving involvement in the Son's life: 3:35; 5:17; 5:20; 10:17; 14:10; 14:15-14:23; 14:31; 15:9-10; 16:32; 17:26.

52. Gruenler says that in John's Gospel not only the Son and the Spirit but the Father too is portrayed as being disposable, in this case to the Son and Spirit as a servant: "While the Father is given pride of place by the Son, he is seen to defer to the Son by honoring and glorifying him as the appointed spokesman on behalf of the divine Family, and by faithfully listening and responding to the Son's requests on behalf of himself and the community of believers" (*Trinity in the Gospel of John*, x-xi).

53. It is true that in John 16:23-33 Jesus tells the disciples that they will pray directly to the Father. But I would argue that here Jesus is eliding himself and the Spirit; for example, the disciples' prayer to the Father will still be mediated by the Holy Spirit, similar to in the case of John 4:23: "But the hour is coming, and is now here, when the true worshipers will worship the Father in spirit and truth, for the Father is seeking such people to worship him."

In the previous section we also saw that the Spirit exercises a certain hierarchy over the Father and the Son in connection with his vocation as the sanctifier. Now we will see that the Spirit in his vocation uses his authority in a kenotic way.[54] In what follows, I will argue that the Spirit in John is kenotic in his relationship to the Father, the Son, and the disciples, appearing not in the dazzling glory of heaven but rather as a quiet, kenotic servant. To do so, I will use John 20:21–22 as a guide:

> Jesus said to them [the disciples] again, "Peace be with you. As the Father has sent me, even so I am sending you." And when he had said this, he breathed on them and said to them, "Receive the Holy Spirit."

As we will see, this text connects the Holy Spirit in unique ways with the Father, the Son, and the disciples.

We will begin with the Spirit's relationship to the Father. John 20:21–22 implicitly connects the Holy Spirit to the sending of the Son by the Father. Just as Jesus sends the disciples by giving them the Holy Spirit, the Father had sent Jesus by giving him the Holy Spirit. We already saw in the previous section how, in John, the Spirit is associated with the Father's sending of the Son, but there we posited a hierarchy of the Father over the Spirit. Now we can look at the Father's utilizing the Spirit to send the Son and say that the Spirit not only exercises a hierarchy over the Father in this task but also exercises this hierarchy kenotically. One key way that the Spirit does this is through his very quietness. The Father would not be able to send the Son without the Spirit, and yet in John we almost always hear about the Father sending the Son with no mention of the Spirit. The Spirit in his mediating work, in this case his sanctifying the Son, is quiet and fosters the dignity of the kenotic Father himself.[55] To use our human analogy from above, the worker sent by the human father to the son at war in a foreign country does not draw attention to himself, but instead focuses on communicating the father's message to the son. Similarly, although the Spirit interacts with the Father in heaven, the Spirit represents

---

54. Supporting the claim that the Spirit is kenotic in John's Gospel is that he is portrayed as so personal in John. In John, he guides, comforts, convicts, speaks, hears, etc. These sorts of activities require empathy and would be implausible for the Spirit if he were merely an impersonal force or overwhelming power.

55. Boff, *Trinity and Society*, 216, says that the Son and Spirit exalted the way of kenosis during the life of Jesus: "What we see is not the dazzle of glory, but simplicity and humility. This means that the mode of being of the immanent Trinity and that of the economic Trinity are not connatural."

the Father in a humble, loving, and kind way to the Son. Here the kenotic Spirit is dignified, largely deferring to the Father.

Next, again beginning with John 20:21–22, I will argue that the Spirit is quiet and kenotic in relation to the Son in his life. If in the previous paragraph, we looked more at what the Spirit was doing outside of and around Jesus on behalf of the Father, here we will look more at what the Spirit does in relation to Jesus as he suffered gloriously on the cross and earned the right to give the Spirit to the world. In 20:22 Jesus says, "Receive the Holy Spirit," words that recall John 19:30, where Jesus at the cross bowed his head down toward the world and gave it his Spirit. Here we see that even though the Spirit has sanctifying human beings as his own proper work, he also allows himself to be sent out by the Son, even while the Spirit also quietly helps and sanctifies the Son in his suffering. Here we should think of Jesus through his suffering at the cross gloriously earning the right to give the Holy Spirit, who allows himself to be more passive here. Here the kenotic Spirit is dignified, largely deferring to the Son.

Finally, again beginning with John 20:21–22, I will now argue that the Spirit in John is kenotic and quiet in his vocation relative to the disciples. 20:21–22 connects the disciples' receiving the Holy Spirit with both Jesus's mission and, in a related way, the mission of the disciples. We have seen that the Holy Spirit worked in a quiet way in Jesus's life as Jesus was the receiver, bearer, and giver of the Holy Spirit. Similarly, disciples are receivers, bearers, and givers of the Holy Spirit as the Holy Spirit works quietly in their lives. For example, just as the Spirit remained on Jesus after his baptism in a hidden manner (1:32), so too the Spirit comes to disciples and remains on them in a hidden manner. They go about their lives in the Spirit so that their words are filled with Spirit and life (John 6:63).[56] Similarly, as John 17 suggests, disciples in the power of the Spirit will bear with persecution through the quiet help of the Spirit; here in John 17 the explicit triad is Father-Son-disciples with no mention of the Spirit even though in John the Spirit is the one who will be with the disciples in the church (14:16–17).[57] Amidst persecution, Christians in the power of the Holy Spirit who accompanies them are to heed Jesus's commandment and example, loving one another, which includes laying

56. See also 11:33 and 13:21, which speak of Jesus being moved in his [S]pirit. My proposal prioritizes the outward working of the Spirit in the Son's life even while also allowing for internal working. Something analogous to this holds for disciples as well.

57. See further Crump, "Re-examining the Johannine Trinity," 395.

down their lives (15:12–13).[58] In all of these things the Spirit does not lord the authority of his vocation over the disciples but rather limits his power so that he may be with the disciples to comfort, help, and serve them.[59] Thus the Spirit exercises his authority in a dignified manner among the disciples.

To conclude and help better illustrate some of this discussion, diagrams 1 and 2 will now be briefly considered again, this time to consider the kenosis of the divine persons. Recall first diagram 1, borrowed from Balthasar:[60]

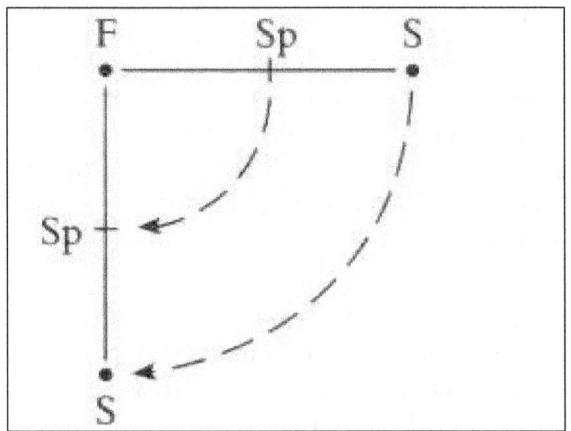

Diagram 1. The Sending of the Son

And recall that diagram 2 illustrates the sending of the Holy Spirit:

---

58. Perhaps also relevant here is John the Baptist's viewpoint in 3:30 that he must decrease so that Jesus can increase.

59. It is also significant that in John there is little mention of glorious angels attending to either Jesus or the disciples (except in 20:12). The Spirit in John is rather typically present among Jesus and the disciples.

60. Balthasar, *Theo-Drama*, 3:191. Used with permission.

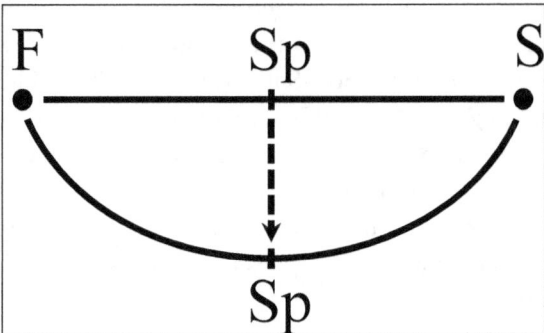

Diagram 2. The Sending of the Spirit

Consider first what these diagrams suggest about the kenosis of the Son. Diagram 1 suggests that the Son experienced the most direct kenosis in the world, as evident in the large vertical distance of the Son from heaven. This fits with the Son being kenotic in connection with his cross and his work as the glorious redeemer of the world. But diagram 2 suggests that the Son also experiences a more indirect kenosis relative to the world as he supports more from a distance the work of the Spirit in the lives of struggling disciples in the world. This looks at Jesus's work as the glorious redeemer more from the perspective of his resurrection victory. Moving now to the Holy Spirit, both diagram 1 and diagram 2 suggest that the Holy Spirit consistently experiences a modest direct kenosis in the world as well as a modest indirect kenosis. This helps illustrate how the Spirit goes about his kenotic work of fostering dignity in his work as the sanctifier of human beings. Finally, both diagram 1 and diagram 2 suggest that the Father as the creator experiences a more indirect kenosis as from heaven he is affected by the more direct kenosis of the Son and the Holy Spirit.[61]

Conclusion

In this section I have argued for a mutual hierarchy framework where each divine person has a unique hierarchical vocation during Jesus's life as evident in John's Gospel so that the divine persons are differentiated even amidst an overall Father-Son-Spirit ordering of the divine persons.

61. In chapter 4 I will introduce diagram 4, which will further illustrate the working of the divine persons and the relationship between the economic Trinity and the immanent Trinity.

In John, the Father is the creator who sends the Son and the Spirit into the world for its sake; the Son is the glorious redeemer who dies and rises for the world; and the Holy Spirit is the sanctifier of human beings in the world. Integral to these differentiated vocations is that each divine person exercises the hierarchy of his vocation in unique kenotic ways that foster mutuality and dignity in the trinitarian co-working. Thus by accounting for both the uniqueness and dignity of the divine persons, my mutual hierarchy proposal argues for the sociality of the economic Trinity in John's Gospel.

CHAPTER CONCLUSION

Both Balthasar and Volf have two sets of opposing statements in their economic trinitarian thought with mediating statements intended to bridge between them. For both Balthasar and Volf, looking at the chief redemptive moment in the economic Trinity especially in the Gospel of John brings the tension involved into relief. Balthasar, in considering Holy Saturday, has one set of statements where the Father exercises great hierarchy over the unconscious Son and another set of statements where the Son exercises a weak conscious obedience toward his hierarchical Father. Here Balthasar's mediating concept that the Son can do the impossible has the effect of further amplifying the hierarchy of the Father over the Son by legitimating the first set of hierarchical statements and connecting the second set of statements to more intense hierarchy. Volf in considering the cross has one set of statements where the divine persons have fully egalitarian relations with each other and another set of statements where the Father has hierarchy over the other divine persons in connection with his having sent them into the world. Volf's mediating concept of perichoresis is highly egalitarian, more associated with the fully egalitarian relations of the divine persons than with hierarchical sending. Thus both Balthasar and Volf have a hierarchy-equality polarity or tension in their understanding of the economic Trinity. Balthasar "resolves" this tension by giving logical priority to the hierarchical pole of the system while Volf gives logical priority to the egalitarian pole, with Balthasar not adequately accounting for dignity among the divine persons and Volf not adequately accounting for the uniqueness of each divine person. Thus neither adequately accounts for the sociality among the divine persons that requires both their uniqueness and dignity.

My mutual hierarchy approach to the economic Trinity had no need for either two opposing sets of statements or mediating concepts. My proposal looked at how in the Gospel of John each divine person has a unique vocation and is hierarchical over the other divine persons in the context of this vocation. In John's Gospel, the Father is the creator who sends the Son and Spirit, the Son is the glorious redeemer, and the Spirit is the sanctifier of human beings. Here the uniqueness of each divine person was accounted for as they work together as a differentiated community, in contrast to especially Volf's proposal. My proposal also looked at how each divine person exercised the power of his vocation in a kenotic way, using his power to serve the other divine persons and the world and to foster dignity and mutuality in the trinitarian fellowship, in contrast to especially Balthasar's proposal. Thus a mutual hierarchy approach identified the differentiated kenotic vocations of the divine persons and adequately accounted for both the uniqueness and dignity necessary for a greater sociality among the divine persons.

4

A Mutual Hierarchy Approach to the Immanent Trinity

THE QUESTION THIS CHAPTER will be trying to answer is "What is the place of the immanent Trinity in a social model of the Trinity?" I will attempt to show that Balthasar and Volf evidence a hierarchy-equality polarity in their understandings of the immanent Trinity in connection with their strong preferences for hierarchy and equality, respectively, among the divine persons. I will also argue that a mutual hierarchy framework for the immanent Trinity entails the *mutual constitution* of the divine persons. Mutual constitution here refers to each divine person possessing a power or hierarchy over the others in connection with his own personal properties, even while each divine person uses this hierarchy in a dignified manner to constitute the other divine persons. Through thus accounting for both the uniqueness and dignity of the divine persons, the chapter will argue for a more fully social understanding of the immanent Trinity.

The chapter will first present the basic contours of Balthasar's hierarchical understanding of the immanent Trinity. Next it will present the basic contours of Volf's egalitarian understanding. After this, the positions of Balthasar and Volf will be compared and evaluated. Finally, I will show how a mutual hierarchy framework that posits the mutual constitution of the divine persons more adequately accounts for the sociality of the divine persons by consistently maintaining both their uniqueness and dignity.

BALTHASAR'S HIERARCHICAL UNDERSTANDING OF THE IMMANENT TRINITY

Central to Balthasar's hierarchical understanding of the immanent Trinity is a distinction between a hierarchical "level of constitution" and a hierarchical "level of relation" among the divine persons. For Balthasar the level of constitution refers to the Father's generation of the Son and the Father and the Son's spiration of the Spirit, which generation and spiration do not entail dialogical relations between the one(s) constituting and the one(s) constituted. The level of relation, on the other hand, refers to the hierarchical relationships among the divine persons (logically) after they have been constituted, where these relationships do not contribute to the constitution of the divine persons.[1] In order to analyze Balthasar's hierarchical understanding of the immanent Trinity, my method in this section will be to first briefly present a couple of key conclusions from Margaret Turek's book *Towards a Theology of God the Father: Hans Urs von Balthasar's Theodramatic Approach*. I will then look at Balthasar's understanding of the immanent Trinity in the "Logos and Logic" chapter of the second volume of *Theo-Logic* in order to critically supplement the work of Turek.[2]

Balthasar's Understanding of the Immanent Trinity as Presented by Turek

In the introduction to her book, Turek lays out her basic thesis for the second half of the book where she discusses the Father generating the Son in Balthasar's thought. Turek writes,

> Part Two of our study will present a schematic ordering and examination of the modalities and aspects integral to the manner of being divine proper to the Father. Preliminarily, we may identify the following: (i) the paternal mode of infinite freedom: unconditioned initiative as self-gift; (ii) the paternal kenosis; (iii) the paternal leaving-free; (iv) the paternal receptivity; (v) the paternal dependence and expectation; and (vi) the paternal affectivity of the immutable God. In regard to each aspect of

---

1. To my knowledge, Balthasar does not explicitly speak of a level of constitution and a level of relation. However, these terms accurately convey his position.

2. See also chapter 1 where I quoted Balthasar's description of his chapter-by-chapter methodology in the second volume of *Theo-Logic*.

the Father's mode of being God, we will develop an understanding in terms of its efficacy to engender its perfect reflection: the Son's begotten, answering mode of infinite love.³

This quotation helps bring out the tension in Balthasar's thought that Turek sees. For example, point (i) shows that for Balthasar, the Father is unconditioned by the Son in begetting him. Thus at the level of constitution, the Father logically precedes the Son.⁴ And yet the Father in begetting the Son also engenders the Son's reflection of the Father's attributes, as the end of the quotation makes clear. For Balthasar, this response of the Son to the Father occurs at the second of his two levels, the level of relation. Here the Father does not logically precede the Son and there is even a certain mutual dependence between the Father and the Son.⁵ But even at this level of relation there is an "asymmetrical relation" of the obedient Son over and against his hierarchical Father.⁶ Thus there is a tension, or "paradox" as Turek calls it,⁷ between these two levels in Balthasar's thought, and at both levels there is a unilateral hierarchy of the Father over the Son.⁸

Balthasar's Understanding of the Immanent Trinity as Evident in the Second Volume of *Theo-Logic*

In the present section I will critically supplement the presentation by Turek on Balthasar's understanding of the immanent Trinity by sampling Balthasar's discussion in the "Logos and Logic in God" chapter from the second volume of *Theo-Logic*. Doing so will confirm Turek's basic position that sees a paradox or tension between a level of constitution and a level of relation in Balthasar's immanent trinitarian understanding. However, it will also critically supplement Turek's presentation by clearly demarcating certain mediating concepts in addition to Balthasar's two

---

3. Turek, *Towards a Theology of God the Father*, xxii.
4. Turek, *Towards a Theology of God the Father*, 96, shows that Balthasar can speak of the Father acting alone in begetting the Son.
5. Turek, *Towards a Theology of God the Father*, 162.
6. Turek, *Towards a Theology of God the Father*, 105.
7. Turek, *Towards a Theology of God the Father*, 106.
8. Turek, *Towards a Theology of God the Father*, 91, 106, also discusses how Balthasar speaks about the unique "super-kenosis" of both the hierarchical Father and the obedient Son in the immanent Trinity.

levels in his immanent trinitarian understanding and by suggesting how these mediating concepts relate to hierarchy in Balthasar's views.

In the "Logos and Logic in God" chapter, Balthasar speaks about the two levels in his immanent trinitarian understanding. For example, he says, "We can talk about the immanent Trinity only using two *countervailing* propositions that resist being welded into a unity."[9] An example of these two countervailing propositions is evident in the following:

> [Balthasar asks] whether God the Father knows himself by virtue of eternally possessing the divine essence or whether he knows himself (as Father) by placing his meaning-word, the Son, vis-á-vis himself? If we opt for the second proposition, the Father would first come to know himself in the Son; if we opt for the first, it appears that his self-knowledge is (at least logically) prior to the generation of the Son, which, supposing we do not fall into Arianism, leads us to ask why such a generation is needed in the first place.[10]

Balthasar goes on to say that each of the two opposing propositions here has some element of truth in it, although neither is sufficient by itself. Balthasar says that certain medieval Roman Catholic theologians like Augustine and especially Anselm held to the second option, which option operates at a level of relation (with the divine persons consistently relating with one another) and is in danger of locating the divine substance above the divine persons. Balthasar seems to have the "Eastern" tradition, or a person-oriented trinitarian model, more in mind with the first option, where the Father (logically) deliberates prior to generating the Son. Thus there is a tension between the level of constitution and the level of relation in Balthasar's understanding of the immanent Trinity.[11]

A little further in the chapter, we can see one of Balthasar's various mediating concepts that he employs to try to bridge between his two levels in tension with each other. Here Balthasar says,

> If we rightly assume that the *taxis* (sequential order) of the processions, while irreversible, is absolutely atemporal—so much that we can and must think of the Persons who proceed, the Son

9. Balthasar, *Theo-Logic*, 2:132, italics original.

10. Balthasar, *Theo-Logic*, 2:128.

11. Balthasar, *Theo-Logic*, 2:133, similarly distinguishes between the processions (level of constitution) and the relations (level of relation) among the diving persons, and Balthasar says these two sets of propositions "resist every attempt to reduce them to one."

and the Spirit, as "letting themselves be brought forth"—does not the divine essence become something that is as much "in motion" as the event of the processions themselves?

Here Balthasar points to the Son and the Spirit's atemporal "letting themselves be brought forth" as a mediating concept.[12] This mediating concept does not really fit with the level of constitution since Balthasar requires of this level that the Father (logically) precede the Son in begetting him, whereas here the Son and the Spirit are aware that they are proceeding from the Father. And it does not fit with the level of relation since Balthasar is explicitly speaking about the processions. Finally, we note that this mediating concept is very hierarchical since the Son and the Spirit merely let the Father constitute them and seem to contribute little to it. This very hierarchical mediating concept has the effect of amplifying trinitarian hierarchy by legitimating somewhat the level of constitution where the Father can be thought of as existing alone by connecting it to the level of relation and by connecting the level of relation to the more intense hierarchy of the level of constitution.[13]

Balthasar goes on to lay out another important mediating concept. He says,

> At the end of this reflection on how the hypostases determine the divine essence, we must mention a paradox that admits of no easy penetration. In all the properties, decrees, and works owing their foundation to the three hypostases, there are two factors that must be given equal weight: the order of the processions and the equal rank of the divine hypostases. We must on no account think that, because the Father is origin, he "commands" the other two; the Son and the Spirit are not, so to say, his obedient executors. The Son and Spirit have proceeded from the Father coeternally with him. Therefore it retroactively affects the origin itself without neutralizing the order of origination. The Son's and Spirit's equality of rank with the Father gives them an equal share in the properties and modes of conduct of the

---

12. Balthasar, *Theo-Logic*, 2:136. It is also noteworthy that Balthasar, *Theo-Logic*, 2:136–37, shows the clear connection between Balthasar's understanding of the economic Trinity and his understanding of the immanent Trinity.

13. Balthasar, *Theo-Logic*, 2:135–36, has another mediating concept, where Balthasar says that the Father "begets before thinking about it." That this mediating statement really does not resolve the paradox between Balthasar's two levels can be seen in Balthasar's statement here that one must bow before this mystery "which thought can neither go behind nor exhaust."

one God; the hypostases determine in their *circumincessio* what God is and wills and does.[14]

Here Balthasar in speaking of the processions refers to the level of constitution and, by speaking of the equal rank of the divine persons, to the level of relation, since he is referring to the divine persons considered (logically) after the processions.[15] The mediating concept here is evident when Balthasar says that the Son and Spirit "retroactively affect" the generating Father. This concept does not fit with the level of constitution since the begetting Father is affected by the Son and Spirit, and it does not fit with the level of relation because the processions are being discussed. Again we have an example of a mediating concept that is hierarchical, mediating between a hierarchical level of constitution and a hierarchical level of relation. The effect of this mediating statement again seems to be to amplify trinitarian hierarchy by attempting to legitimate the hierarchy of the level of constitution where the Son and Spirit are not logically present and to amplify the hierarchy of the level of relation by connecting it to the greater hierarchy of the level of constitution.

Having spoken about the generation of the Son and the processions more generally, Balthasar goes on to speak specifically of the spiration of the Spirit, and in the process the tension between Balthasar's hierarchical level of constitution and hierarchical level of relation is again evident. For example, Balthasar says that the fruitfulness of the mutual love of the Father and the Son issues in the Spirit, which finds an analogy in a human child's "issuance from its parents."[16] Here one must understand how Balthasar utilizes the analogy from the human nuclear family: the Spirit appears between the Father and the Son just as a child appears "between" his or her parents.[17] For even though as one reads from left to right in a Father-Spirit-Son structure of the Trinity the Spirit seems to precede the

14. Balthasar, *Theo-Logic*, 2:147-48.

15. It is important to note here that even though Balthasar says that the divine persons are of "equal rank," he also mentions the "order of the processions" in the same phrase. The divine persons may only equally determine the divine essence because the Son and Spirit proceed from the Father who (logically) precedes them and is hierarchical over them. This mention of equality is unintelligible apart from its integral connection to Balthasar's hierchical view of the processions.

16. Balthasar, *Theo-Logic*, 2:163.

17. See also chapter 3 where I discussed diagram 1, a diagram borrowed from Balthasar that shows that the Holy Spirit is located between the Father and the Son in both the economic Trinity and the immanent Trinity. Diagram 1 is taken from Balthasar, *Theo-Drama*, 3:191.

Son, logically the Spirit comes after the Father and Son just as the father and mother relate first, and only *after* procreation does the child appear between them. Thus, for Balthasar the Spirit may only be between the Father and the Son at the level of relation by being (logically) after the Father (and the Son) at the level of constitution.[18] In connection with the tension between Balthasar's two levels, Balthasar uses a mediating concept and says that the Spirit paradoxically pervades "the entire event of the Son's origination from the Father." This pervading does not fit into the level of constitution because at this level the Spirit comes (logically) after the Father (and the Son), and it does not fit into the level of relation since constituting activity is being spoken of. Again we have an example of a mediating concept that is hierarchical, mediating between the hierarchical level of constitution and the hierarchical level of relation, and amplifies hierarchy.[19]

Conclusion

Margaret Turek clearly demonstrates that Balthasar has a tension in his understanding of the immanent Trinity. For Turek, this tension is between a hierarchical level of constitution where a divine person or persons logically precede the other(s) and a hierarchical level of relation where the divine persons consistently interact with one another. My reading of Balthasar's discussion in the "Logos and Logic in God" chapter from the second volume of *Theo-Logic* confirmed this tension and also critically supplemented Turek's work by reflecting on mediating statements in Balthasar that seek to bridge between his two trinitarian levels. The main thrust of these statements is that the impossible is nevertheless somehow accomplished. The effect of these mediating statements was to

---

18. Sachs, who is an otherwise quite sympathetic interpreter of Balthasar, says the following about the great hierarchy in the husband-wife trinitarian analogy in Balthasar's usage: "The 'masculine-feminine' typology is an example of a gender-symbolism which, widely present in patristic theology, is developed in a highly idiosyncratic way by Balthasar that is hardly credible today. Many of the underlying points are valid and can be made without appealing to questionable gender stereotypes" ("Holy Spirit and Christian Form," 388). See also Sachs, "Deus Semper Major," for more discussion of Balthasar's understanding of the spiration of the Spirit.

19. Balthasar, *Theo-Logic*, 2:153, shows that the tension between Balthasar's two levels can also be seen in the Son's role in spiration as Balthasar can speak of him both as unconscious and as conscious in this spiration. Balthasar, *Theo-Logic*, 2:156, asserts that the Spirit proceeds principally from the Father.

try to legitimate how, at the level of constitution, some divine persons can be thought of as not yet (logically) constituted, and to amplify the sense of hierarchy among the divine persons at the level of relation by connecting it to the even-more-hierarchical level of constitution. Finally, this is connected to a hierarchy-equality polarity in Balthasar's thought as Balthasar conceives of the relationships between the divine persons in the immanent Trinity as unilaterally hierarchical with the Father at the top, with his hierarchy greatly emphasized and the notion of equality among the divine persons stigmatized by rarely being mentioned or being interpreted hierarchically.

VOLF'S EGALITARIAN UNDERSTANDING OF THE IMMANENT TRINITY

Volf's understanding of the immanent Trinity is generally egalitarian, although he also allows for a certain limited hierarchy among the divine persons that is in tension with this. As we will see, here Volf stresses a fully egalitarian level of relation in the immanent Trinity even while also teaching a hierarchical level of constitution. In this section, my method will be to look at the general contours of Volf's egalitarian understanding of the immanent Trinity as evident predominantly in the "Trinity and Church" chapter of *After Our Likeness*.

Volf explicitly refers to a level of constitution and a level of relation in his trinitarian thought. This can be seen in the following from a footnote in the "Trinity and Church" chapter:

> Wolfhart Pannenberg, who disputes the distinction between the level of constitution and that of relation, understands the constituting of the persons as strictly reciprocal. This leads him to insist on the *future* monarchy of the Father, for otherwise one could not distinguish between the persons.[20]

This is the only passage in Volf's works that I am aware of where he explicitly rejects the view that the processions (generation and spiration) are mutual relations, although Volf's constructive proposal also clearly differs from the view that holds that the processions involve mutual relations.[21] In the present instance, Volf ties the view that sees processions

---

20. Volf, *After Our Likeness*, 216, italics original.

21. However, Volf does not consistently reject seeing the processions as mutual relations. For example, consider the following where Volf quotes Colin Gunton

as mutual relations with what Volf sees as Pannenberg's Hegelian view where the immanent Trinity is allegedly absorbed into the economic Trinity.[22] Volf does not consider the possibility that one could see the processions as mutual relations and not deny the ontological distinction between God and the world.[23] Nevertheless, Volf here helpfully distinguishes the view that sees the processions as mutual relations from his own view that holds to a level of constitution and a level of relation.

A little further on in the chapter, Volf, in a passage we also looked at in chapter 3, roots his two-level view of the immanent Trinity in the economy of salvation and relates it to the categories of hierarchy and equality. Volf says,

> Within salvation history they [the divine persons] do appear as persons standing in reciprocal relationships to one another. With regard to the immanent Trinity, salvation history thus allows us to infer the fundamental equality of the divine persons in their mutual determination and their mutual interpenetration; even if the Father is the source of the deity and accordingly sends the Son and the Spirit, he also gives everything to the Son and glorifies him, just as the Son also glorifies the Father and gives the reign over to the Father (see Matt 28:18; John 13:31–32; 16:14; 17:1; 1 Cor 15:24). Moreover, within a community of perfect love between persons who share all the divine attributes, a notion of hierarchy and subordination is inconceivable. Within *relations* between the divine persons, the Father is for that reason not the one over against the others, nor "the First," but rather the *one among the others*.[24]

---

approvingly: "As Gunton points out in *The One, the Three, and the Many*, 'the persons [of the Trinity] do not simply enter into relations with one another, but are constituted by one another in the relations'" ("Trinity Is Our Social Program," 409). See further Volf, "Trinity Is Our Social Program," 407–13, for more discussion on this issue.

22. I critiqued Pannenberg in chapter 1 for having elements in his thought that do not adequately account for the ontological distinction between God and the world.

23. Other theologians besides Pannenberg also hold to the divine processions involving mutual relations, but differ from Pannenberg and more resemble Balthasar and Volf in stressing the clear need for the immanent Trinity not to be dependent upon creation for its eternal existence. For example, Gunton holds that the processions involve mutual relations but maintains the integrity of the immanent Trinity: "The objection to an attempt to restrict theology to the economy alone is not that it involves the world of becoming, decisively not, but rather that, as it stands, it does not allow for an ontological distinction between God and the world to be securely maintained" (*One, the Three, and the Many*, 161).

24. Volf, *After Our Likeness*, 217, italics original.

Here Volf argues for the close relationship of the economic activities of egalitarian glorification and hierarchical sending with the level of relation and the level of constitution, respectively. For Volf, the level of relation is fully egalitarian and the level of constitution is fully hierarchical with the Father (logically) preceding the other divine persons. The tension between the two levels is thus evident.[25] However, Volf in his book does not often mention the hierarchical level of constitution just as he rarely mentions hierarchical sending. This further points to the tension in Volf's trinitarian understanding since Volf has little place in his doctrine of the immanent Trinity for hierarchy among the divine persons, largely only using the hierarchical level of constitution in an attempt to preserve the distinctness of the divine persons.[26] In the hierarchy-equality polarity associated with Volf's view of the immanent Trinity, Volf clearly emphasizes equality: "within a community of perfect love . . . a notion of hierarchy and subordination is inconceivable." Finally, Volf in the quotation also references perichoresis ("mutual interpenetration"), which, like in his economic trinitarian views, is his chief mediating concept, and he explicitly associates it with the equality of the divine persons.

More should now be said about Volf's mediating concept of perichoresis. Consider the following statement by Volf:

> When O'Donnell writes that the "union which Moltmann describes is only a moral union" . . . he overlooks precisely the decisive point, namely, that the divine persons *are* in one another. While this being in one another does presuppose the constitution of the persons . . . the persons are constituted as being mutually internal to one another; they do not only later become mutually internal to one another.[27]

Volf here connects perichoresis with the hierarchical level of constitution. And yet Volf places distance between perichoresis and the level of constitution. The level of constitution is referred to as a presupposition

---

25. Del Colle, "Communion and the Trinity," 315, critiques Volf by saying that his two levels of the Trinity do not necessarily inform one another.

26. Volf, *After Our Likeness*, 216–17, explicitly associates hierarchy with distinguishing among the divine persons. That Volf sees the egalitarian relations of the person in the immanent Trinity as primary also may clearly be seen in his lack of any mention of hierarchy among the divine persons in such trinitarian works as "Being as God Is: Trinity and Generosity" and "Trinity, Unity, Primacy: On the Trinitarian Nature of Unity and Its Implications for the Question of Primacy."

27. Volf, *After Our Likeness*, 210, italics original.

for perichoresis. Perichoresis is still chiefly connected with mutuality, a mutuality not possible in the hierarchical level of constitution but rather connected to the egalitarian level of relation.

The egalitarian thrust of perichoresis can be more clearly seen in other parts of the chapter. For example, Volf says,

> In their mutual giving and receiving, the trinitarian persons are not only interdependent, but also *mutually internal*, something to which the Johannine Jesus repeatedly refers: "so that you may know and understand that the Father is in me and I am in the Father" (John 10:38; cf. 14:10–11; 17:21). This mutually internal abiding and interpenetration of the trinitarian persons, which since Pseudo-Cyril has been called περιχώρησις, determines the character both of the divine persons and of their unity.[28]

Here Volf associates the "mutual giving and receiving" of the divine persons, which is a part of the fully egalitarian level of relation, with perichoresis. But Volf here is only suggestive, at most, of the hierarchical level of constitution by saying that perichoresis "determines the character of the divine persons and of their unity," which statement may have certain connotations of the distinctness of the divine persons obtained at the level of constitution. The effect of this usage of perichoresis in Volf's immanent trinitarian understanding is to strengthen the sense of the equality of the divine persons by providing some minimal way to try to account for the uniqueness of the divine persons and by providing another way—in addition to the egalitarian level of relation—that the divine persons are highly egalitarian relative to one another.

Finally, we return to a statement by Volf dealing with perichoresis as a mediating concept that we also looked at in the previous chapter. Volf says,

> Perichoresis refers to the reciprocal *interiority* of the trinitarian persons. In every divine person as a subject, the other persons also indwell; all mutually permeate one another, though in so doing they do not cease to be distinct persons. In fact, the distinctions between them are precisely the presupposition of that interiority, since persons who have dissolved into one another cannot exist in one another. Perichoresis is "co-inherence in one another without any coalescence or commixture." This is why both statements can be made: "Father and Son are in one another," and "Christians are in *them*" ("in us"—plural!; John

---

28. Volf, *After Our Likeness*, 208, italics original.

17:21). Being in one another does not abolish trinitarian plurality; yet despite the abiding distinction between the persons, their subjectivities do overlap.²⁹

The mediating concept perichoresis is ambiguous here, even if it is mostly associated with the egalitarian level of relation. For perichoresis somehow involves the level of constitution, since Volf brings up the "distinctions" among the divine persons, which distinctions we have seen for Volf arise from the level of constitution. Accordingly, here Volf says that these distinctions are the presuppositions for the mutual indwelling. But Volf mainly associates perichoresis with the fact that the divine persons "mutually" permeate one another, which mutuality we have seen is excluded in the hierarchical level of constitution and rather denotes the fully egalitarian level of relation. Thus in perichoresis the largely egalitarian divine persons permeate one another and their subjectivities "overlap," a concept that raises the question of whether Volf adequately accounts for the distinctness of the divine persons in connection with perichoresis. Perichoresis here for Volf is ambiguous, but he emphasizes its association with the egalitarian level of relation.³⁰

In this section I have thus shown that Volf exhibits a tension between hierarchy and equality in his understanding of the immanent Trinity. Utilizing *After Our Likeness*, I laid out the basic shape of this tension as Volf pits a fully egalitarian level of relation against a hierarchical level of constitution and greatly emphasizes the former while showing reticence toward the latter. This tension also involves a stark contrast between the consistent mutual interaction of the divine persons in Volf's preferred level of relation in comparison to the Father (logically) preceding the Son and the Spirit at the level of constitution. Volf also uses perichoresis as a mediating concept between these two levels. He clearly connects perichoresis most with the egalitarian level of relation and emphasizes this connection, but sometimes, especially when Volf is concerned to preserve the distinctness of the divine persons, he also vaguely associates

---

29. Volf, *After Our Likeness*, 209, italics original.

30. See Volf, "Spirit and the Church," 396–98, where Volf stresses the perichoresis, equality, and love of the divine persons as those aspects of the Trinity that are especially relevant for the church in its imaging of the Trinity. Here Volf associates perichoresis with equality and sees this as relevant for ecclesiology.

Moltmann, Volf's doctoral advisor, associates perichoresis with the fully egalitarian level of relation to such an extent that he precludes associating it with the hierarchical level of constitution: "Through the concept of perichoresis, all subordinationism in the doctrine of the Trinity is avoided" (*Trinity and the Kingdom*, 175).

perichoresis with the hierarchical level of constitution. The result of this is that perichoresis is ambiguous in Volf's proposal, usually being associated with the equality of the divine persons, but sometimes associated with hierarchy. The effect of this usage of perichoresis is to try to legitimate the fact that the level of relation has no hierarchy whatsoever by providing it a buffered contact to a minimal amount of hierarchy in order to distinguish among the divine persons. Volf thus minimizes the amount of hierarchy present in his understanding of the immanent Trinity, seemingly as much as possible. In this way we see how Volf "resolves" the hierarchy-equality polarity or tension in his immanent trinitarian understanding by giving logical priority to the egalitarian pole of the system.

A BRIEF COMPARISON OF AND EVALUATION OF BALTHASAR AND VOLF

Various similarities and differences are evident in the immanent trinitarian understandings of Balthasar and Volf. Both Balthasar and Volf distinguish in the immanent Trinity between a level of constitution, where the Father (logically) precedes the Son and the Spirit, and a level of relation where the divine persons consistently relate. In Balthasar there is a tension between a hierarchical level of constitution and a hierarchical level of relation. In both levels, Balthasar stresses the hierarchy of the Father over the Son and makes little mention of their equality. Volf, on the other hand, has a tension between a hierarchical level of constitution and an egalitarian level of relation, with Volf overwhelmingly emphasizing the latter over the former. The tension between hierarchy and equality is thus more explicit in Volf than in Balthasar since Volf explicitly contrasts hierarchy and equality (and chooses the equality pole of the polarity) whereas Balthasar simply talks about and emphasizes hierarchy and does not often mention equality (and chooses the hierarchy pole of the polarity).

Both Balthasar and Volf also employ concepts that seek to mediate to some extent between their two levels in tension with one another. However, these mediating statements function differently in the two theologians. The effect of Balthasar's hierarchical mediating concepts is to intensify the hierarchy of the Father over the Son in the immanent Trinity both by attempting to legitimate his level of constitution where the Father can (logically) appear alone by connecting it with the level of relation and by connecting the obediential relationships evident in the level of relation to the more intense hierarchy of the level of constitution. But the effect of Volf's mediating concept of perichoresis is to intensify the equality of the divine persons by trying to legitimate the fact that his level of relation has no hierarchy whatsoever by providing it a buffered contact to a minimal amount of hierarchy in the level of constitution in order to try to distinguish among the divine persons.

Finally, both Balthasar and Volf do not adequately account for the sociality of the divine persons, for a maximally social understanding of the Trinity, since they do not adequately account for both the uniqueness and dignity of the divine persons necessary for this sociality. In the case of Balthasar, his manner of stressing hierarchy in the level of constitution, the level of relation, and his mediating concepts is largely oppressive in nature. For in the hierarchical level of constitution the Father appears (logically) prior to the Son and Spirit so that the Son and Spirit are undignified in being able to contribute anything to the Father, and the Father is undignified for not involving them. Added to this is that, in the hierarchical level of relation and the mediating concepts, the Father in an undignified way commands obedience from the Son and the Spirit, and the Son and Spirit's main contribution to the relationship is merely to obey the Father, which is likewise undignified. In the case of Volf, in Volf's fully egalitarian level of relation there is nothing present that would distinguish among the divine persons, and in his understanding of perichoresis the subjectivities of the divine persons are said to overlap. In summary, Balthasar accounts for the uniqueness of the divine persons but does not adequately account for their dignity, while Volf accounts for dignity but does not adequately account for uniqueness. In this way, neither Balthasar nor Volf adequately accounts for the sociality of the divine persons, which requires both the uniqueness and dignity of the divine persons.[31]

---

31. An argument could be made that, largely due to the hierarchy-equality polarity present in each, the two theologians in the end are not as different from one another as one might think. For example, Balthasar's conception of the relations between the Father and Son is largely oppressive; however, the Son appears as almost the mirror image of the Father, which could call into question how unique the Son is. Similarly, Volf at the level of relation homogenizes the divine persons. But an argument could be made that in so doing he detracts from their dignity.

A MUTUAL HIERARCHY APPROACH TO THE IMMANENT TRINITY

In this section, I will argue for a mutual hierarchy framework in the context of a revised social trinitarian understanding of the immanent Trinity. In doing so, I will argue for the mutual constitution of the divine persons. Here the word *hierarchy* from the mutual hierarchy framework in the context of the immanent Trinity points to the fact that each divine person has *unique* personal properties that involve *hierarchical* power over the others as part of their *constitution*. Furthermore, the word *mutual* from the mutual hierarchy framework in the context of the immanent Trinity points to the fact that each divine person limits the use of his power relative to the others to foster *dignity* in their mutual constitution.[32]

In what follows, I will first utilize a mutual hierarchy framework to argue for the unique personal properties and unique powers of each divine person. And then I will again utilize the mutual hierarchy framework to argue that each divine person limits his power as they mutually constitute each other. At the outset it must be emphasized that how this mutual constitution occurs in many ways remains a mystery, and I am presenting sketches that are certainly open to the supplementation by others. Accordingly, in order to help in the presentation, analogies from the realms of family life and drama will be offered, which things are appropriate considering that human communities were originally made in the image of the Trinity (Gen. 1:26–27) and such analogies are used in the New Testament as well (e.g., John 17:21).[33] In proceeding thus I hope to show that such a mutual hierarchy understanding of the immanent Trinity accounts for the uniqueness and dignity of the divine persons needed for a more fully social conception of the immanent Trinity.

---

32. For more background on the mutual constitution of the divine persons, see chapters 1 and 3 where I briefly discuss Pannenberg and his views on seeing the processions as mutual relations.

33. Balthasar makes extensive use of the author, director, actor analogy for the Trinity in *Theo-Drama*. See especially Lösel, "Murder in the Cathedral," 427–39, for a discussion of this.

Mutual Hierarchy as a Framework for Understanding the Unique Personal Properties of the Divine Persons

In the previous chapter I utilized two diagrams in order to help illustrate the differentiated vocations of the divine persons as evident in John's Gospel according to a mutual hierarchy framework. Here we will again utilize these diagrams as well as some human community analogies in order to argue that each divine person has unique personal properties in the immanent Trinity.

The first diagram presented in the previous chapter was from Balthasar on the sending of the Son:[34]

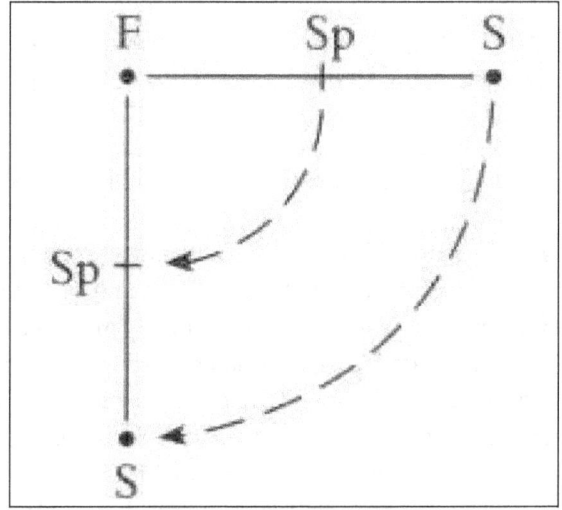

Diagram 1. The Sending of the Son

The previous chapter noted how in John's Gospel the Son during his life on earth was located a great distance from the Father in heaven, as evident in diagram 1, and that this was connected to his being ordered second in the Trinity behind the Father. In harmony with the axiom that the economic Trinity reveals the immanent Trinity, diagram 1 is now helpful for illustrating the immanent Trinity, which is represented by the horizontal line. The Father in the diagram remains in heaven and is the pivot or anchor that does not move as one shifts between the economic Trinity and the immanent Trinity. And around this pivot of the Father, the great

---

34. Balthasar, *Theo-Drama*, 3:191. Used with permission.

distance between the Father and the Son remains constant, so that in the immanent Trinity the Son is the one divine person most associated with responding to the Father and is ordered second behind the Father.[35]

If diagram 1 from chapter 3 helps us better understand especially the Son in the immanent Trinity, diagram 2 helps us better understand especially the Holy Spirit. Again we should look at this second diagram on the sending of the Spirit by the Father and the Son:

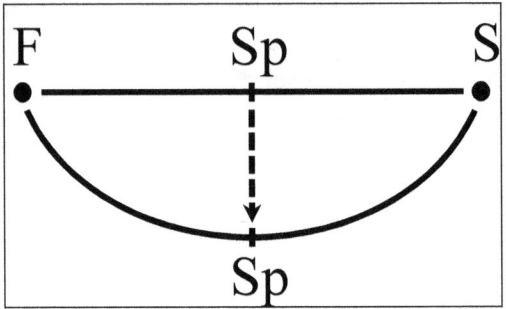

Diagram 2. The Sending of the Spirit

The previous chapter noted how, in John's Gospel, the Spirit as the third person of the Trinity was located between heaven and earth in the economy, a modest distance from each as he continually mediates between the two. This coordinated with his being ordered third in the economic Trinity, located between the Father and the Son. In harmony with the axiom that the economic Trinity reveals the immanent Trinity, diagram 2 is now helpful for illustrating the immanent Trinity, which is represented by the horizontal line. Just as the Spirit in the economy always intimately dwells between heaven and earth and dwells intimately between the Father and the Son who now dwell in heaven, in the immanent Trinity the Spirit always dwells intimately between the Father and the Son, closer to them than they are to each other.[36] Thus the two diagrams help illustrate the Father-Son-Spirit ordering of the immanent Trinity.

> 35. It may also be added that if the Son would have become incarnate even if the Fall into sin never occurred, which I personally believe, then the economic Trinity still would have revealed and corresponded to the immanent Trinity as the distance between the Father in heaven and the Son on earth would have still been present, only without the need for the cross.
>
> 36. Again, even if sin had never occurred, the Spirit could have dwelt between heaven and earth, between the Father and the Son in heaven, and between the Father and the incarnate Son on earth once the incarnation had taken place. The economic

An illustration from a human family can help illustrate how the Spirit can be ordered third in the immanent Trinity and yet be located between the Father and the Son, something that Balthasar also asserted. For example, Ephesians 5:21—6:4 points to a husband as the leader in a Christian family, to the wife as second and his complement, and to their child as ordered third. Here even though the child is ordered third in the family, he or she is best thought of as between his or her father and mother since they have the responsibility of nurturing and taking care of him or her.[37] Analogously, the Spirit is ordered third in the immanent Trinity but is located between the Father and the Son. Here the Spirit has a closeness to the Father and the Son analogous to a child in key respects being closer to his or her parents than the parents are to each other. For example, the child shares the DNA of both parents whereas the parents do not share each other's DNA. Similarly, the Holy Spirit can intimately mediate between the Father and the Son.

An illustration from drama can further illustrate the importance of each divine person having unique personal properties. Consider three human beings who wanted to put on a play. If all three were playwrights but they could not act, or if all three were actors but they could not write a play, it would be difficult for the show to go on. But if one person was an author, one was a director, and one was an actor, they would complement one another and the play could be performed. In the case of the immanent Trinity, each divine person is unique in connection with his position relative to the other persons and has associated hierarchical personal properties so that the divine persons can truly complement and constitute one another.[38]

The two diagrams drawn from the economic Trinity in John and the succeeding discussion now put us in a position to try to describe

---

Trinity still would have revealed and corresponded to the immanent Trinity, only without the need for the groaning of the Spirit in the face of human misery.

37. See also 1 Corinthians 11:3 where Paul ultimately grounds his analogy from the human family in the Trinity: "But I want you to understand that Christ is the head of every man, and the man is the head of a woman, and God is the head of Christ."

38. This discussion suggests a certain spatial dimension of the divine persons. Moltmann associates perichoresis with the mutual indwelling of the divine persons (*circuminsessio*). But my proposal especially argues for perichoresis in the sense of *circumincessio* (notice the difference in spelling between *circuminsessio* and *circumincessio*, the letter "s" versus the letter "c"), which refers to the "face-to-face" encounter of the divine persons, such as connoted in the English words "interceding" and "processions."

the unique, hierarchical personal properties each divine person has. Based on the discussion thus far, the Father as the first divine person is marked by unique personal properties in the areas of leadership, structural grounding ability, and stability. The Son as the second divine person at the greatest "distance" from the Father is marked by unique personal properties in the areas of responsiveness, complementarity, and fostering completion. And the Holy Spirit as the third divine person between the Father and the Son is marked by unique personal properties in the areas of intimacy, mediation, and fostering fellowship.

Mutual Hierarchy as a Framework for Understanding the Mutual Constitution of the Divine Persons

Having described the unique, hierarchical personal properties of each divine person in connection with a mutual hierarchy framework, we now will look at how each divine person limits the use of the hierarchy associated with his personal powers in connection with mutual constitution in the immanent Trinity. Here we will also introduce two additional diagrams as well as some human community analogies in order to better describe this mutual constitution.

Diagrams 1 and 2 in the previous section showed the relative positions of the divine persons and helped illustrate their personal properties in the immanent Trinity. Consider now a third diagram that illustrates the mutual hierarchy of the divine persons in the immanent Trinity:

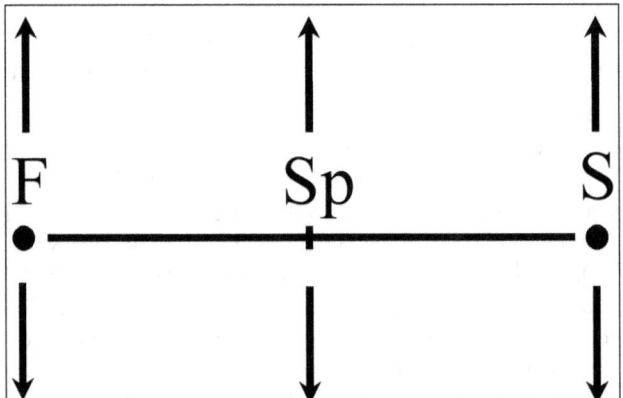

Diagram 3. The Mutual Hierarchy of the Divine Persons

Diagram 3 first illustrates how each divine person has a certain hierarchy over the others in the context of his personal properties. This may be seen in the up-facing arrow above each divine person, which illustrates each person's power. Thus, for example, the arrow pointing up above the Father in diagram 3 points to a certain hierarchy the Father has as the first person of the Trinity over the Son and the Spirit in connection with his unique personal properties. In this context, the arrows of Son and the Spirit point down.

However, besides illustrating the hierarchy of each divine person over the others in connection with his personal properties, diagram 3 also illustrates how a divine person limits his power as the divine persons mutually constitute each other and foster each other's personal properties. We saw a sort of extension of this in chapter 3 where each divine person in connection with the hierarchy of his vocation limited his power in order to foster the vocations and dignity of the other divine persons. This reveals that in the immanent Trinity each person in connection with his personal properties exercises his powers in such a way that he also limits his power over the other divine persons and fosters their dignity. For example, although the Father has a certain hierarchy over the Son and the Spirit in connection with his unique personal properties, the Father also exercises this hierarchy in such a way as to foster the personal properties and dignity of the Son and the Spirit. In this context, as the Father exercises his powers the arrow of the Father moves from up to down as he utilizes his personal properties in such a way as to build up the Son and Spirit (and move the arrows of the Son and the Spirit from down to up).[39] This same procedure that we have applied to the Father with his personal properties holds true for the Son and the Spirit as well. As the divine persons thus utilize and limit the power of their personal properties to mutually constitute each other, their dignity is also fostered.[40]

---

39. This is not to say that any divine person is ever passive. All are continually utilizing the powers associated with their personal properties even as they also always defer to the other divine persons on things more proper to them. While none are ever passive, there are varying degrees of prominence of each divine person in their dynamic fellowship.

40. Grenz in his book *The Social God and the Relational Self* makes the helpful point that true community is not possible if persons, whether human or divine, are thought of as either completely centered selves in the sense of isolated selves or if persons are thought of as completely de-centered selves that only receive their identity from others and in this way have no individual identity of their own.

An illustration from a human family—husband, wife, and child—can help illustrate how each divine person limits his power in connection with his personal properties amidst the mutual constitution of the divine persons. Each family member simultaneously forms the identity of the others and has his or her own identity formed by them. But a major difference in the case of the immanent Trinity is that rather than merely having one's identity partially formed by others in a family, each divine person continually constitutes the very existence of the others and is constituted by them.[41] But there is still at least an analogy here. For example, a wife exercises her unique gifts in relation to her husband, but in so doing she also limits her power and leaves room for him to exercise his unique gifts.[42] Aspects of the mutual constitution of the divine persons in the immanent Trinity can be illuminated by a mutual hierarchy framework and a family analogy, but its mystery nevertheless remains.[43]

An illustration from drama can further illustrate the mutual constitution of the divine persons. Again, utilizing our analogy from a play put on by three human beings, consider that an author, a director, and an actor want to put on a play. But now consider that the playwright works hard to sabotage the director and actor, the director works hard to sabotage the playwright and actor, and the actor works hard to sabotage the playwright and director. When the time for the play comes, it would not

---

41. Even in procreation in a human family, the father and mother's very existence is not dependent upon their child. At most a child was dependent for his or her existence at one point in time in the past. Furthermore, in a human family, even though a child comes into being through the mediation of his or her parents, a child's most fundamental identity—his or her relation to God—is clearly distinct from the child's relation to his or her parents.

42. Ephesians 5:21—6:4 is marked by a mutual hierarchy framework. Here Ephesians 5:21 ("and be subject to one another in the fear of Christ") provides the overall framework for the entire pericope. Each family member serves the others through his or her gifts, as all live together under Christ.

It is also noteworthy that familial trinitarian themes are extensive in John's Gospel. For example, Erickson, *God in Three Persons*, 205, cites Vincent Taylor to show that "Father" occurs 121 times in John's Gospel and 16 times in his letters, compared to 123 times in the rest of the New Testament. From this Erickson concludes, "This certainly suggests that for John the Father-Son relationship was the dominant category for a description of the relationship."

43. This discussion of mystery in God is a good place to mention debates about the meaning of the term "substance" in reference to the divine substance. Numerous commentators have noted that the teaching that the Son is *homoousios* with the Father from the Council of Nicea is somewhat ambiguous. For example, see Davis, *First Seven Ecumenical Councils*, 61.

be pretty! For the best chance at a successful play, a playwright needs to use his skills to bring out the best in the director and actor and then leave them room to use their skills. The same is true in the case of the director and actor. In the case of the immanent Trinity, each divine person relates to the others in such a way as to build them up, forming them in a dignified manner and allowing himself to be formed by them. This dignified use by each divine person of the powers associated with his personal properties is thus necessary for their mutual constitution.[44]

We will now conclude this section by doing our best to utilize the springboard of the economic Trinity to speak about the divine processions as part of the mutual constitution of the divine persons. First, consider again diagram 1 borrowed from Balthasar:[45]

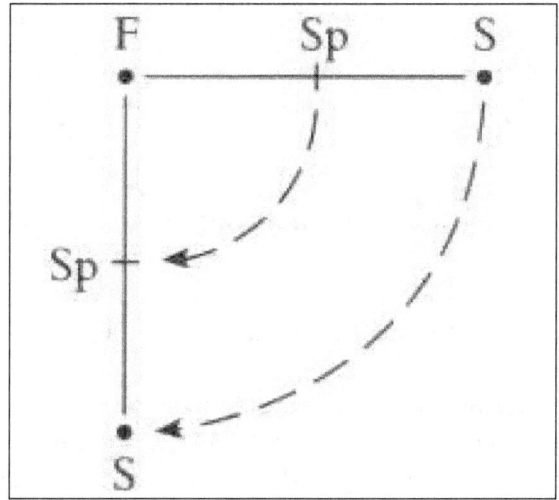

Diagram 1. The Sending of the Son

The vertical line in diagram 1 illustrates the "distance" of the Son from the Father in connection with the Father sending him into the world. Now we can posit more concretely that the incarnation as illustrated in

---

44. The mutual constitution of the divine persons includes some "durative" consideration. The spontaneity of the divine persons refers to the persons dynamically relating to one another in such a way that the freshness of the divine communion is never exhausted. However, the spontaneity of the divine persons also requires and involves the stability of the divine communion. The divine communion is always stable yet always spontaneous, always fresh yet always familiar.

45. Balthasar, *Theo-Drama*, 3:191. Used with permission.

diagram 1 corresponds to the Father's generation of the Son. Thus it is not surprising that both the incarnation and the generation of the Son have often both been associated with the term "birth." Diagram 1 also helps illustrate that the Son in his life responded to the Father's sending him. Here the Son completed a mission by doing what was most proper to him. The chief locus of this is Jesus's cross and resurrection. This economic activity of the Son in fulfilling the Father's will corresponds to the Son eternally responding in love to the generation of the Father.

The spiration of the Spirit will now be considered, again beginning with the economic Trinity. Consider again diagram 2 on the sending of the Spirit by the Father and the Son:

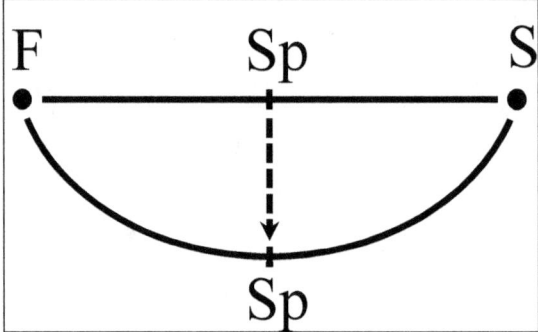

Diagram 2. The Sending of the Spirit

The curved line in this diagram illustrates how the Father and the Son in the economy of salvation send the Holy Spirit into the world to do his most proper sanctifying work in the church. Now we can say that this work of the Spirit in the church corresponds in the immanent Trinity to the Spirit's response to the Father and the Son's spiration of him. The Spirit in the church does what is most proper to him, and this corresponds to his most proper identity and activity in the immanent Trinity.

In order to better illustrate and integrate these things, we will now introduce diagram 4, which will be explained more fully in chapter 6. Consider diagram 4, which illustrates the prominence of the divine persons in Matthew's narrative:

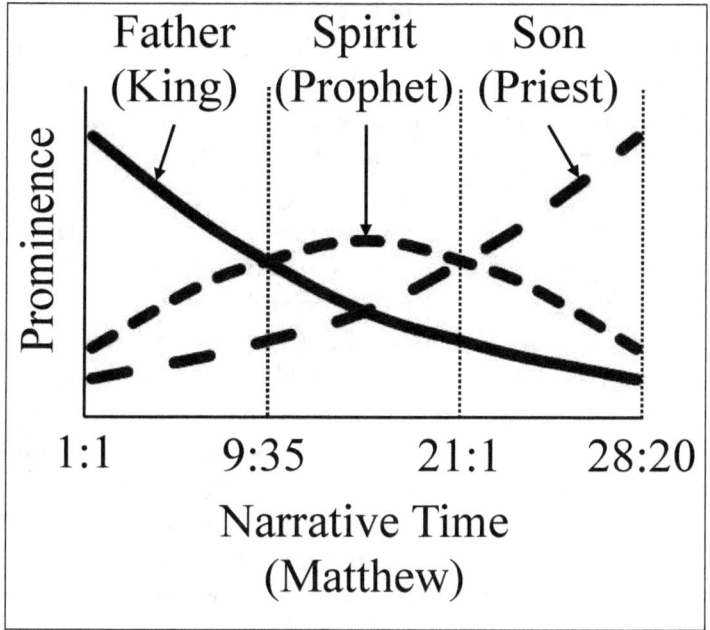

Diagram 4. The Prominence of the Divine Persons in Matthew

Diagram 4 looks at the prominence of the vocation of each divine person as the narrative time in the Gospel of Matthew proceeds.[46] As will be explained further in chapter 6, prominence refers to how much a divine person's work stands out or is conspicuous at a given time. For example, in a play a character is often more prominent in connection with such things as being in the middle of the stage, having the spotlight on him or her, and speaking an important line. So too in the Gospel of Matthew, the prominence of each divine person varies with narrative time. The basic flow of the graph is that the Father's vocation is most prominent at the beginning of Matthew at the incarnation and then decreases until the end of the Gospel; the Spirit's vocation is most prominent in the middle of Matthew as Jesus is most active training the disciples for ministry in the church; and the Son's vocation is least prominent at the beginning

46. A graph for the Gospel of John would be very similar to diagram 4. It would be connected to the Father as the creator being most prominent at the beginning of John, the Spirit as the sanctifier being most prominent at the middle of John, and the Son being most prominent at the end of John. The three sections of John arguably are tied to the progression in the Jewish religious year from Passover to the Feast of Tabernacles to Hanukkah, but this is outside of the scope of this book.

and then builds to a climax at Jesus's cross and resurrection. The reason for bringing this diagram up now is the same as utilizing diagrams 1 and 2: the economy of salvation reveals the immanent Trinity. For example, the far left of diagram 4 illustrates the Father's most prominent work in the economy being the incarnation, which corresponds in the immanent Trinity to his prominence in begetting the Son. The far right of diagram 4 shows the reverse of this. Here the Son is the most prominent in his crucifixion and resurrection. This corresponds in the immanent Trinity to the Son responding to the Father's begetting of him. And so the far left and the far right of diagram 4 illustrate the Father's begetting of the Son and the Son's response to this begetting, respectively, which is what we also saw in diagram 1. Finally, the middle of diagram 4 illustrates the Holy Spirit's most prominent work in the economy, his sanctifying work in the church. This corresponds to his response to his spiration the immanent Trinity, which is also what we saw in diagram 2.[47]

More may now be said about the personal properties of the divine persons in connection with the dynamics of the processions. We begin with the Father. The Father is the divine person who uses his unique personal properties to help generate the Son in the Spirit as well as help spirate the Spirit with the Son. The Father is the one who exercises a certain initiating leadership in the divine life and in this context has authority over the Son and the Spirit. The Father is the one around whom the Trinity is organized or structured, a sort of stabilizing ground or anchor. And yet the Father in his unique first position in the immanent Trinity uses his powers in order to foster the dignity of the Son and the Spirit in the midst of generation and spiration. Here as the Father exercises his powers and leads the generation of the Son and the spiration of the Spirit, he also limits his powers, which leaves room for the responses of the Son and the Spirit and amplifies their personal properties. The Father's powers in such areas as leading, grounding, and stabilizing are the basic forms the

---

47. Various other trinitarian conclusions may also be drawn based on diagram 4. The far left of the diagram shows that the Spirit plays a more minor role (in comparison with the Father) in begetting the Son, and the far right of the diagram shows that the Spirit plays a more minor role (in comparison with the Son) in the Son's response to being begotten by the Father. The far left and far right of the diagram also depict the most active spiration of the Spirit by the Father and the Son, respectively. Finally, the fact there are varying degrees of prominence for each divine person suggests that the processions are dynamic, perhaps analogous to the dynamics of a human conversation where each person does things like listen, prepare to speak, begin to speak, and prepare to end speaking and begin listening.

Father's love takes as he uses his personal properties to contribute to the processions in the mutual constitution of the divine persons.[48]

The Son is the divine person who uses his unique personal properties to respond to the Father's generation of him in the Spirit and to spirate the Spirit with the Father. The Son is thus the divine person who is most associated with such things as response, complementarity, and completion. And yet the Son in his unique position in the immanent Trinity uses his powers in order to foster the dignity of the Father and the Spirit in the midst of responding to his generation and in the midst of complementing and completing the spiration of the Spirit. Here as the Son exercises his powers in responding to generation and aiding in spiration, he also gradually limits his powers, which leaves room for and amplifies the personal properties of the Father and the Spirit. The Son's powers in such areas as responsiveness, complementing, and fostering completion are the basic forms the Son's love takes as he uses his personal properties to contribute to the processions in the mutual constitution of the divine persons.

Finally, the Spirit is the divine person who uses his unique personal properties to respond to the Father and the Son's spiration of him and to aid, in a modest manner, in the Father's generation of the Son and the Son's response to the Father's generation.[49] The Spirit is thus the divine person who is most associated with simultaneous intimate response to two divine persons (in spiration) and with his ability to uniquely and modestly complement both of the other two divine persons in connection with their personal properties (in generation and responding to generation). And yet the Spirit in his unique position in the immanent

---

48. See also Sánchez, *Receiver, Bearer, and Giver of God's Spirit*, 65–85, for an extended discussion of the Father's generation of the Son in the Holy Spirit (*in spiritu*). See also Sánchez, *Pneumatología*, 110–22.

49. I say modest here because of the large vertical distance of the line of the Spirit from that of the Father at the far left of diagram 4 and because of the same vertical distance of the line of the Spirit from that of the Son at the far right of diagram 4. Ultimately this (relatively) large distance seems to be connected to the fact that the Holy Spirit by being between the Father and the Son is always nearer to them than they are to each other; note that the Spirit's vertical distance from the Father and the Son in diagrams 1 and 2 is less than the vertical distance of the Son from the Father in diagram 1 (see also the Spirit's nearness to the Father and the Son in diagram 4 even doing his most prominent work). However, it also should be noted from the middle of diagram 4 that the Holy Spirit here helps in a more prominent way in the Father's generation of the Son and in the Son's response to generation (in comparison to the Holy Spirit's prominence at the far left and far right of diagram 4).

Trinity limits his powers in the midst of his exercising of them to amplify the Father and the Son. The Spirit's powers in such areas as intimacy, mediation, and fostering fellowship are the basic forms the Spirit's love takes as he uses his personal properties to contribute to the processions in the mutual constitution of the divine persons.

Conclusion

In this section I have argued for a mutual hierarchy framework in the context of the immanent Trinity. Building upon my analysis of the economic Trinity as evident in John's Gospel from chapter 3, I argued that each divine person has hierarchy over the others in connection with his unique personal properties within an overall Father-Son-Spirit ordering of the immanent Trinity, with the Spirit being located between the Father and the Son. I went on to argue that each divine person in utilizing the hierarchy associated with his personal properties also limits his powers in order to foster the dignity of the other divine persons. I argued that this is integral to how the divine processions should be understood as the divine persons mutually constitute one another. Thus, by accounting for both the uniqueness and dignity of the divine persons, my mutual hierarchy proposal accounted for the sociality of the immanent Trinity.

CHAPTER CONCLUSION

Both Balthasar and Volf in their understandings of the immanent Trinity have a level of constitution where the Father (logically) precedes the Son and the Spirit and a level of relation in tension with this where the divine persons consistently relate. The level of constitution is very hierarchical in both Balthasar and Volf, although Volf places little emphasis upon it. Balthasar's level of relation is quite hierarchical as well, while Volf's level of relation is fully egalitarian. In connection with these things, Balthasar's hierarchical mediating statements have the effect of further amplifying trinitarian hierarchy, while Volf's largely egalitarian mediating concept of perichoresis has the effect of amplifying the equality of the divine persons. In this way both Balthasar and Volf have a hierarchy-equality polarity or tension in their respective understandings of the immanent Trinity, with Balthasar giving logical priority to the hierarchical pole of the system in such a way that the dignity of the divine persons is not adequately accounted for, and Volf giving logical priority to the equality pole in such a way that the uniqueness of each divine person is not adequately accounted for.

My mutual hierarchy approach to the immanent Trinity had no need for two divided levels, and hence also did not need any mediating concepts. Instead, my proposal looked at how each divine person has hierarchy over the others in connection with his unique personal properties within the overall Father-Son-Spirit structuring of the immanent Trinity. This accounted for the uniqueness of the divine persons, in contrast to especially Volf's proposal. Furthermore, I argued that each divine person in utilizing the hierarchy associated with his personal properties also limits his power in order to foster the dignity of the other divine persons as they mutually constitute one another. This fostering of dignity was in contrast to especially Balthasar's proposal. Thus a mutual hierarchy approach identified the mutual constitution of the divine persons and more adequately accounted simultaneously for both the uniqueness and dignity necessary for a greater sociality among the divine persons.

5

Mutual Hierarchy as a Framework for Ecclesiology

IN WHAT FOLLOWS, THE potential fruitfulness of a mutual hierarchy framework will be explored and compared to both a hierarchical and an egalitarian framework in the area of ecclesiology. Here a mutual hierarchy framework will be applied to three particular areas of ecclesiology: the relationship between a pastor and a congregation, trans-congregational relations, and relations between the church and the mission field.[1] Finally, I will summarize the conclusions of this chapter.

---

1. By trans-congregational relations in the second area, I mean relations between Christians outside of their relations within a congregation. For a helpful attempt at a definition and description of the trans-congregational church by another Lutheran theologian, see Kloha, "Trans-Congregational Church in the New Testament," 172–190. Kloha sees three main definitions of church (*ecclesia*) in the New Testament: a congregation, a clustering of congregations, and the one holy Christian church (*una sancta*). While I agree that these usages of church are central in the New Testament, there also is typically a certain looseness in its way of speaking. For example, when Paul writes to a particular church (or group of churches), he does not typically specify whether he is just addressing only believers or also the unbelievers in their midst (the "mixed" church). From a slightly different perspective, when the New Testament speaks of the trans-congregational church in a region (e.g., Acts 9:31), this does not have to only refer in a formal manner to the congregations in that region living and working together as congregations, but can also include diverse groupings of Christians working together more informally across congregational boundaries. This is even more so the case for the one church on earth (*una sancta*). Small groups of Christians who are part of the one holy Christian church but are from different congregations and even different denominations can certainly say together "We are Christ's church," although one should not for this reason neglect the importance of such things as

SOME BASIC CONTOURS OF BALTHASAR'S HIERARCHICAL ECCLESIOLOGY AND VOLF'S EGALITARIAN ECCLESIOLOGY

As discussed in previous chapters of this book, Balthasar emphasizes the hierarchy of the Father over the Son in the doctrine of the Trinity. Ultimately Balthasar's hierarchical doctrine of the Trinity is the foundation for his entire theology, where all things may be divided into pairs, with one element of the pair hierarchical over the other in a unilateral manner. For example, consider the following ecclesiological statement by Balthasar:

> If Church can be defined as communio, her "constitutive elements" must be "totally immanent in each other" in such a way that they "cannot be separated from one another. This is evident, for instance, in the reciprocal structural relationship between sacrament and Word, between the general priesthood of the faithful and the ministerial priesthood, between the faithful and the Church, between duty and law, between the whole Church and the local or national Church, between the pope and the college of bishops, between the bishop and the presbyterium." It is this reciprocal immanence of elements, themselves structurally distinct and unconfused, that makes Christ's Church a reflection of the Trinity; thus, too, it renders the operation of the Holy Spirit in her a valid and salvific interpretation of the unity and distinction between the Father and his incarnate Son, in which God shows his nature as love, and love is manifested as the "law of grace."[2]

Here Balthasar, after the pattern of the Father and the incarnate Son, divides various ecclesial members into pairs in such a way that love is defined in terms of the "law of grace" where the lesser in each pair owes strict obedience to the greater. For Balthasar, combining these pairs together leads to a pyramidal shape for the church with the pope at the top: bishops owe the pope obedience, priests owe bishops obedience, and laity owes priests obedience.[3]

---

congregational structure, doctrinal confession, and corporate sacramental worship.

2. Balthasar, *Theo-Logic*, 3:357–58. Here Balthasar quotes Corecco, "Ekklesiologische Grundlagen," 169.

3. For a discussion of the church lacking a sufficient critical principle vis-à-vis the magisterium in Balthasar's ecclesiology, see Lösel, "Conciliar, not Conciliatory," 23–49.

Balthasar in his discussion in the "Spirit: Subjective and Objective" section of the third volume of *Theo-Logic* further explains his ecclesiological framework. Here he distinguishes between "objective Spirit" and "subjective Spirit" and establishes this conceptual pair as the paradigm for his entire ecclesiology.[4] For Balthasar, objective Spirit refers to the Spirit's work associated with the pastoral office and is symbolized by Peter, while subjective Spirit refers to the Spirit's work among the laity and is symbolized by Mary. For Balthasar, objective Spirit is hierarchical over subjective Spirit and never vice versa. Or stated in terms of Balthasar's Peter and Mary symbolism, within the church on earth Peter is always hierarchical over Mary and never vice versa.[5]

Balthasar's hierarchical ecclesiological framework is problematic in the three ecclesial areas chosen for this chapter. First, at the congregational level, it locates all authority with the priest, inadequately accounting for the contribution and dignity of the laity. Second, it makes the magisterium hierarchical (in a unidirectional way) over individual congregations, problematizing congregational contribution.[6] And third, it ultimately places Spirit-led mission work at the bottom of the pyramid, making believers hierarchical over unbelievers in a unilateral way and calling into question the latter's value and the value of mission work (if unbelievers have little value).[7] Balthasar's ecclesiology encourages a choice of pastor over laity, trans-congregational church over congregation, and maintenance over mission.

Moving now to Volf, in previous chapters of this book we saw that Volf stresses the fully egalitarian relations of the divine persons while he

---

4. Balthasar, *Theo-logic*, 3:307–18. See Nichols, *Say It Is Pentecost*, 1–22, which shows that Balthasar's hierarchical ecclesiological framework is cast in terms of an object-subject philosophical framework. In a given pairing, an object is unilaterally hierarchical over a subject.

5. Balthasar can also speak of Peter submitting to Mary, but this refers to Mary only in her exaltation in heaven. See Saward, "Mary and Peter in the Christological Constellation," 105–33.

6. Volf, *After Our Likeness*, 113–23, critiques the Eastern Orthodox theologian John Zizioulas in a way that would largely apply to Balthasar as well. Volf questions why, for Zizioulas, an individual congregation and even an individual Christian can only be connected to the apostolic church, and hence Christ, through a priest's ordination by a bishop (apostolic succession).

7. Doyle, *Communion Ecclesiology*, 100, in a brief survey of Balthasar's ecclesiology, assesses, "Balthasar may not be the best theological voice available when it comes to the relation of the Church to various cultures, to science, to other religions, or to the plight of the poor."

minimizes and sometimes stigmatizes the thought of hierarchy among them. The case is similar in Volf's ecclesiology as he stresses egalitarian relations among Christians while minimizing and stigmatizing the thought of ecclesial hierarchy. Volf's ecclesiology will now be analyzed through looking at the final three sections of the important "Trinity and Church" chapter in *After Our Likeness*.[8]

In the "Trinity and Church" chapter, Volf's three trinitarian categories have counterparts in three ecclesiological categories. First, in the "Relational Personhood" section[9] of the chapter, Volf argues that just as the egalitarian face-to-face relations of the divine persons are most important in the doctrine of the Trinity, the face-to-face relations of Christians are fully egalitarian in nature and are the principle means through which Christ works in the church. Here is the chief basis for Volf's congregationalism since, according to Volf, Christians within a congregation generally interact face to face with one another more than Christians among different congregations do. But here at the heart of Volf's ecclesiology, Volf does not adequately account for the uniqueness of Christians, for by saying they relate in a fully egalitarian manner it becomes difficult to distinguish differences among them. Second, in the "Perichoretic Personhood" section,[10] Volf, corresponding to his trinitarian category of perichoresis, argues that Christians in a congregation can in a highly egalitarian manner "mutually indwell" one another—in a figurative sense—by learning about the personal characteristics of one another. Such highly egalitarian "mutual indwelling" again tends to blur how Christians differ from one another. Third, in the "The Structure of Trinitarian and Ecclesial Relations" section[11] Volf, corresponding to his third trinitarian category, allows for a minimal amount of hierarchy in his ecclesiology. Here Volf greatly minimizes how much hierarchy a pastor has over a congregation and does not mention any hierarchy, whether of pastors or otherwise, in the trans-congregational church. As Volf relates his ecclesiology to the equality of the divine persons in his doctrine of the Trinity, Volf's ecclesiology strongly emphasizes the equality of Christians in such a way that the uniqueness of ecclesial members relative to one another is not adequately accounted for.

8. For background on Volf's ecclesiology, see Bidwell, *Church as the Image of the Trinity*; Kärkkäinen, *Introduction to Ecclesiology*, 134–41.
9. Volf, *After Our Likeness*, 204–8.
10. Volf, *After Our Likeness*, 208–13.
11. Volf, *After Our Likeness*, 214–20.

An excerpt from Volf's "Trinity and Church" chapter should help further illustrate his ecclesiological views. Volf says,

> The symmetrical reciprocity of the relations of the trinitarian persons finds its correspondence in the image of the church in which all members serve one another with their specific gifts of the Spirit in imitation of the Lord and through the power of the Father. Like the divine persons, they all stand in a relation of mutual giving and receiving.[12]

Here Volf emphasizes fully egalitarian relations of Christians with one another. By saying all members serve one another, Volf implicitly critiques hierarchical systems where only clergy serve laity in the church in connection with exercising authority over them. For both the Trinity and the church, Volf emphasizes his first category of fully egalitarian mutual relations and views his hierarchical category as less-desirable, paradoxical, and an exception.

Volf's egalitarian ecclesiology is problematic in the three ecclesial areas chosen for this chapter. First, in the area of life within a congregation, Volf's egalitarian framework leads to a minimizing of the pastoral office through seeing the church as constituted chiefly through the egalitarian charismatic gifts of all Christians. For example, in the chapter "Structures and the Church" in *After Our Likeness,* Volf sees the pastoral office as a subset of the charismata of all Christians and only discusses hierarchy in connection with the pastoral office, not in connection with the gifts of the laity.[13] In this way the pastoral office is associated with generally undesirable hierarchy. Second, Volf's egalitarian framework provides the rationale for his overwhelming emphasis on an individual congregation over the trans-congregational church. Christians within a congregation are much more capable of egalitarian, face-to-face, relations with one another than Christians or congregations in the trans-congregational church.[14] And third, Volf's emphasis on the egalitarian relations of Christians through the power of the Holy Spirit tends to foster a choice of church maintenance over mission. For example, Volf's book *Exclusion and Embrace* is based on his egalitarian understanding of the Trinity and deals with how the church as the image of the Trinity

---

12. Volf, *After Our Likeness*, 219 (italics original).
13. Volf, *After Our Likeness*, 221–57.
14. See, for example, Volf's discussion in "The Catholicity of the Local Church" in *After Our Likeness*, 270–78.

should nonviolently respond to injustice in the world.[15] Here Christians chiefly relate to the world by having egalitarian relations with it. Volf emphasizes that all people are egalitarian in the sense that God equally loves all people and Christ has equally died for the sins of all. Volf here also tends to make people who do not have the Holy Spirit capable of truly egalitarian relationships with Christians, although Volf also sometimes allows that Christians have certain hierarchical relations over non-Christians.[16] Thus, similar to in other areas of his theology, Volf's missiology has a tension between egalitarian relations among human beings, which Volf emphasizes, and hierarchical relations of Christians over non-Christians, which Volf tends to minimize.[17] In the end, Volf tends to choose the egalitarian relations of Christians within a congregation over egalitarian relations that extend to unbelievers outside of the congregation, similar to how he tends to choose the egalitarian relations of Christians within a congregation over egalitarian relations between members in the trans-congregational church. Volf emphasizes that all human beings have egalitarian relations with one another, but practically speaking, relations among Christians within a congregation are the most feasible to practice in a consistent face-to-face manner in the image of the

---

15. Volf, *After Our Likeness*, 7, says that *Exclusion and Embrace* is grounded in the same egalitarian view of the Trinity as *After Our Likeness*. *Exclusion and Embrace*, 290–95, summarizes Volf's proposal to deal with violence in the world. For Volf, Christians should be nonviolent, absorbing violence through self-giving love, pointing out wrongs but standing with arms wide open in the hope that the other will reciprocate, accept what he already has been declared in Christ, and then be embraced. Lacking here is much of the positive action of the church, a concern that Volf himself acknowledges in these pages. For a discussion of Volf's pacifism that allows for eschatological violence by God and its contrast with the pacifism of Stanley Hauerwas, see Coker, "Peace and the Apocalypse," 261–68.

16. See, for example, Volf, *Allah: A Christian Response*, where Volf on the basis of his egalitarian understanding of the Trinity takes as his point of departure that Christians and Muslims have more in common than in difference.

17. Volf can allow a certain hierarchy in connection with mission: "I have argued that the social vision based on the doctrine of the Trinity should rest primarily on the downward movement in which God, in a sense, comes out of the circularity of divine love in order to take godless humanity into the divine embrace" ("Trinity Is Our Social Program," 417). There is thus a tension in Volf's missional thought here in connection with a hierarchy-equality polarity that sees hierarchy and equality as opposites. A related tension in Volf's thought occurs in the area of God's work of creation. Was God's creation of the world a fully egalitarian act or did it involve unfortunate hierarchy? For Volf, was the act of creation egalitarian, which calls into question God's distinctness from creation, was it chiefly hierarchical and hence against God's true nature, or did it involve both of these things in uneasy tension?

Trinity. Thus Volf's ecclesiology that prioritizes face-to-face egalitarian relations of Christians within a congregation encourages a choice of laity over pastor, congregation over trans-congregational church, and maintenance over mission.

In both Balthasar and Volf, ecclesial community is not accounted for as fully as it could be. In Balthasar's hierarchical framework, the distinctness of different ecclesial entities is accounted for, but less so dignity. In Volf's egalitarian framework, dignity is accounted for, but less so uniqueness. In both cases, unnecessary ecclesial choices are fostered. Balthasar's ecclesiology encourages a choice of pastor over laity and of trans-congregational church over congregation, while for Volf's ecclesiology it is the opposite, a choice of laity over pastor and of congregation over trans-congregational church. Ironically, the end result logically for both theological frameworks is a choice of maintenance over mission, with the mission field being neglected due to insufficient dignity in Balthasar and due to insufficient distinctness in Volf.

A MUTUAL HIERARCHY APPROACH TO ECCLESIOLOGY

Genuine ecclesial community can be better discerned and fostered by utilizing a mutual hierarchy framework. Mutual hierarchy means not having to decide for or against something just because it is egalitarian or hierarchical. In contrast especially to Volf's ecclesiology, in a mutual hierarchy framework each ecclesial member has hierarchies over the others in connection with that member's own unique gifts, offices, and responsibilities. Each ecclesial member has unique powers, with varying levels of complementarity with the powers of others. And yet, in contrast especially to Balthasar's ecclesiology, each member should use these hierarchies in a dignified manner, limiting powers as necessary, to foster mutuality and the dignity of others. A mutual hierarchy framework involves far more than strict lordship/obedience relationships and rather involves such relational categories as friendship, mentoring/discipleship, instruction, encouragement, consolation, forgiveness, and especially love. Here each member should use their hierarchies to serve others and complement their fellow Christians in the work of God's kingdom. In what follows, the fruitfulness of a mutual hierarchy ecclesiological framework will be explored in the three ecclesiological areas surveyed above, first by way of contrast with the corresponding thought of Balthasar and Volf, and then by further constructive elaboration.

The fruitfulness of a mutual hierarchy ecclesiological framework may now be explored in the three ecclesial areas surveyed above in Balthasar and Volf. First, a mutual hierarchy framework yields a different conception than in Balthasar or Volf of the relation between a pastor and a congregation. Unlike in Balthasar and Volf's systems, a mutual hierarchy framework does not tend toward a choice between a pastor (Balthasar) and laity (Volf). The two do not have to be mutually exclusive but rather should complement one another. Whereas in Volf the hierarchy of a pastor within a congregation is minimized and the charismatic gifts of the laity do not involve hierarchy, in a mutual hierarchy framework a pastor can be clearly distinguished from laypeople in terms of their respective vocations, even while the vocations of all involve hierarchy. A pastor has hierarchy over his congregation in connection with his work as a pastor. But members of the congregation also have hierarchies over the pastor and over one another in connection with their unique characteristics, abilities, and vocations. By recognizing that each person has hierarchy over others, the unique gifts of each person can more intentionally be explored and cultivated. In this regard, the complexity and depth of the gifts of each person can be better appreciated. For example, a pastor may have duties more remote from the more proper duties of the pastoral office—for example as a husband and father—and his unique perspective for these other tasks can be a source of enrichment for a congregation. Similarly, a layperson may have certain gifts in one area of ministry in the church where his or her unique perspectives from a job and family can be a source of enriching for the congregation. Here a mutual hierarchy framework accounts for the uniqueness of each Christian.

But a mutual hierarchy framework not only teaches that a pastor and laypeople each have unique gifts that involve hierarchy, it also teaches that these hierarchical gifts should be used not to lord authority over one another, but rather to serve one another in a dignified manner. This is in contrast especially to Balthasar's ecclesiology where the pastor exercises all authority in a congregation. Here a mutual hierarchy ecclesiological framework has great promise for fostering true community in a congregation. For it encourages members of a congregation to work together and sacrifice for one another so that their gifts can complement each other and enable greater tasks to be accomplished. In this regard it also fosters apprenticeship in a congregation. For example, certain tasks, perhaps like a building project, may require more lay expertise while other tasks, perhaps like certain mission programs, may require more pastoral expertise. And yet in each of these tasks the one with more proficiency can help teach others new skills. Again, a newly ordained pastor just arriving at his first call will likely learn much about the workings of a congregation from the laity, even as he will also likely contribute skills flowing from studying recent scholarship and mentoring. As such projects and mutual working proceed and members train each other using their gifts, new skills will be developed even while those being apprenticed will have new contributions to make so that a certain "reverse apprenticeship" will also take place in an apprenticeship project as the one being trained will also complement and teach the trainer in various ways since they each have unique gifts. Recognizing all of these things can also increase the capability and flexibility of a congregation. Tasks that otherwise may have seemed too large or too complex may be able to be accomplished because of the recognition of the mutual hierarchy abundantly present in a congregation. The multifaceted gifts of people working together and training one another in a congregation can meet a greater array of needs and have greater opportunities for growth. In this way dignified teamwork and community can be fostered within a congregation.

A mutual hierarchy framework also yields a different conception than in Balthasar or Volf of trans-congregational relations. Unlike in Balthasar and Volf's systems, a mutual hierarchy framework does not tend toward a choice between an individual congregation (Volf) and the larger church (Balthasar). The two do not have to be mutually exclusive but rather should complement one another. Whereas in Volf very little hierarchy is allowed in the trans-congregational church in an attempt to protect the primacy of the individual congregation, in a mutual hierarchy framework a congregation can be clearly distinguished from other congregations and other trans-congregational entities because all of these have unique hierarchical properties, gifts, and functions relative to one another. A unique individual congregation is typically required for Christians to be baptized in and gather together in a specific place as the people of God to receive God's gifts. This unique congregation has its own unique gifts in connection with the unique gifts of its members. But this does not prevent other congregations and other trans-congregational entities from having their own unique gifts. By recognizing that each trans-congregational entity has hierarchy over the others, the unique gifts of each can more intentionally be explored and cultivated. In this regard, the complexity and depth of the gifts of each trans-congregational entity can be better appreciated. For example, some congregations may be better at working with the homeless, some congregations may be better at fostering relationships in the neighborhoods and communities of their members, some congregations may be better at providing devotional and educational resources to their communities, a seminary may be better at educating pastors in preparation for service, and a missionary organization may be better at reaching out to an unchurched area.[18] Here a mutual hierarchy framework accounts for the uniqueness of each trans-congregational entity.

But a mutual hierarchy framework not only teaches that trans-congregational entities each have unique gifts that involve hierarchy over the others, it also teaches that these hierarchical gifts should be used not to lord authority over each other but rather to serve each another in a dignified manner. This is in contrast especially to Balthasar's ecclesiology where the church hierarchy with the pope at the top exercises all authority. Here a mutual hierarchy ecclesiological framework has great promise for fostering true community in the larger church. For it encourages trans-congregational entities to work together, and sacrifice for one another, so that their gifts can complement each other and enable greater tasks to be accomplished. For example, it recognizes that congregations are dynamic entities. Each congregation and its members form and have also been formed by other congregations and their members. There is fluidity between congregations as congregations send pastoral candidates away from themselves to seminary, Christians move and change congregations, Christians become missionaries in other places, and pastors change congregations. Trans-congregational entities recognizing that they form one another can help them to deliberately reach out to one another and serve and help one another. Here trans-congregational entities can also serve the more critical function of serving as checks and balances on each other's power to help prevent the abuse of power. Trans-congregational entities recognizing the mutual hierarchy among them is also important as they work together in such things as the formation of pastoral candidates, large-scale service work, and large-scale mission work. Thus, recognizing the mutual hierarchy of trans-congregational entities can help them to recognize, develop, and maximize their gifts,

18. Mancini, *Church Unique*, is a great resource to help a congregation assess and develop its own identity and vision.

and help them navigate the complex problems of the church and world by utilizing the flexibility of trans-congregational entities working together in a strategic way. In this way, dignified teamwork and community can be fostered in the trans-congregational church.

A mutual hierarchy framework also yields a different conception than in Balthasar or Volf of the relationship between the church in general and the mission field. Unlike in Balthasar and Volf's systems, a mutual hierarchy framework does not tend toward a choice of maintenance over mission. The two do not have to be mutually exclusive but rather should complement one another. Whereas in Volf, little hierarchy is allowed to distinguish the church from the mission field, a mutual hierarchy framework consistently incorporates the concept of hierarchy necessary to mark off Christians as distinct from non-Christians because each of these groups have unique hierarchical properties, gifts, and functions that can be helpful to one another.[19] Christians are the unique children of God who strive to do his mission in the world through the power of the Holy Spirit, and this mission work requires hierarchy if God is to be the one who ultimately will convert others. But this does not prevent non-Christians from being dearly loved by God and capable of doing all sorts of things that can help the world in such areas as fostering peace and lawfulness, economics, and service. By recognizing that Christians and non-Christians have hierarchy over each other, the unique gifts of each human person can more intentionally be explored and cultivated. In this regard, the complexity and depth of the gifts of the human world can be better appreciated. Thus a mutual hierarchy framework accounts for the uniqueness of each human being.

But a mutual hierarchy framework not only teaches that Christians and non-Christians each have unique gifts that involve hierarchy over

19. A mutual hierarchy ecclesiological framework is compatible with the Lutheran core "two kinds of righteousness" framework. The problems the two kinds of righteousness guards against can easily be defined in terms of hierarchy and equality. If only vertical or passive righteousness were allowed (a danger of a law-gospel framework if law is only understood in its "second" use as a mirror to reveal sin and vocation/mission is neglected), God would only be defined in hierarchical terms, not caring about human fellowship and vocation. On the other hand, if only horizontal or active human righteousness were allowed (a danger of "social gospel" thinking), the hierarchy of God over creation would disappear, resulting in an egalitarian understanding of the God-world relationship. But this two kinds of righteousness framework does not have to choose between vertical righteousness alone or horizontal righteousness alone, but rather views these two as both distinct and complementary. See Kolb, "Luther on the Two Kinds of Righteousness," 449–66.

each other, it also teaches that these hierarchical gifts should be used not to lord authority over each other but rather to serve each other in a dignified manner. This is in contrast especially to Balthasar's missiology where the church tends to have a unilateral hierarchy over the non-Christian world. Here a mutual hierarchy framework has great promise for fostering true community in the world. For it encourages Christians and non-Christians to work together and sacrifice for each other so that their gifts can complement each other and enable greater tasks to be accomplished. For example, it fosters teamwork and flexibility in relationships between Christians and non-Christians. If all hierarchy proceeded from the church to the world, then strictly speaking, non-believers would not be able to really contribute anything helpful to believers, and non-Christians could easily be offended by Christians' views about them. One could not benefit from a non-believing friend, family member, business owner, government official, etc. But when Christians recognize and appreciate the genuine contributions of their non-believing neighbors, it greatly multiplies Christians' capacity to benefit from these things and grow. Similarly, non-Christians can receive many benefits from Christians, not to mention the added benefit of being offered the gospel through both word and deed. Christians can love non-Christians, serve them through their deeds, and share the gospel with them explicitly as occasions arise, while non-Christians can love Christians, serve them through their deeds, and engage in conversations with them. If non-Christians see that Christians treat them with respect and care and work for and with them, non-Christians may be more likely to befriend Christians, work with them, share their thoughts and worldviews with them, and even be open to hearing about Jesus. Similarly, if Christians see that non-Christians have dignity in God's sight and that they too can work for good purposes in the world, Christians can be in a better position to value them, work with them, and further develop relationships with them that could slowly flower into opportunities to share the gospel with them in an explicit manner. Genuine personal growth, teamwork, solving complex problems in the world, more worldly harmony, a more missional mindset of the church, and kingdom growth all can result from appreciating the relationships between Christians and non-Christians, as a mutual hierarchy framework encourages. Thus a mutual hierarchy framework has the potential to foster dignity in the relationships between Christians and non-Christians in the world.[20]

This section has shown that in comparison to the corresponding frameworks of Balthasar and Volf a mutual hierarchy ecclesiological framework has great potential for good in the three ecclesiological areas surveyed. In the relation between a pastor and a congregation, it allows for both a distinct pastoral office and yet a genuine contribution by laity and the maximization of gifts through the flexibility and teamwork of the entire congregation. A mutual hierarchy framework also yields a different conception of trans-congregational relations as congregations, Christians, and other trans-congregational entities are encouraged to work together beyond the confines of the individual congregation. Finally, a mutual hierarchy framework also allows Christians and non-Christians to live and work together in a more fruitful manner, a way more mutually beneficial for all involved, so that the complex problems of the world may be better addressed and the gospel be given more opportunities for advancing.

CHAPTER CONCLUSION

This chapter has argued that a mutual hierarchy framework is preferable to both a hierarchical framework and an egalitarian framework in the realm of ecclesiology. An analysis of the hierarchical ecclesiological framework of Hans Urs von Balthasar has shown that for him all relationships are hierarchical in one direction so that the church has a pyramidal structure with the pope at the top. This tended to reduce the sort of vocation one exercises to commanding those lower down the pyramid or obeying those higher up. An analysis of the egalitarian ecclesiological framework of Miroslav Volf has shown that for him hierarchy becomes a typically negative exception so that it is difficult to account for the differences

---

20. Free-market capitalism involves Christians and non-Christians working together on a large scale; here reflecting on a mutual hierarchy framework could be helpful in considering economics. There is also potential in a mutual hierarchy framework to address the issue of denominationalism. Here the framework has the potential to help show that amidst ongoing debates there is a need for distinct denominations as well as dignified ecumenism and joint mission work. See also Sánchez, "Toward an Ecclesiology of Catholic Unity and Mission in the Borderlands," 17–34, as Sánchez similarly argues that a Christian should not have to choose between confession (or, in the broader term of the article, unity) and mission, but rather each mutually informs the other.

among Christian and even among human beings. For Volf, the sort of vocation one should exercise was diminished since the ideal becomes all doing nearly the same thing. In both cases, unnecessary ecclesiological choices were fostered, toward hierarchical elements in Balthasar, toward egalitarian elements in Volf, and toward maintenance over mission in both. In both cases ecclesial community was not accounted for as fully as it could be.

But a mutual hierarchy ecclesiological framework accounted for the uniqueness of ecclesial members, a concern of Balthasar, as well as for the dignity of ecclesial members, a concern of Volf. Here uniqueness was better accounted for than in Volf since each ecclesial member should exercise distinct hierarchies over the others. And dignity was better accounted for than in Balthasar since recognizing that all possess hierarchies also fosters recognizing that hierarchy, power, and vocation should be used to help and serve others rather than to try to lord power over or usurp the powers of others. Recognizing this mutual hierarchy fostered such things as the following: recognizing the complexities of situations, enabling flexibility to meet this complexity, fostering checks and balances against abuses of power, encouraging people and congregations to work to identify their own unique gifts, assessing how diverse gifts can complement each other, and better recognizing how the church lives in the image of the Trinity. The chapter thus briefly demonstrated these things through looking at the benefits of mutual hierarchy in the three ecclesial areas: relations between a pastor and a congregation, trans-congregational relations, and relations between the church and non-Christians.

6

Mutual Hierarchy amid the Triadic Macrostructure of the Gospel of Matthew

THE BIBLICAL BASIS FOR the doctrine of the Trinity in the previous chapters has chiefly been various verses from the Gospel of John that often seem to speak about this doctrine in an explicit manner. The question may now be asked, do the Scriptures have a more systematic way of teaching the doctrine of the Trinity? The present chapter will look at this question in the context of the Gospel of Matthew and do so in three basic steps. First, various structural proposals for the Gospel of Matthew and other biblical books and collections of biblical books will be surveyed, and a new triadic structure for Matthew connected to the three offices of Christ will be proposed. Second, the three thirds of Matthew identified will be analyzed in greater detail to show how each third emphasizes Christ exercising a distinct king-prophet-priest office in connection with an emphasis on the work of the Father, the Holy Spirit, and the Son, respectively. Finally, having established an emphasis on the distinct work of one divine person in each third of Matthew, I will show that each divine person (one divine person emphasized most in each third of Matthew) fosters the dignity of the other two rather than competing with them. By thus establishing the uniqueness and dignity of each divine person in connection with the three thirds identified in Matthew, the mutual hierarchy of the divine persons at a macro-level in Matthew will be evident. Finally, the chapter will briefly discuss how this mutual hierarchy reading of the Gospel of Matthew is potentially very fruitful for such practical matters as hermeneutics, sermon preparation, and personal Christian devotion.

A TRIADIC MACROSTRUCTURE IN MATTHEW

In this section, triadic structural proposals for various non-Matthean biblical books and collections of biblical books will be surveyed first. Following this, various major structural proposals for the Gospel of Matthew will be briefly considered. Next, the question will be asked of whether a triadic structuring of Matthew is plausible in light of the structural proposals considered. Finally, the broad outlines of this paper's triadic structural proposal for Matthew will be laid out.

The question should first be treated briefly of whether a triadic macrostructure can be found in non-Matthean biblical books or collections of biblical books. Probably the most well-known triadic grouping in the Old Testament is the one that sees three parts to the Old Testament as a whole. Although the Hebrew Scriptures and the Septuagint had different orderings of books, a triadic grouping of the Old Testament something like the following was common in biblical times, including by Jesus himself (Luke 24:44): the Law, the Prophets, and a third category of the Writings, Psalms, or History.[1] Even the Torah itself has a certain triadic character to it to the extent that Genesis clearly deals with matters long before the other four books, and Deuteronomy, as its name meaning "second law" suggests, was clearly distinguished from the first giving of the law where Israel remained at Mount Sinai in the books of Exodus, Leviticus, and Numbers.[2]

In the New Testament, each Gospel has holy week as a distinct concluding section, raising the question of whether there might also be a similar earlier division that would result in three thirds in a given Gospel. Here the Gospel of Luke has been widely accepted as triadic, with holy week at the end, a travel narrative near the middle that commences with the sending out of disciples near Luke 9:51, and other material preceding the travel narrative.[3] While not as obvious or definitive as in the Gospel

---

1. See, for example, Grabbe, "Law, the Prophets, and the Rest," 319–38.

2. On the relative independence of the book of Deuteronomy in the Torah see Sonnet, *Book within the Book*.

3. Denaux, "Delineation of the Lukan Travel Narrative," 3–37. Spivey and Moody, *Anatomy of the New Testament*, 156, sees a striking similarity between the structure of Luke and Acts. The order of Luke is Galilee, journey to Jerusalem, Jerusalem, while the

of Luke, the Gospel of Mark also has a conspicuous sending out of the disciples in Mark 6:6 after Jesus has called and appointed them earlier in the Gospel, which at least leaves open the possibility of a triadic structure of Mark.[4] John's Gospel is a strong candidate for having a middle third, for the heart of John's Gospel has a "festival cycle" in the Jewish calendar year prior to holy week as the scene moves conspicuously from Passover (John 6) to the Feast of Tabernacles (John 7:1—10:21) to Hanukkah (John 10:22—12:11).[5]

Given these precedents and possibilities for triadic proposals, might the Gospel of Matthew have a triadic structure? The most prominent structural proposal for Matthew is Benjamin Bacon's pentateuchal theory, which posits in Matthew, after the pattern of the Pentateuch, five discourses with preceding narratives, where each discourse is immediately followed by a variation of the formula "when Jesus had finished these sayings."[6] Charles Lohr built upon Bacon's observation of alternating narrative and discourse material in Matthew and posited a chiastic "book" structure where earlier sections of Matthew match up with later sections. Given that the Pentateuch can conceivably be divided into three sections, the Pentateuch-based Matthean proposals of Bacon and Lohr can conceivably harmonize with a triadic structuring of Matthew.[7] A third structural proposal, that of Jack Kingsbury in connection with the phrase "From that time Jesus began" in Matthew 4:17 and 16:21, is explicitly triadic, but it is unclear how this proposal should relate to

---

order of Acts is Jerusalem, journeys of missionaries, Rome.

4. Moloney, *Gospel of Mark*, while seeing the commonly-held major division of Mark occurring at Mark 8:31 nevertheless sees smaller divisions in Mark as well, with the fourth division being 6:6b—8:30 ("Jesus and the Disciples") and thus seeing 6:6 as structurally significant. Witherington, *Gospel of Mark*, has 6:6b—8:38 as a distinct section entitled "The Tests of Discipleship; the Trials of God's Anointed One." See also Byrne, *Costly Freedom*, 107–33, where Byrne provides commentary on Mark 6:6b—8:21, which section he entitles "Jesus Extends His Ministry."

5. Scholars are increasingly noting the centrality of feasts in John. See, for example, Bauckham, "Holiness of Jesus and His Disciples in the Gospel of John," 95–113; Coloe, *God Dwells with Us*; Wheaton, *Role of Jewish Feasts in John's Gospel*; and Yee, *Jewish Feasts and the Gospel of John*.

6. Davies and Allison, *Matthew*, 1:58–72, surveys some of the major structural proposals for Matthew. See also Luz, *Matthew 1–7: A Commentary*, 1–13.

7. Luz, *Matthew 1–7*, 9, concludes on the basis of his survey of Matthew's structuring methods that "a similarity of Matthean compositional devices with those of Old Testament and Jewish literature is prominent."

Bacon's pentateuchal-based structure, as Davies and Allison note.[8] Davies and Allison also note the structural significance of sending in Matthew 9:35—10:4, which sending, as seen in the previous paragraph, has a structural parallel in Luke (and perhaps also Mark) as sending is closely associated with the transition from the first third to the middle third of Luke's Gospel (and perhaps also Mark's).[9] A triadic proposal for the Gospel of Matthew is thus far conceivable based on other triadic structural proposals for Matthew's Gospel and other biblical narratives.[10]

Another important background work for considering Matthew as triadic is Robert Sherman's book *King, Priest, and Prophet: A Trinitarian Theology of the Atonement*. Sherman argues that a key way that Jesus fulfills the Old Testament is through fulfilling the three key leadership roles of the Old Testament: king, priest, and prophet. Although Sherman surveys the New Testament as a whole, his thesis obviously holds for the Gospel of Matthew, which heavily emphasizes Jesus fulfilling the Old Testament.[11] For Sherman, the categories of king, priest, and prophet are important, albeit not exhaustive, biblical categories for describing the work of the Trinity and have a special connection to the Father, Son, and Spirit, respectively, as well as to the classical theories of the atonement: the *Christus victor*, the vicarious sacrifice, and the empowering exemplar theory, respectively.[12] As will be seen further especially in the next section, the offices of king, priest, and prophet figure very prominently

---

8. Davies and Allison, *Matthew*, 1:61–72, 85–87, also note another structural foundation in Matthew: the pervasiveness of triads in his text. Luz, *Matthew 1–7*, 5–9, makes a similar point and notes various other structural methods used repeatedly by Matthew.

9. On the structural significance of Matthew 9:35—10:4 see Davies and Allison, *Matthew*, 2:143.

10. Luz, *Matthew 1–7*, 2, notes that while there appears to be broad agreement in scholarship that Matthew can be divided into sections, there is little agreement over how to divide it.

11. Allison, *New Moses*, argues that, in Matthew's Gospel, Moses is a type for Jesus in his royal and prophetic offices. That Moses was also a priest can be seen in Moses's authority over Aaron in Exodus 4:16 (see also Lev 9:23, 10:1–3). See also Exodus 32:11–14 where Moses intercedes with God in a priestly manner after the golden calf episode led by Aaron the high priest.

12. Sherman, *King, Priest, and Prophet*, 23, has a chart summarizing Sherman's views. See further chapter 1 where Sherman situates his views among various current proposals for understanding the atonement.

in Matthew, making Sherman's work potentially very fruitful for understanding this Gospel.[13]

How then might the Gospel of Matthew be structured triadically? The most easily recognizable third of Matthew is the final one, the holy week narrative (Matt 21–28). Here Jesus's priestly work comes to the fore culminating in his death and resurrection on behalf of all human beings. Key to demarcating the other two thirds in Matthew is Jesus's sending out his disciples/apostles, beginning in 9:35—10:4 in the lead-up to Jesus's second sermon.[14] Before this time, the disciples had largely been spectators of Jesus's powerful activity, for example witnessing his authoritative miracles in chapters 8 and 9. But 10:2 changes the disciples' title to apostles (the only occurrence of this word in Matthew), 10:2–4 contains the only instance in Matthew where the Twelve are listed together by name, and Jesus's sending them out on a limited mission in 10:5 denotes a more active role for them than before, a sort of deliberate apprenticeship.[15] Reminiscent of the prophets being sent out in the Old Testament, the apostles in 9:35—20:34 are new prophets sent out by Jesus. Finally, 9:35 as a boundary for the beginning of the middle third of Matthew (9:35—20:34) can harmonize with Bacon's pentateuchal theory for Matthew if Jesus's second discourse (9:35–10:42), third discourse (13:1–52), and fourth discourse (Matt 18), each considered as a unit with the succeeding narrative, are grouped together after the pattern of Exodus, Leviticus, and Numbers in the Torah.[16]

---

13. Sherman himself recognizes a strong tie between the Gospel of Matthew and the king, priest, and prophet categories. The index at the back of the book has more entries for Matthew than any other biblical book.

14. Luz, *Matthew 1–7*, 10, argues that that the summary statements in 4:23 and 9:35 form a decisive inclusio containing the Sermon on the Mount and the two miracle chapters of Matthew 8–9. For Luz, the sending discourse of Matthew 10 inaugurates the ecclesial continuation of Jesus's activity.

15. Sherman, *King, Priest, and Prophet*, 235–36, asserts that Matthew 9:35 indicates that the disciples' work after they are sent out by Jesus will be a recapitulation of Christ's own activity of proclaiming the gospel and doing miracles up to this point in Matthew. Luz, *Matthew 8–20*, 59–60, sees various connections between what Jesus did prior to Matthew 10 and what the disciples are commissioned to do in Matthew 10.

16. Clark and Waard, "Discourse Structure in Matthew's Gospel," 1–97, sees the following three thirds in Matthew: chapters 1–9, 10–18, and 19–28. This proposal is very similar to mine, only mine sees the second major transition occurring at the beginning of holy week, which is arguably a more natural dividing point that occurs in the other Gospels as well.

Further supporting my triadic proposal for Matthew's Gospel is the symmetry that it supports, a symmetry quite reminiscent of Lohr's chiastic book proposal. Consider the following outline that looks at Matthew's five discourses and the major narratives in Matthew, with chapter locations in parentheses:

1. *The First Third of Matthew (1:1—9:34)*
   Narrative (1–4)
   First Discourse (5:1—7:27)
   Narrative (7:28—9:34)

2. *The Middle Third of Matthew (9:35—20:34)*
   Second Discourse and Succeeding Narrative (9:35—12:50)
   Third Discourse and Succeeding Narrative (13–17)
   Fourth Discourse and Succeeding Narrative (18–20)

3. *The Final Third of Matthew (21-28)*
   Narrative (21–22)
   Fifth Discourse (23–25)
   Narrative (26–28)

A number of things should be noted here. The first third and the final third each have the same structure: narrative, discourse, narrative. And in both of these thirds, the sermon is about three chapters long and is flanked by narratives of near the same length. This structuring also accounts for Lohr's chiastic structuring seeing the initial narrative (Jesus's birth and beginnings in Matt 1–4), prior to the first discourse, having a certain structural parallel with the concluding narrative (Jesus's death and resurrection in Matt 26–28) after the fifth discourse.[17] There is also considerable symmetry in the middle third of Matthew. Here each of the three sections begins with a discourse about a chapter long and is followed by a narrative. Thus the middle third has three sections that are similar in length. In fact, all nine of the total proposed sections of

---

17. Lohr's initial three sections are nearly identical with mine. His final three sections are the same except that he sees chapters 19–22 as a section whereas I have chapters 21–22 as a section. But in between these six sections Lohr has the following five sections: 10, 11–12, 13, 14–17, 18; here Lohr has simply continued to divide the text into alternating discourses and narrative sections in keeping with his structural method. See Lohr, "Oral Techniques in the Gospel of Matthew," 427.

Matthew are similar in length, which adds further nuance to the fact that each of Matthew's three thirds is similar in length.

A final initial argument for Matthew containing three thirds in the way that has been described comes from statistics. In the New Testament forms of the words "king" (βασιλεύς or βασιλεία) and "prophet" (προφήτης) occur in Matthew more than in any other book, and some form of the term "priest" (ἱερεύς, ἀρχιερεύς, ἱερατεία, or ἱερωσύνη) occurs only slightly more in the Book of Hebrews (thirty-nine) than in Matthew (twenty-eight). Clearly these terms are central to Matthew's Gospel. And if Matthew is divided in the triadic manner just described, the dispersion of these terms supports the proposed structure. For example, in Matthew's telling of holy week in Matthew 21–28, the word priest occurs twenty-three times, far more than in either of the other two proposed thirds. Similarly, the word for prophet occurs thirteen times in the middle third of Matthew (9:35—20:34), more than in either of the other two thirds. Finally, although a form of the word king occurs the same number of times (twenty) in the final third of Matthew as it does in the first third, it must be kept in mind both that there is intense irony in holy week where Jesus is largely called a king by his opponents as a form of mockery and that Matthew has many other ways to depict Christ as a king than just explicitly referring to him as one, for example, by including him in the listing of numerous kings in the genealogy at the beginning of the book (1:1–17). In this way, the statistical dispersion of the terms king, prophet, and priest supports the proposed triadic structure.

A UNIQUE WORK OF CHRIST MOST PROMINENT IN EACH THIRD OF MATTHEW

This section will look in greater detail at the proposed three thirds of Matthew and how each third emphasizes a different work of Christ and a different divine person. An explanation will first be given as to what it means that one divine person is emphasized most in each third of Matthew. Following this, each third will be analyzed independently. For each third, the thought of Robert Sherman on the king-prophet-priest category with its corresponding divine person for that third will first be summarized and critically appropriated, and then the text of Matthew will be analyzed in light of this.

What does it mean to say that one work of Christ, and one divine person, is emphasized more than the others in each third of Matthew? Terminology is important here, as can be seen by briefly considering the cross. A divine person's vocation does not necessarily mean that that divine person is exercising more "brute power" than another. For example, Jesus sees the cross as central to his own work, and yet he does not exercise much brute power at the cross. Jesus at the cross exercises a very powerful love, and exhibits a tremendous ability to voluntarily suffer, but this is distinguished from power in the sense of doing miracles, for example. A helpful term for gauging the vocation of a divine person in a Gospel narrative is "prominence." Prominence refers to how much a divine person's work stands out or is conspicuous at a given time. For example, in a play a character is often more prominent in connection with such things as being in the middle of the stage, having the spotlight on him or her, and speaking an important line. At the cross, the Son stands out; his work especially highlights the fact that only he as incarnate, and not the Father or the Spirit, can die on a cross for sin. Another helpful term is "properness." The Son at the cross does what is most proper to him. A Christian can to a certain extent prophetically proclaim the gospel in the power of the Spirit so that it is somewhat proper to him or her as a Christian, but only the Son could have as his proper priestly work dying for sin at the cross and leading creation to completion in his resurrection.[18] With these things said, the following points should be clarified: each divine person always works to his capacity, the divine persons always work together, and the total prominence of the divine persons always remains constant. Nevertheless, the prominence or properness of the vocation of each divine person varies at different points in the narrative of Matthew.

Matthew 1:1—9:34

Coming now to consider the royal first third of Matthew, Robert Sherman asserts that Christ in his life is a king who acts on behalf of God the Father, the great king and creator from the Old Testament.[19] Here there

---

18. Sherman, *King, Priest, and Prophet*, 63, 251–52, uses the language of appropriateness, which is nearly the same as properness, to describe both the vocation of each divine person and the corresponding office of Christ.

19. On God being the great king of the Old Testament see, for example, 1 Samuel 10:19 where Israel's asking for a king is a rejection of God (see also Deut 17:14). Sherman, *King, Priest, and Prophet*, chapter 4, contains Sherman's main treatment of the

is a dual character to Christ's royal office as, on the one hand, Christ is authorized by God the Father to be a king and, on the other hand, Christ actually acts like a king on behalf of the Father. Here Sherman associates the royal office with a *Christus victor* view of the atonement in such a way that Christ the king speaks and acts with authority, especially for the purpose of defeating the devil and oppressive forces in the world. Finally, intrinsic to these things is that the office of king is associated primarily with the past.

The first third of the Gospel of Matthew, Matthew 1:1—9:34, emphasizes Jesus's vocation as a king in a way that largely agrees with Sherman's definition of this office, as can be seen by looking at the first four chapters of Matthew. The genealogy in 1:1-17 has a strong royal theme as it mentions various patriarchs and kings of Israel from the distant past, culminating in the final king, or Christ, Jesus.[20] In 1:18-25 God the Father, in arguably the greatest miracle since the creation of the world, ultimately is the one who sends his Son into the world, as can be seen in the name Immanuel, God with us.[21] In Matthew 2, the Magi come to worship Jesus as king, and then the corrupt king Herod seeks to kill him.[22] A new exodus theme is present here in the deliverance of the holy family, as evident in the quotation in 2:15 referring to God calling his son out of Egypt.[23] Here it is crucial to keep in mind a point extensively taught by

---

royal office.

20. Davies and Allison, *Matthew*, 1:161-90, emphasize the royal theme in the genealogy and assert that "David the King" plays a central role. See also Kennedy, *Recapitulation of Israel*, 81-102, which argues that the movement from Abraham to David in the genealogy is an ascent to kingship that is rooted in the great promise of nationhood that was first given to Abraham. The subsequent descent in the kingship theme after David and especially after the exile to Babylon points forward to the coming true king. Fretheim, "Reclamation of Creation," 360, asserts that Abraham's call is tied to God's creational work and involves all the families of the earth.

21. Davies and Allison, *Matthew*, 1:197-98, sees a parallel between the juxtaposition of Matthew 1:1-17 and 1:18-25 with the juxtaposition of Genesis 1 and Genesis 2. If so, God as the creator is recalled or recapitulated.

22. Davies and Allison, *Matthew*, 1:224-84, argues that Matthew 2 in various ways asserts the kingship of Jesus against the false kingship of Herod. See also Deut 17:15, where God says that a foreigner may not be set up as king of Israel; Herod's father was an Edomite, and Herod was a client king of Judea on behalf of Rome as a foreign power.

23. See Quarles, *Theology of Matthew*, 73-96, for a helpful discussion of Matthew 2 stressing Jesus as a Davidic king and Matthew's developing the new David theme generally. Kennedy, *Recapitulation of Israel*, 103-53, looks at numerous ways that Matthew 2 has the exodus as its primary background.

Terrence Fretheim that creation themes were intricately intertwined with exodus motifs in Jewish thought as the latter recapitulated and partially fulfilled the former.[24] In Matthew 3, Jesus at his baptism is anointed with the Holy Spirit by the Father, recalling the repeated mention of the royal titles Christ and king in the genealogy.[25] Here John the Baptist is associated with the advent of "the kingdom of heaven (3:2)," and the Father's words at Jesus's baptism are likely partially based on Psalm 2:7, which references the royal Messiah, and thus make the familiar Old Testament equation of Israel's king being God's son.[26] God's anointing Jesus with his Spirit in connection with water and a hovering dove also involves a new creation theme as it hearkens back to Genesis 1:2 and the Father's working through water and the Spirit hovering over the newly created world.[27] There also seems to be a new exodus/creation theme here in the sense that Jesus is one with his people, like Moses of old, delivering them as a "son" (Exod 4:22–23, 19:6; Matt 2:15) through water in the midst of powerful enemies. In 4:1–11, Jesus at his miraculous forty-day temptation defeats the devil, an obvious *Christus victor* theme, by repeatedly quoting Scripture and appealing to the Father as the true king and God who is to be worshipped.[28] This also again contains a clear new exodus/creation theme, recalling Israel being tempted for forty years in the desert

---

24. Fretheim, *Exodus*, deals extensively with exodus and new exodus themes being new creation themes, for example by seeing God bringing light amidst the chaos and darkness of the plagues in Egypt recalling similar themes in the first few verses of Genesis 1. My thanks to Chad Bird for pointing me to Fretheim's commentary in personal correspondence. See also Davies and Allison, *Matthew*, 1:345.

25. Barber, *Jesus as the Davidic Temple Builder*, 937–38, argues that David or the Davidic king were strongly associated with the anointed one, or Christ, in the Old Testament. In connection with Matthew 3, Barber mentions that when David was anointed king the Spirit of the Lord came upon him (1 Sam 16:13) and that when Solomon, the son of David, was anointed king he was taken down to a river (1 Kings 1:38–40).

26. Davies and Allison, *Matthew*, 1:336–40. The allusion to Psalm 2:7 in Matthew 3 also suggests that the mentioning of God's son in the Hosea quotation in Matthew 2:15 has royal connotations. See also Barber, "Jesus as the Davidic Temple Builder," 938, which lists various biblical and extra-biblical texts that connect divine sonship to the royal son of David.

27. Davies and Allison, *Matthew*, 1:331–34, 345.

28. Sherman, *King, Priest, and Prophet*, 111, mentions the view of Morna Hooker that the temptation is part of a cosmic confrontation between God and the devil. Luz, *Matthew 1–7*, 144, asserts that a main idea in both Jesus's baptism and temptation is that Jesus submits to God's will.

after the exodus.²⁹ There is also an abundance of Scripture quotations at Jesus's temptation, continuing the strong tendency to quote Scripture in the first few chapters of Matthew, which recalls such themes that Sherman associates with the royal office as the importance of the past and the recapitulation of the Father's will as expressed in the Old Testament.³⁰ Thus the first four chapters of Matthew strongly emphasize the office of king through such things as repeatedly referencing the term king and actual kings, Jesus being authorized as king by God the Father, new exodus/creation themes, the *Christus victor* theme of Jesus defeating the devil, the incarnation being a great miracle recalling God's creation of the world, and emphasizing the past through formula quotations of Scripture and recapitulating God's will from the Old Testament.

Jesus's first discourse, the so-called Sermon on the Mount (Matt 5:1—7:27), also emphasizes Jesus's office as king, even if perhaps not quite as prominently as the first four chapters of Matthew. For example, the setting of the sermon points to the Father's leadership of Jesus, such as through Jesus ascending a mountain, reminiscent of Moses ascending Mt. Sinai to see God and receive the law (Exod 19:3).³¹ The beginning of the sermon stresses blessings that come from the Father (Matt 5:8-9), which blessings are structured around access to the kingdom at the beginning and end of the beatitudes (5:3, 10-11).³² Jesus goes on to recapitulate and authoritatively interpret some of the Ten Command-

---

29. Davies and Allison, *Matthew*, 1:344-45. Allison in discussing reasons why Jesus appears both as the new Moses and the new Israel in Matthew 1-4, notes, "The Messiah was, at least in rabbinic sources, to be both like Moses and a king; but in ancient thought a king represented, could indeed be said to be, his people: so why imagine that Matthew was unable to equate the Messianic king like Moses with true Israel" (*New Moses*, 142). See further ibid., 137-72. Kennedy, *Recapitulation of Israel*, 153-215, argues that Jesus's Baptism and subsequent testing in the desert mirrors Israel's exodus through the Red Sea followed by wandering in the wilderness; this would make Jesus's baptism and temptation in the wilderness together have a new exodus/creation theme.

30. Goulder, "Sections and Lections in Matthew," 79, notes the bunching of formula citations of Scripture in the first four chapters of Matthew. For more on a new creation theme in Matthew 1-4 see Allison, *New Moses*, 200-207.

31. For further reflections on the setting of the Sermon on the Mount recalling Moses see Allison, *New Moses*, 172-180; Davies, *Setting of the Sermon on the Mount*; and Scaer, *Sermon on the Mount*, 49-70.

32. Consider also the doxology: "Praise God from whom all blessings flow." See also Sherman, *King, Priest, and Prophet*, 161. Allison, *New Moses*, 180-82, connects the beatitude on meekness with Moses's meekness and Jesus's being a meek king in the sense of clemency.

ments, which is a new exodus/creation theme since Moses's receiving of the law came in the context of the exodus.[33] Here Jesus also seems to refer to the Father as the great king of Jerusalem (5:35) and explicitly speaks of the Father as complete (5:48). In Matthew 6, Jesus teaches that prayer should be addressed to the Father and that the Father is trustworthy to provide for needs. Here disciples are to seek God's kingdom and righteousness (6:33), which suggests that earlier mentions of these terms in Matthew should be associated with the Father (3:2, 3:15, 4:17). Finally, given the focus on the Father in the sermon, the crowds' astonishment at the authority of Jesus's teaching after the sermon suggests this authority is ultimately associated with the Father (7:29).[34] Thus the Sermon on the Mount emphasizes the office of king through such things as repeatedly referencing the terms "king" and "kingdom" and associating them with the Father, stressing the Father's care as creator in connection with prayer and new exodus/creation themes, and stressing the Father's authority.

The narrative material after the sermon (7:28—9:34) also has the Father's kingship as a prominent theme as Jesus does a series of powerful miracles. Sherman sees the office of king evident in these chapters in such things as Jesus doing a miracle for a gentile centurion who like Jesus was under the authority of another (8:5–13),[35] being a master of the sea like God in the Old Testament (8:23–27),[36] driving out demons (8:28–34),[37] and healing a paralytic so that the crowds glorified God who had given such authority to human beings (9:1–8).[38] The account of Jesus and the centurion (8:5–13) not only has the centurion allude to Jesus being under the authority of another, bringing God to mind, it also twice references the kingdom in this context. When Jesus then heals the paralytic, the crowds who saw it feared and glorified God, who had given such authority to men (9:8), which recalls the reactions by the crowd to

---

33. On Jesus's words' relation to the Ten Commandments and the Torah see Gibbs, *Matthew 1:1–11:1*, 276–79. On a new exodus theme in connection with Jesus's words see Allison, *New Moses*, 182–90. See also Sherman, *King, Priest, and Prophet*, 224–25; and Fretheim, "Reclamation of Creation," 354–65.

34. Allison, *New Moses*, 268, 276, argues that Jesus's primary attribute in Matthew is probably authority and that Matthew's first seven chapters are a chief illustration of this.

35. Sherman, *King, Priest, and Prophet*, 132.

36. Sherman, *King, Priest, and Prophet*, 119, 128.

37. Sherman, *King, Priest, and Prophet*, 118–19, 126–27.

38. Sherman, *King, Priest, and Prophet*, 130–31.

Jesus's authority at the conclusion of the Sermon on the Mount (7:28–29). Jesus's healing of two blind men in 9:27–31 also references Jesus as the Son of David, recalling the last use of this royal appellation in the infancy narrative with its strong royal themes (1:20).[39] Through these and the other powerful miracle accounts in 7:28—9:34, Jesus's authority is seen not just in his being authorized as a king or speaking as a king like before, but now especially in his acting like a king.[40] Thus Matthew 7:28—9:34 emphasizes the office of king through such things as referencing royal terms in the context of Jesus being closely associated with the Father and doing powerful miracles, and Jesus powerfully demonstrating his authority over demons and the effects of evil in agreement with a *Christus victor* theme.

Matthew 9:35—20:34

Moving now to the office of prophet, Sherman asserts that Christ in his life is a prophet on behalf of the Holy Spirit.[41] Here there is a dual character to Christ's prophetic office. On the one hand, Christ is an object of spiritual prophecy *empowering* disciples in line with the Spirit empowering the prophets of old. On the other hand, Christ in the power of the Spirit works spontaneously as a prophet to provide an *example* to the disciples. Here Sherman associates the prophetic office with an empowering exemplar view of the atonement in such a way that Christ the prophet does such works as the following: remedy human weakness, ignorance, finitude, and uncertainty about the meaning or purpose of life. Finally, whereas Sherman primarily associates the office of prophet with a future time frame, this chapter will instead associate it with the present.

The middle third of Matthew (Matt 9:35—20:34) emphasizes Jesus's vocation as a prophet in a way that largely agrees with Sherman's

---

39. Barber, *Jesus as the Davidic Temple Builder*, 938, argues that Jesus's exorcisms and healings are particularly tied to his Davidic identity, for example since both David and Solomon were known for such things. France, *Matthew*, 284, notes that "son of David" occurs more frequently in Matthew's Gospel than in the whole of the rest of the New Testament, and that seven of his nine uses of it are peculiar to his Gospel.

40. See Quarles, *Theology of Matthew*, 85, for a listing of Old Testament descriptions of the Davidic messiah, many of which involve powerful works. See also Allison, *New Moses*, 207–13, for possible connections between Jesus's ten miracles in this section and Moses's ten plagues at the exodus.

41. Sherman, *King, Priest, and Prophet*, chapter 6, contains Sherman's main treatment of the prophetic office.

definition of this office, as can be seen in 9:35—12:50. Jesus's sending out of the disciples on a limited mission with his second sermon in Matthew 10 is a new kind of task for Jesus, one that especially reveals the proper work of the Spirit, who similarly empowered the prophets of old (9:37-38; 10:19-20).[42] Jesus's sending the disciples out is part of an apprenticeship where the disciples are commissioned to do the sort of works (10:1) that he himself had been doing (9:32-35).[43] 10:5 is the first time in Matthew's Gospel that the important term "send" (ἀπέστειλεν) is used in reference to the disciples; this word send especially fits with the office of prophet, as prophets were known for being mobile in the Old Testament in comparison to kings and priests, who were generally considered more stationary.[44] Jesus repeats the word prophet three times in connection with his sending of the disciples (10:40-41), and Jesus refers to himself as the prophet Jonah a little later (12:39-40).[45] Significantly, Jesus associates this new prophetic work with shepherding (ποιμένα, 9:36) and being a laborer (ἐργάται, 9:37-38), both of which terms are associated with pastors in the New Testament (e.g., Eph 4:11, 1 Pet 2:25, 2 Cor 11:13, 1 Tim 5:17-18). This points to a specific vocation of the disciples being emphasized in contrast to the term disciple itself, which can be used as a designation for new Christians more in the context of faith than of specific vocations

42. Sherman, *King, Priest, and Prophet*, 235-36, argues that Christ's sending his disciples out in Matthew 9:35—10:41 is an especially helpful illustration for Christ's prophetic office. Here Sherman asserts that the details that Matthew recounts in 10:16-20 make especially clear the connection between the wisdom the disciples receive and Christ's role as teacher. Similarly, Sherman in reference to 10:19-20 says that "the Spirit uses Christ as the mediator or conduit for reaching his followers" (ibid., 252). Basser and Cohen, *Gospel of Matthew and Judaic Traditions*, 245-46, see 9:36 referencing Numbers 27:16-18 where Moses just after being told he is about to die worries about his people being like sheep without a shepherd in the context of the Lord commanding Moses to lay hands on Joshua.

43. Gibbs, *Matthew 1:1-11:1*, 500, argues that Jesus's authority over unclean spirits and disease in Matthew 8-9 is the foundation for the disciples having similar authority in 10:1. See also Luz, *Matthew 1-7*, 10.

44. In the Old Testament the prophets especially seemed to be of the people, more "grassroots" as we might say today, in comparison to the royal office ruling over the people, often in connection with a throne, and the priestly office that mediated between the people and God and that was centered at the tabernacle or temple. In various ways the prophets critiqued Israel's kings and priests and appealed directly to the people.

45. Sherman, *King, Priest, and Prophet*, 235, argues that the sending out of the disciples in the second sermon to preach and do miracles anticipates the events of Pentecost in Acts; Sherman also cites Matthew 10:40-41 to refer to the disciples as "deputy prophets."

(28:19). Following Jesus's instruction in Matthew 10, the narrative that follows shows Jesus illustrating the commissioning instructions he has just given the disciples, beginning with the very next verses that speak about the teaching, preaching, and deeds of Jesus himself (11:1–2).[46] Like Jesus, the disciples will be empowered to serve others in their vocations as a sort of conduit of the Spirit as the Spirit will speak through them (Matt 10:16–20, 12:31–32).[47] Thus 9:35—12:50 emphasizes the office of prophet in general agreement with Sherman through such things as repeatedly mentioning prophets, Jesus empowering disciples in the power of the Spirit, and Jesus helping to remedy human uncertainty about the purpose of life by giving his disciples concrete vocations and explaining these vocations.

Jesus's prophetic work seems to reach its climax in his third sermon and the narrative material following it (Matt 13–17). Jesus's third sermon begins by speaking in practical terms about sowing the seed of the gospel in the world (13:1–9, 24–30) and seems to reach its climax in the two parables about the growth of the kingdom (13:31–33). This growth is the ultimate goal of Jesus's prophetic work, and the agricultural language of the parables seems to fulfill Jesus's language about workers and harvesting that Jesus used in the introduction to his second sermon (9:36–38). The parables near the end of the sermon also begin to anticipate the fact that sacrifice will be needed for the kingdom's growth, such as in a man selling all that he has in order to purchase treasure (13:44–46). Five times in the context of this sermon there is a reference to either prophets or prophecy (13:14, 13:17, 13:35, 13:57, 14:5). Following Jesus's sermon emphasizing the growth of the kingdom, the narrative shows the kingdom's growth and the disciples working harder than at any other point in the Gospel. Here Jesus delegates to the disciples the task of helping him to distribute food to huge crowds at the feeding of the 5,000 (14:13–21) and the feeding of the 4,000 (15:32–39). At the same time Jesus also empowers Peter to do the only miracle that Matthew explicitly records as done by a disciple (14:28–33). Following Jesus's intense training of and mission

---

46. The subordinate nature of the disciples' work in comparison to Jesus's can be seen in the fact that Matthew nowhere in the subsequent couple of chapters records any of the things the disciples did when they were sent out. See, for example, Morosco, "Matthew's Formation of a Commissioning Type-Scene," 553. See also Luz, *Matthew 1–7*, 12. One reason for the disciples not actually going out after the second sermon may be that Matthew is still narrating the commissioning of the disciples, with the mission proper not beginning until the third sermon and following narrative.

47. Sherman, *King, Priest, and Prophet*, 220–22, 235–36, 252.

work with the disciples, Jesus speaks of building the church in connection with Peter's great confession (16:18), although Jesus soon afterward makes clear that the growth of the church will also be accompanied by bearing a cross (16:24).[48] Thus Matthew 13–17 emphasizes the office of prophet in general agreement with Sherman through such things as repeatedly mentioning prophets and prophecy, Jesus fostering the growth of the kingdom by continuing to empower his disciples and more clearly providing them an example to follow, and Jesus helping to remedy human weakness and ignorance through training the disciples in the midst of mission work to large crowds of people.

Jesus's fourth sermon (Matt 18) and the narrative material following it (Matt 19–20) provide an intimate example for Jesus's disciples to imitate of being a merciful prophet. Jesus in the fourth sermon mentions the kingdom four times (18:1, 3, 4, 23) and calls for mercy, which sheds further light on the kingdom that had been mentioned often in the third sermon in Matthew 13 (verses 11, 19, 24, 31, 33, 38, 41, 43, 44, 45, 47, and 52).[49] Jesus then goes on to illustrate his words through actions. For example, after Jesus sternly warns in his sermon that the disciples must show mercy to little children (18:6), he has mercy on them as they quickly fail to do so (19:13–15). Similarly, after Jesus has warned against false greatness (18:1–4), he has patience with James and John selfishly wanting to have the best seats in the kingdom in a worldly sense (20:20–28).[50] Thus Matthew 18–20 emphasizes the office of prophet in general agreement with Sherman through such things as Jesus fostering the growth of the Spirit-led kingdom by giving his disciples an example of mercy and sacrifice to follow and by training his disciples to remedy human weakness.

Matthew 21–28

Moving now to the office of priest, Sherman asserts that Christ in his life is most properly a priest in connection with a vicarious sacrifice view of

---

48. Davies and Allison, *Matthew*, 2:649, asserts that Matthew 13:53—18:35 is the portion of Matthew where the theme of the church dominates as Jesus formally establishes the church and gives it instruction.

49. Sherman, *King, Priest, and Prophet*, 226, asserts that Jesus is a prophet who turns worldly wisdom on its head in the context of Matt 18:12–14 and Matt 20:1–16.

50. Here the disciples are "little" in a much less innocent sense than they were at their commissioning in 10:40–42. See also Sherman, *King, Priest, and Prophet*, 149.

the atonement.⁵¹ Here there is a dual character to Christ's priestly office as he is both a priest and a sacrifice. Just as in the Old Testament there were certain qualifications to be a priest, so too with Jesus, only in his case he had the ultimate qualification of being divine, which was necessary to make the ultimate sacrifice. As for Jesus being an actual sacrifice, negatively his sacrifice removes the separation between God and humans, and positively it establishes a new covenant between God and human beings and anticipates the fellowship of heaven. Finally, whereas Sherman primarily associates the office of priest with a present time frame, this chapter will instead associate it with the future.

The narrative section Matthew 21–22 that initiates holy week (Matt 21–28) emphasizes Jesus's vocation as a priest in a way that largely agrees with Sherman's definition of this office. The temple dominates the final third of Matthew as it is the place where Jesus debates with his opponents (21:12–17, 23; 26:55), where he delivers his final discourse (24:1), and in the passion narrative it is key to the charges against Jesus (26:61; 27:40) and to his death (27:51).⁵² This is significant because the temple was the chief place of work for priests in the Old Testament. And so the beginning of holy week contains various debates by Jesus against his opponents at the temple over his qualifications to do the things that he is doing.⁵³ For example, at the beginning of holy week, Jesus accuses those in the temple of turning it into a den of robbers, whereas Jesus seems to call the temple his own house and calls it a house of prayer (21:13). A little later Jesus has a series of debates with messengers from the Pharisees (22:15–22), the Sadducees (22:23–33), and the Pharisees themselves (22:34–46) over who Jesus is and what he does.⁵⁴ Jesus as the true priest wins the argument

---

51. Sherman, *King, Priest, and Prophet*, chapter 5, contains Sherman's main treatment of the priestly office.

52. Thirteen out of the sixteen occurrences of the word temple (ναός) in Matthew occur during holy week.

53. Davies and Allison, *Matthew*, 162–63, 168–69, note that in Jesus's debates with his opponents in Matthew 21–22 his opponents asked him questions that were traps in spite of the obvious facts testifying to who Jesus was; in spite of skill in setting traps, these opponents also easily fell into traps themselves, and their responses to Jesus's questions show no creativity or wit, especially compared to Jesus's responses.

54. Jesus's qualifications in terms of what he does seem to revolve around the fact that Jesus loves God (who was most prominent in the first third of Matthew) and loves human beings (who were subjects of the Spirit's training work in the middle third of Matthew). See, for example, 22:34–40, which speaks of love of God and love of neighbor and associates these with the Law and the Prophets.

about credentials against false priests, as can be seen in his pronouncing judgment on his opponents in Matthew 23.[55] Jesus also does the last of his miracles at the beginning of holy week, cursing the fig tree in 21:18-22. There is irony here in that Jesus in holy week does his most proper work and yet does few miracles, an irony that will intensify as Jesus's suffering increases as holy week proceeds and is fitting for Jesus laying down his life as a vicarious sacrifice.[56] Thus Matthew 21-22 emphasizes the office of priest in general agreement with Sherman through such things as its setting (largely at the temple) and Jesus demonstrating his qualifications against priestly opponents.

Jesus's last sermon, Matthew 23-25, also contains priestly themes, alluding again to Jesus's qualifications as a priest and anticipating his sacrifice. The opening of the sermon (Matt 23) shows that Jesus's qualifications greatly exceed those of his opponents. Here Jesus distinguishes himself from his persecutors in the context of the temple and priestly things associated with it like the altar and throne room (23:16-22), tithing (23:23-24), ceremonial purity regulations (23:25-28), and blood guilt in the context of the sanctuary and altar (23:29-36). This last sermon of Jesus also agrees with the priestly theme of association with the future. The apocalyptic language of the sermon points to a near future where Jesus will bear apocalyptic suffering (24:44), a more distant future where the disciples will testify about the gospel of Jesus (24:14), and a remote future, even the end of the world (25:31-46).[57] Thus Matthew 23-25 emphasizes the office of priest in general agreement with Sherman through such things as judging against the qualifications of Jesus' priestly opponents, a setting at the temple with various articles of furniture in the temple mentioned, and Jesus looking to the future and alluding to suffering and the atonement.

---

55. That Matthew groups together Jesus's opponents as false priests is supported by the fact that the chief priests are almost always listed first in groupings of Jesus's opponents. See 2:4; 16:21; 20:18; 21:15; 21:23; 21:45; 26:3; 26:47; 26:59; 27:1; 27:3; 27:12; 27:20; and 27:41.

56. Sherman, *King, Priest, and Prophet*, 123-24, also notes the irony in holy week. Helpful is one of the definitions for irony in Merriam-Webster's online dictionary: "incongruity between the actual result of a sequence of events and the normal or expected result."

57. For the fifth discourse having fulfillment in the near future and the distant future, see Gibbs, *Jerusalem and Parousia*; and Cooper, "Adaptive Eschatological Inference," 59-80.

Priestly themes build to a climax in the passion narrative in Matthew 26–28. Immediately following Jesus's last sermon, Jesus reminds the disciples of his earlier passion predictions, assuming that they should know that his crucifixion is connected to the current Passover (πάσχα) feast (26:2). Matthew goes on to deliberately portray the Last Supper as a Passover meal (26:17–19).[58] Here Jesus recalls the sacrificial system (e.g., Exod 24:8) as he interprets the cup as "my blood of the covenant, which is poured out for many for the forgiveness of sins (Matt 26:28)," suggesting that he himself is the true Passover lamb, and anticipates communal blessings flowing from his sacrifice in speaking about drinking with the disciples in the Father's kingdom (26:29).[59] In the aftermath of the Supper, the disciples fail three times to keep watch, recalling Jesus's predictions that his disciples would betray and deny him (26:21, 26:25, 26:34) and suggesting that the disciples who are supposed to sacrifice for others (e.g., 10:38, 16:24) are more like the chief priests opposing Jesus. Here again we see an example of irony in holy week, only in this case it is intensified as Jesus is not only not doing any miracles but is also having his disciples whom he has trained now begin to turn away from following him. Following this, we see a more concrete example of a disciple of Jesus acting like a false priest and associating with false priests.[60] Judas, who had betrayed Jesus to the chief priests (26:14)—the same chief priests who had gathered at the house of the high priest and plotted to stealthily

---

58. 26:5 and 27:15 also refer to Passover.

59. Allison, *New Moses*, 256–61, asserts that Matthew patently connects the Last Supper with Passover and Exodus 24:8. Sherman, *King, Priest, and Prophet*, 170–76, asserts that 26:28 teaches Christ's expiation of sin and 26:29 refers to restored communion in Christ and anticipation of the eschatological kingdom.

That Passover may be thought of as involving a priestly sacrifice may be seen by its inclusion in Leviticus 23 with the other main Jewish feasts. Although Passover could be celebrated in a person's home, Leviticus 23 associates it with the temple in Jerusalem, where the main Jewish feasts and the temple sacrifices were centered. See also Exod 23:14–17 and Exod 34:18–23.

60. Luz notes that Judas's emergence on the scene in Gethsemane is so abrupt that "the events overtake one another" (*Matthew 21–28*, 412). This suggests a connection between Judas's betrayal and the failures of the disciples in Gethsemane. Luz, *Matthew 21–28*, 359, notes that the church fathers as well as most interpreters prior to the twentieth century held that the other apostles as well as Judas had reached into the dish with Jesus in 26:23 so that they could not recognize with certainty who the betrayer was. Davies and Allison, *Matthew*, 3:461, argues that 26:23 deliberately leaves open which disciple would betray Jesus.

kill Jesus (26:3)—comes with a crowd from the chief priests (26:47) to arrest Jesus and deliver him over to the high priest (26:57).

Jesus's trials point to Jesus as a priestly sacrifice especially through an ironic juxtaposing of the guilt of Jesus's (false priestly) opponents and Jesus's innocent bearing of this guilt. A foundation for this seems to be the book of Leviticus where in the sacrifices at the temple the guilt of the worshipper was exchanged for the innocence and value of a sacrifice in connection with the activity of a priest.[61] In Jesus's trial in the court of the high priest, the trial itself is dubious as it is carried out at night, and Matthew records that the priests deliberately seek and find false witnesses who testify falsely about Jesus in connection with the temple, the place of sacrifice and the central place of their priestly power.[62] In contrast to this guilt of the priests is the innocence of Jesus, who in fulfillment of Isaiah 53:4–7 and the Passover feast remains silent as a sacrificial lamb and suffering servant in spite of the false allegations against him (26:62–63).[63] Near the end of the trial the high priest tears his robes, which seems to symbolize such things as his status as a false priest and the coming to an end of the Old Testament office of priest. Juxtaposed with Jesus's unjust trial in the court of the high priest is Peter's quasi-trial in the high priests' courtyard (26:69–55) where Peter denies Jesus and in his guilt resembles the guilty priests inside at Jesus's trial.[64] Next Jesus is unjustly led to Pilate

---

61. Words like atonement (כָּפַר) and forgive (סָלַח) occur regularly in Leviticus in connection with the various sacrifices that are described. Barber, "Jesus as the Davidic Temple Builder," 951, lists Leviticus 4, which mentions forgiveness four times (verses 20, 26, 31, 35), as an example of Leviticus emphasizing forgiveness of sins in a cultic context and says that in the Old Testament only priests were commonly linked with the forgiveness of sins.

62. Davies and Allison, *Matthew*, 3:537, says that the chief literary feature in the trial before the high priest is irony. Boxall, *Discovering Matthew*, 156, says that in comparison with Mark's Gospel, Matthew's heightens the negative role of the chief priests, as the chief priests explicitly seek false testimony against Jesus (26:59), are associated with blood money (26:14–16; 27:3–10), and persuade the crowds to have Jesus destroyed (27:20).

63. In the trial before Pilate, Jesus again remains silent when the chief priests accuse him (27:14), again recalling Isaiah 53, as does Jesus's remaining silent at the cross except for his cry of dereliction (27:46).

64. Davies and Allison, *Matthew*, 3:543–44, make a similar point and argue that Peter's denials of Jesus also seem to be an answer to why Jesus was struck by those with the high priest (26:68). It is also conceivable that Peter's bitter weeping recalls the bitter herbs and weeping in the Passover meal.

(27:1-2),⁶⁵ which is juxtaposed with Judas's quasi-trial with the priests at the temple resulting in Judas's suicide (27:3-10). The main thrust of this account is that Judas and the priests are guilty,⁶⁶ but Jesus is innocently bearing their guilt.⁶⁷ At the trial before Pilate (27:11-26), the guilt of the chief priests is evident in their accusing Jesus before Pilate in private (27:12), in the note of their having delivered Jesus out of envy (27:18), and in their persuading the crowd to call for the notorious prisoner Barabbas to be released rather than Jesus (27:20).⁶⁸ At the same time, all involved—Barabbas, the crowd, and Pilate—follow the chief priests and resemble them.⁶⁹ All the while Jesus's innocence remains (27:19), as Jesus silently sacrifices himself as Isaiah's suffering servant and the paschal lamb (27:12, 14) so that his blood might cover all sin (27:25).⁷⁰

65. This may recall Isaiah's suffering servant being unjustly led to the slaughter in Isaiah 53:7.

66. Davies and Allison, *Matthew*, 3:564, suggests that the money Judas returns to the temple also originated from there, which suggests such things as the chief priests' guilt, Judas's association with them and their guilt, and the temple's connection to all of this guilt.

Boxall, *Discovering Matthew*, 156, agrees with some patristic commentators in seeing a parallel with Joseph being handed over for 20 pieces of silver by his brother Judah (Gen 37:25-28). Boxall also notes that the chief priests in rejecting the silver from Judas ironically are also rejecting their priestly ministry to forgive sins.

Perhaps also relevant here is that Leviticus 8:35 explains that one of the reasons that Aaron and his sons were ordained as priests was "so that you [they] may not die (8:35)," which is in fact what happened to Aaron's sons Nadab and Abihu moments later as they made an improper offering (10:1-2). Leviticus 27 may also be relevant here as it speaks in the context of a votive free-will offering of various weights of silver, including thirty shekels (27:4), of fields, and even of the necessity of one "devoted for destruction from mankind" to "surely be put to death (27:29)."

67. Luz, *Matthew 21-28*, 470-73, argues that the remorse of Judas was genuine and that Judas rightly saw that his delivering up innocent blood to death was deserving of the physical death penalty. Davies and Allison, *Matthew*, 3:562, leaves open the possibility that Judas repented spiritually. Boxall, *Discovering Matthew*, 159, says that among the Gospels, Matthew's portrayal of Judas is the most positive, leaving his spiritual fate ambiguous.

68. Davies and Allison, *Matthew*, 3:593, argues that the main theological theme of 27:11-26 is responsibility, but the literary method is irony.

69. Davies and Allison, *Matthew*, 3:555, 583, notes the irony in the chief priests seeming to be in charge at Jesus's trial before Pilate rather than Pilate the ruler himself.

70. Boxall, *Discovering Matthew*, 161, sees some irony involved with Pilate to the extent that his character seems ambiguous. Barber, "Jesus as the Davidic Temple Builder," 951, suggests that being seated and pronouncing judgment, such as Jesus says the disciples will do in 19:28, is a priestly activity. With this in mind, the fact that Pilate washes his hands and sits on the judgment seat (27:19) while Jesus stands (27:11)

At the cross itself, the irony reaches its climax as Jesus voluntarily pays the punishment that all false priests deserve. The greatest irony seems to be associated with the relation between the terms king and priest as Jesus's opponents, who may be grouped together as false priests, are overly concerned about worldly kingship and Jesus's claims to be a king. Thus the soldiers, who on the surface are representatives of a ruler, Pilate, are actually representatives of a false priest since Pilate has subordinated himself to the chief priests.[71] The soldiers keeping watch over Jesus mock Jesus by dressing him up as a king and then put a charge over his head that says, "This is Jesus, the King of the Jews."[72] Here the soldiers are working at only a secular level, valuing human definitions of kingship, while in actuality at a spiritual level they are guilty of being false priests helping to put Jesus to death.[73] But Jesus is actually a priest having his head anointed with his own blood after having already had his head anointed with oil in preparation for his burial by the woman at the house of Simon the leper (26:6–13),[74] for in the Old Testament only priests were

---

seems to point to Pilate as a false priest making a false judgment about Jesus's innocence or cleanness, even while these same things point to Jesus as a priestly sacrifice since he bears human guilt, even though he is innocent. See also 26:64 where Jesus's speaking about himself being seated in the future likely contrasts with the high priest being seated at Jesus's trial in a false manner, although this is not explicitly stated.

71. Davies and Allison, *Matthew*, 3:608–9, notes the centrality of Psalm 22, a Davidic lament in the passion narrative. Boxall, *Discovering Matthew*, 154–55, sees Jesus's death as very "un-Davidic" in character and sees Jesus as a righteous sufferer being a major theme of the passion as evident in Matthew's use of Psalms 22 and 69, which he calls "psalms of lament." Here priestly suffering seems to outweigh royalty. Barber, "Jesus as the Davidic Temple Builder," 939–40, notes that Jesus's passion is consistently linked with imagery from the Davidic psalms and that like in Jesus's case David was betrayed by a confidant (1 Sam 15:21); David went up to the Mount of Olives when his life was being sought (1 Sam 15:23); David's betrayer hanged himself (1 Sam 17:23); and David was associated with temple building. Note also that the chief priests in 27:42 mock Jesus as a king like the soldiers do.

72. Davies and Allison, *Matthew*, 3:598, points to the irony of Jesus actually being a king as he is mocked for it.

73. Davies and Allison, *Matthew*, 3:603, argues that the scarlet robe put on Jesus is a soldier's garb, not a king's. Luz, *Matthew 21–28*, 514–15, says that the soldiers give Jesus imitations of three insignias of a Near Eastern client king—a scarlet cloak instead of a purple robe, a crown made of thorns rather than a golden laurel-berry crown, and a reed staff instead of a wooden or golden scepter. Luz sees this as a very deliberate mocking of Jesus and accordingly notes that a deep irony pervades the scene. This irony tends to deconstruct the royal theme.

74. Davies and Allison, *Matthew*, 3:443, notes that lepers did not act as dinner hosts and that Jesus through entering into contact with a leper would have entered a

ordained by being anointed with both oil and blood.[75] Since Jesus is the soldiers' priest, ironically he offers to transform their worship of him as king from mockery to the reality that they are forgiven sinners, forgiven priests, truly capable of recognizing Jesus as the one sent by the royal Father.[76] Similarly, Jesus endures the soldiers' casting of lots for his clothing, with them not realizing that this casting of lots was a priestly activity, where such priestly activity had as its goal that people might be clothed in the righteousness of Jesus's blood (see 26:28, 27:25).[77] Similarly, Jesus

---

state of uncleanness immediately before the Passover. But this would cause a difficulty of Jesus being an unclean king. The difficulty is resolved if Jesus is being anointed as a priest who is bearing human uncleanness in himself through his vicarious sacrifice. Davies and Allison, *Matthew*, 3:448, in the context of Jesus's being anointed at the house of Simon the Leper also notes that anointing in the Old Testament was not just for kings but also priests. That Jesus's anointing with oil was for the purpose of his burial, which Jesus in his passion predictions said would follow crucifixion, also tends to tie it to his priestly rather than royal work.

75. The priestly function of Jesus's scarlet robe and crown of thorns can be seen in such things as their being used to mock Jesus, the robe's color being the color of blood, and the crown and robe causing Jesus to be covered in blood, with blood connoting a sacrifice. Jesus's being stripped and then re-clothed recalls the ordination of priests in Leviticus 8, where the high priest and other priests were washed with water and then dressed with priestly clothing that was anointed with oil and blood (Lev 8:12, 23, 30), whereas kings were only anointed with oil (e.g., 1 Samuel 10:1, 16:1). Matthew's connecting of Jesus's clothing with his anointing with oil and blood is also significant in that anointing (26:12) and clothing figure prominently at Jesus's burial, as Jesus's dead body is covered with a clean linen garment (27:59). Jesus's burial garment here contrasts with the high priest's torn garment and has a priestly connotation both through its being "clean," for priests declared entities clean or unclean (Leviticus 11–15), and through its being made of linen, a fabric repeatedly mentioned in Exodus 28 with its description of the clothing of the priests and the high priest. Barber, "Jesus as the Davidic Temple Builder," 945, cites Zech 6:11 and other early Jewish sources to show that the high priest was also "crowned." See also the turban worn only by the high priest (Lev 8:9).

76. Seeing Jesus as a king at the cross has truth to it insofar as Jesus continues to reveal what God the Father's will for the world is. However, Jesus is more a priest than a king at the cross. For he is not so much revealing what the Father's will is for the world, which he has already abundantly done, as he is fulfilling that will through his own proper work as a priest.

77. Casting lots in the Old Testament was associated with the Urim and Thummim that the high priest was dressed with at the same time he was dressed with his four layers of clothing (Exodus 28, Lev 8:8). Barber, "Jesus as the Davidic Temple Builder," 950, asserts that the judging role of the priest seems especially tied to the Urim and Thummim. For the casting of lots in the Old Testament was associated with the Urim and Thummim that the high priest not only wore but also used for judging the people (Exod 28:30; Lev 8:8; Num 27:21). Leviticus 16:8–10 also connects the casting of lots

patiently and quietly endures the soldiers' worldly keeping watch over (a form of the verb τηρέω) him so that as a vicarious sacrifice he might transform this into a godly, priestly keeping watch over Jesus, which is what indeed happens in the confession of faith that Jesus truly is the Son of God by "the centurion and those who were with him, keeping watch over Jesus (27:54).".[78]

Matthew juxtaposes this guilt of the false priestly soldiers with the false priests themselves at the cross. The group led by the chief priests have the most to say at the cross as they expand upon the mockery of the soldiers and the passersby (27:41-43). They mock Jesus for saving others but not being able to save himself. Salvation here is defined in very secular terms as saving a person from dying, like a king might triumph in a secular battle.[79] These words of the chief priests about salvation are also tied to the temple. For they are continuing the mockery of the passersby, who said, "You who would destroy the temple and rebuild it in three days, save yourself!" Again, the chief priests are flaunting their own power that is centered in the temple and are mocking Jesus for not being able to save himself from physical death, let alone save others from physical death or destroy the physical temple. Similarly, the chief priests

---

with one goat being sacrificed while a second goat is atoned for and released into the wilderness on the Day of Atonement. Here Jesus judges by allowing himself to be judged in place of his executioners.

78. The Hebrew word for keeping is שָׁמַר, a word that was not only used for guarding the tabernacle/temple, but also for Adam and Eve keeping the Garden of Eden (Gen 2:15) as well as for the cherubim guarding the Garden of Eden after the Fall (Gen 3:23). Here we recall that in the Old Testament the tabernacle/temple was associated with the Garden of Eden, for example in having cherubim embroidered on the curtain into the Most Holy Place (Exod 26:31). Priests were responsible for keeping watch over the temple (e.g., Lev 8:35, Num 3:5-13). Barber, "Jesus as the Davidic Temple Builder," 947-51, speaks extensively about the guarding and judging duties of the priests in the temple. Priests were responsible for declaring people and things clean or unclean; being the principal teachers of the law and determining what was "bound" or "loosed," including members in the community; having juridical authority in the community, including to forgive sins; and having ruling authority in Hellenistic times. Priests at the time of Moses and even at Jesus's time were associated with judging in Israel seeing that there was no true Jewish king (Deut 17:8-20). The priestly theme of judgment thus ties together the soldiers' keeping watch over Jesus and their casting lots for his clothing. Barber also adds that Pharisees were sometimes also priests and that after the destruction of the temple rabbis inherited the responsibility to do such priestly things as declaring things clean or unclean and loose or bound.

79. Davies and Allison, *Matthew*, 3:586, says that Matthew 27:18 shows that the real motive for the Jewish leaders handing over Jesus into death is not supposed blasphemy but rather desire for power over the populace.

mock him for calling himself the king of Israel when he cannot even save himself from physical death,[80] and they mock Jesus by saying that God will have to rescue Jesus from death, if God even desires him, for Jesus is unable to save himself from death. The chief priests are false priests who think not in the spiritual terms of forgiveness and atonement but rather in the selfish materialistic way a corrupt king might. But the irony is that Jesus is silently bearing all of this guilt as a priestly sacrifice. And the further irony is that because of Jesus's vicarious sacrifice, the words of the chief priests are capable of being true, though opposite of the way that the chief priests intended. The chief priests' words that Jesus saved others but cannot save himself are ironically true.[81] Jesus has and is saving people spiritually from their sins, but to do so he cannot save himself in the sense of saving himself from physical death.[82] Similarly, Jesus is bringing salvation not by physically destroying the temple, but rather by destroying the temple in the sense of making it obsolete as a place of sacrifice by allowing the temple of his body to be sacrificed so that the new spiritual temple of the church might be built in connection with his resurrection.[83] Similarly, although they have intended to mock Jesus as

---

80. We might even say that the chief priests could not be more wrong, for they view him as a king at the cross, not as a priest, and they completely pervert what the true king should be.

81. Davies and Allison, *Matthew*, 619, similarly notes that Jesus can only save people by staying on the cross, by losing his kingship, and by acting through humble obedience and service as the true Israel.

Davies and Allison, *Matthew*, 3:592, says that the people's cry in Matthew 27:25 for Jesus's blood to be on them and their children is full of irony but that it would be excessively subtle to say that they were crying out for Jesus's blood to cover their sins. Boxall, *Discovering* Matthew, 158, connects the words in 27:25 to 26:28 so that Jesus's blood ironically embraces the Jewish people under the atonement and the promise of forgiveness. I generally agree with Boxall. My point is not that those at the cross were crying out for the atonement but rather that Jesus's atonement was ironically forgiving their cry and offering the means of transforming it into the cry of faith.

82. Davies and Allison, *Matthew*, 3:647, notes that based on what has preceded in the passion narrative, one might expect that Jesus would have been given a dishonorable burial, but instead he is given an honorable one. This helps demonstrate more clearly the irony that has preceded, and that Jesus's sacrifice has been efficacious. Sherman, *King, Priest, and Prophet*, 177, sees Matt 27:62 pointing to a continued priestly context at Jesus's burial through the mention of the Passover feast.

83. For an exhaustive treatment of the tearing of the temple curtain in Matthew 27:51 see Gurtner, *Torn Veil*. Gurtner argues among other things that the veil in question was likely the inner veil that had cherubim woven into it, recalling the cherubim's guarding roles in Genesis 3:24; with the tearing of this veil, access is now open to God in heaven, which helps explain why apocalyptic signs followed upon the tearing.

a king, in a highly ironic way he really is a king, for his death recalls the Father's will that Jesus revealed earlier in the Gospel. And even more so, the priests' actions have made him look like he most properly is, a priest, and through the atonement he has opened up the possibility for them to live up to their name, priest, through being forgiven of their sins. Finally, truly God the Father does care for Jesus and will vindicate him and all who believe in him because he is completing the priestly work that is most proper to him as the Son of God.[84]

The events of Easter Sunday continue to emphasize Jesus's priestly work, in this case especially its efficacy (see also Rom 4:25). To take just one example, the Great Commission at the end of Matthew's Gospel (28:16–20) in one sense highlights the disciples' guilt, as it is the first time the disciples as a group have seen Jesus since they fled in Gethsemane. At the cross, they had to at best be vaguely alluded to by the saints that rose from their tombs to go testify in the holy city after Jesus's resurrection (27:52–53). The women, who had not been as closely trained by Jesus, have understood the resurrection to some extent prior to the disciples. Even some of the unbelieving chief priests have some cognitive understanding of the significance of Jesus's death and resurrection since they have to plot against it (Matt 28:11–15). And now the saintly disciples, when they finally see Jesus at the end of the Gospel, all doubt (in spite of

---

Sherman, *King, Priest, and Prophet*, 180, similarly sees in the rending of the temple curtain a sign that Jesus's priestly mediation has opened access to God and fulfilled the Day of Atonement. Barber, "Jesus as the Davidic Temple Builder," 939–43, speaks extensively about the building of the temple and its relevance for Matthew's Gospel. For example, Barber notes that various mentioning of rocks and stones in holy week have a connection to the temple (e.g., 21:42; 24:1–2, 27:51, 27:60, and 28:2). Again, Barber notes that the same word for build is used in Jesus speaking about building his church in connection with Peter's confession in Matthew 16:18 and in Jesus's being accused of destroying and rebuilding the temple; Barber also notes that both of these occurrences of building come in the context of Jesus being called the son of God, which appellation in the Old Testament was associated with David, who is associated with building the temple. Barber also notes that the rebuilding of the temple after the exile had eschatological and messianic implications.

84. This suggests that the title "Son of God" in Matthew goes through a sort of transformation. At Jesus's Baptism, his being God's son is tied to his royal status. Here the focus is on Jesus's looking up to God the Father, or perhaps better, on the Father's looking down on him. But at the cross, the term Son of God, while still obviously recalling Jesus's relationship with the Father, now emphasizes Jesus's unique identity as the Son who sacrifices himself for sin. This is also suggested in the confession of the centurion in 27:54, where after witnessing the cross, this centurion accurately identifies Jesus as the Son of God.

what some English translations say). The irony is that those who should have known Jesus best are the last to see him, and even when they do they all doubt, confirming that Jesus needed to be their priest. But the other side of this irony is that the disciples' doubt, more clearly than perhaps anything in the Gospel, shows how great Jesus's sacrifice was, for it shows how Jesus has already atoned for their sins so that he immediately forgives them when he sees them.[85] Jesus's forgiveness is so strong and efficacious that he is even able to commission them for spreading the gospel in spite of their great sin and to assure them of his fellowship with them until the end of the world (28:16-20).[86] Thus Matthew 26-28 emphasizes the office of priest through such things as having a priestly setting at the temple at Passover with numerous priests present, Jesus instituting the Lord's Supper as a new Passover, Jesus sacrificing himself as a vicarious atonement in the context of priestly themes, and Jesus establishing his fellowship with his disciples until the end of the world.

This section first showed in general agreement with Sherman's description of the royal office that Jesus in Matthew 1—9:34 is a king authorized by God the Father who goes on to act as a king in very powerful ways on behalf of the Father. In Matthew 9:35—20:34, Jesus is chiefly a prophet who on behalf of the Holy Spirit empowers disciples for ministry and vocations amidst the kingdom and goes on in the power of the Holy Spirit to give them an example of mercy and sacrifice to emulate. In Matthew 21-28, Jesus does his most proper priestly work, first establishing

---

85. That many of the chief priests do not believe at this point in the gospel seems less surprising than just how slow the disciples are to believe. Even one of the soldiers who helped put Jesus to death was quicker to confess Jesus than the disciples (27:54). And at least Jesus's opponents who plotted against him after the cross (27:62-66, 28:11-15) had some cognitive understanding of the significance of his cross and resurrection.

86. Davies and Allison, *Matthew*, 3:679, notes a connection of Matthew 28:16-20 with God (in connection with Moses) commissioning Joshua in Deuteronomy 31:14-15, 23 and Joshua 1:1-9. Here there is the thought that Moses has been a faithful servant of God and that Joshua should emulate this; or to state it another way, it is because of what Moses has done that Joshua can now be commissioned. Something similar is true in Matthew 28:16-20 as it highlights the fact that it is because Jesus has been successful that he can forgive and commission the disciples in spite of themselves (although in Joshua's case there is not a stress on his shortcomings). The emphasis is put upon the success of the predecessor. Here we may also add the eschatological note that 1 Corinthians 15:24 relates that it is only at the end of time that the successful Son will finally deliver over the kingdom to the Father. On this see also Moltmann, *Trinity and Kingdom*, 90-94.

his priestly qualifications and then sacrificing himself for all people in a vicarious sacrifice.

MUTUAL HIERARCHY AMONG THE THREE THIRDS OF MATTHEW AND ITS PRACTICAL SIGNIFICANCE

The previous chapters had uniqueness and dignity as the two main categories for a mutual hierarchy framework in the context of a social model of the Trinity. The previous section especially emphasized that each third of Matthew emphasizes a unique divine person and his unique work. What about the dignity of the divine persons and their work? There were already hints of these things in the discussion of each third in the previous section. For example, even though the Father is emphasized in the first third, his working also fostered the vocations of the Son and Spirit. For example, in the first four chapters of Matthew, the Father's work was at the fore, and yet the Father sent the Son into the world through the Spirit (1:18), anointed him for ministry at his baptism through the Spirit in the presence of great crowds (3:16), and led him to his temptation through the Spirit to inaugurate his ministry (4:1), all of which things helped pave the way for the Spirit's prophetic work in the middle third of Matthew. Furthermore, the Son himself was obviously involved in all of these events and prepared to suffer and even already began to suffer (2:13, 3:15, 4:2), foreshadowing his future cross. Thus the Father's work doesn't stifle the work of the other divine persons but serves it and leads to it. As important as such a discussion of the dignity of the two divine persons less prominent within each third is, it is beyond the scope of the present work. Instead, this section will look briefly at the interrelations among the three thirds of Matthew. Each third with its emphasis on one divine person will be shown to support the other two thirds with their emphasized divine persons, and this will be further illustrated through imagining if the third of Matthew in question were absent. Finally, a diagram that helps summarize the mutual hierarchy of the divine persons in Matthew will be provided, and it will be used to help lay out some of the practical significance of mutual hierarchy in such areas as hermeneutics, sermon preparation, and personal Christian devotion.

Jesus representing the Father as king in the first third of Matthew is not only unique and important in its own right, it also supports the Holy Spirit's work in building the kingdom in the middle third and Jesus's own most proper work in holy week. Because the Father sent Jesus into the world and promised to help his work, the Son is situated to and equipped to train disciples and spread the kingdom in the power of the Spirit in the middle third. Similarly, because the Father has sent Jesus into the world and nurtured him, the Son is in a position to have confidence to sacrifice himself completely in the final third, knowing that his Father will sustain him and raise from the dead. To put both of these points negatively, if Jesus didn't exist in this world in the first place or couldn't rely on the Father's care in his life, he couldn't effectively teach the disciples in the power of the Spirit to spread the message of this care to others and, similarly, couldn't sacrifice himself for sin because he wouldn't be able to trust in the Father's rescuing him.

Similarly, Jesus's prophetic work in the Spirit in the middle third is not only unique and important in its own right, it also supports Jesus's own priestly work in holy week as well as the Father's royal work as creator and sender of the Son. Part of the Father's plan for creation in the beginning was for the Spirit to help human beings grow together in the image of God. Jesus doing such prophetic work in the power of the Spirit is the chief instance in history both of individual human growth and of a human being helping others grow. The Son's prophetic work in the Spirit also supports his own most proper priestly work in holy week. Here the Spirit's growing of the kingdom is the necessary complement of the Son's death and resurrection so that the message of these things may benefit human beings. To put both of these points negatively, if the Spirit didn't work through people in their vocations, the Father's will for human relationships with himself and each other would go unfulfilled and the Son's redemption and preparation of eternal life would be of no avail.[87]

Finally, Jesus's own priestly work as emphasized in holy week in Matthew is not only unique, it also supports the work of the other divine persons in the other thirds. Here the Son's work fulfills the royal work of the Father as creator, as recapitulated in the first third of Matthew. Part of the Father's plan for creation in the beginning, and recalled in the first third of Matthew, was for the Son to bring creation to fulfillment.[88] Here the Son's priestly work in holy week highlights the work of the Father by fulfilling his will, both atoning for the sins of a now-fallen human race that the Father made in the beginning and ushering in new and heavenly

---

87. See also Sherman, *King, Priest, and Prophet*, 250–52.
88. See also Sherman, *King, Priest, and Prophet*, 210.

possibilities through his resurrection in agreement with the Father's will from the beginning.[89] The Son's priestly work in holy week also provides the forgiveness and destiny necessary to give meaning to the Holy Spirit's prophetic work of expanding the kingdom. To put matters negatively, without the Son's unique priestly work in holy week, the Father's royal will would forever remain unaccomplished and the Spirit's prophetic work would have no future due to a lack of forgiveness and a lack of eternal destiny.

Diagram 4, which was briefly introduced in chapter 4, will now be considered again to help illustrate the mutual hierarchy of the divine persons in Matthew and bring out some of the practical implications of this. Recall that diagram 4 illustrates the prominence of the divine persons in Matthew's narrative:

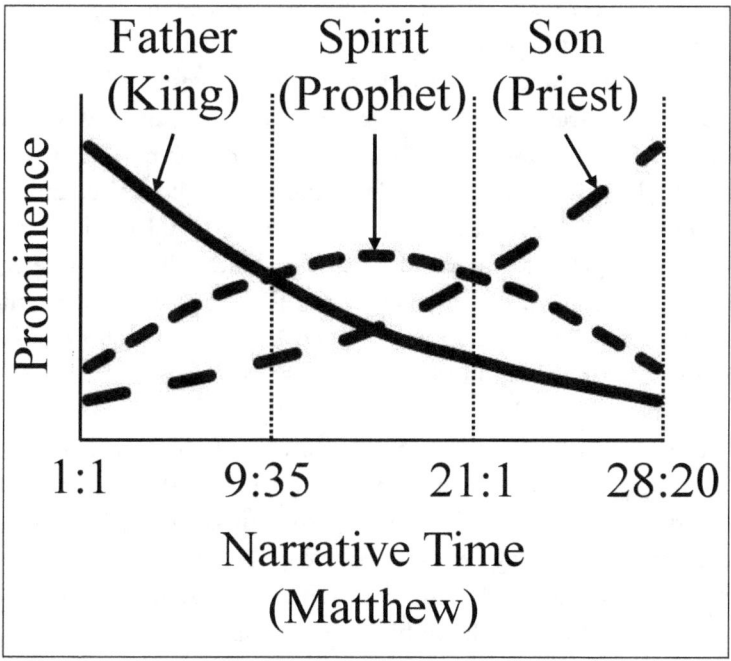

Diagram 4. The Prominence of the Divine Persons in Matthew

Diagram 4 looks at narrative time in the Gospel of Matthew and shows the prominence of the vocation of each divine person as the narrative proceeds. Thus, in agreement with what has been said in this chapter, the

---

89. See also Sherman, *King, Priest, and Prophet*, 213.

Father is most prominent in the first third of Matthew, the Holy Spirit is most prominent in the middle third, and the Son is the most prominent in the final third. Diagram 4 also suggests that a divine person's work is always changing in prominence. For example, in the first third, the more that the Father performs his most proper work, the less prominent the Father's work becomes and the more prominent the work of the Son and the Holy Spirit becomes. As the Father exercises his vocation in the first third of Matthew, he increasingly limits his power, which fosters the work of the Spirit and the Son in the final two thirds of Matthew, respectively.

This diagram helps illustrate some of the practical significance of the divine working in Matthew. Here it especially helps in the area of hermeneutics. Rather than needing to rely on proof texts scattered around the biblical narrative, as was somewhat the case in chapter 3 in connection with the economic Trinity in the Gospel of John, diagram 4 shows that there is a relatively systematic presentation of themes in the Gospel of Matthew. This is not to say that the exact shape of diagram 4 is correct. More work would be required to establish this. But we can say that diagram 4 provides a reasonable picture of how each third of Matthew emphasizes a unique work of one divine person, while not excluding the work of the other divine persons in that third, and while helping foster the work of the other divine persons in the rest of Matthew. Matthew's Gospel is not an atomistic and sporadic collection of verses or pericopes where the divine persons erratically struggle for the spotlight; rather Matthew is a narrative with a relatively smooth plot progression, having some parallel with (and likely exceeding) various great works of literature or drama today.

The mutual hierarchy of the divine persons in Matthew as illustrated in diagram 4 also is important for the practical matter of sermon preparation. In sermon preparation, a pastor could look at diagram 4 and have a map to help navigate where a pericope is situated in Matthew and what sorts of themes to look for. For example, if a pericope is from Jesus commissioning the disciples in his second sermon (9:35—10:42), a pastor could look at diagram 4 and see that since this sermon comes at the beginning of the middle third of Matthew, the Holy Spirit's work is most prominent, closely followed by the Father's work, with the Son's work less prominent. This means that the sermon chiefly deals with Jesus training his disciples in the power of the Holy Spirit, but the initial commissioning of this training is deeply reliant upon the authority and the promised victory of the Father, while the Son's suffering has not yet ramped up to the higher levels of later in the Gospel.

Similarly, the mutual hierarchy of the divine persons in Matthew as illustrated in diagram 4 is potentially very helpful for the practical matter of Christian devotions. A Christian, and even a newer Christian, does not have to approach the Gospel of Matthew with no idea about how the story proceeds. Here diagram 4 helps provide a sort of map for the basic story of Matthew. In a Christian devotion, the person can see the simple contours of what happens in Matthew. The story proceeds from the Father providing for Jesus, to the Holy Spirit helping Jesus grow the kingdom, to the Son dying for sins and fulfilling the Father's will. Over time Christians could also make more advanced use of diagram 4 where they could see the development of different themes as Matthew proceeds.

This section has thus briefly shown that each third of Matthew, by having its own distinctive emphasis, is not a threat to the other two thirds but rather fosters their dignity. The three thirds with their distinctive themes require and complement each other (Matthew 28:19). If any of the thirds were missing, the theology of Matthew would fall apart, including Matthew's doctrine of the Trinity. Finally, this mutual hierarchy of the divine persons in Matthew can be illustrated in diagram form, which helps bring out the great practical potential of this mutual hierarchy in such areas as hermeneutics, sermon preparation, and Christian devotion.

CHAPTER CONCLUSION

This chapter began by asking the question of whether the Scriptures have a more systematic way of teaching the doctrine of the Trinity than using proof texts not fully related to the biblical narratives they were taken from. The present chapter has argued on the basis of the Gospel of Matthew that they do. In the first section it looked at some of the other major structural proposals for the Gospel of Matthew and biblical works closely related to the Gospel of Matthew and found that a proposed triadic structure for Matthew was plausible. The second section looked at the proposed triadic structure in greater detail and found a confluence of various unique trinitarian terms and themes within each third that was coherent in connection with the categories of king, prophet, and priest. Finally, the third section looked at how the emphasized trinitarian theme in each third does not compete against the trinitarian theme most prominent in the other thirds but rather complements them and fosters mutual dignity. In connection with each third of Matthew being unique and yet fostering the dignity of the other thirds, the mutual hierarchy of the divine persons in Matthew was evident in a systematic way at a macro-level. This mutual hierarchy of the divine persons in Matthew was illustrated in diagram form, which helped bring out the great practical potential of mutual hierarchy in such areas as hermeneutics, sermon preparation, and Christian devotion.

7

Mutual Hierarchy and Discipleship in the Gospel of Matthew

THE PREVIOUS CHAPTER LAID out how the triadic macrostructuring of Matthew's Gospel helps teach the three offices of Christ and the coworking of the divine persons of the Trinity. Thinking about discipleship in connection with this raises a key question. Is there a discipleship-centered reading of Matthew's Gospel that complements the christocentric (and trinitarian) reading from the previous chapter? This chapter will try to answer this question by utilizing a mutual hierarchy framework to argue for a trinitarian-based discipleship reading of the Gospel of Matthew in connection with the categories of king, prophet, and priest. It will do so in three basic steps. First, it will give some background on the literature on discipleship in Matthew's Gospel and introduce my basic proposal. Second, it will look in more detail at the most prominent form of discipleship in each third of Matthew in connection with the king, prophet, and priest categories, respectively. Third, it will argue that the most prominent discipleship form in each third of Matthew also fosters the dignity of the other two discipleship forms in the other two thirds of Matthew rather than competing with them. By thus establishing both the uniqueness and the dignity of the discipleship forms, mutual hierarchy will be evident. Finally, the chapter will briefly discuss how this mutual hierarchy discipleship-centered reading of the Gospel of Matthew is potentially very fruitful for such practical matters as hermeneutics, sermon preparation, and mentoring disciples.

DISCIPLESHIP AND THE GOSPEL OF MATTHEW

In this section, portions of the work of Ben Cooper will be adduced to summarize some of the main issues in the recent literature on discipleship in the Gospel of Matthew. Next, Cooper's own "pragmatic-critical" approach to Matthean discipleship will be briefly summarized. Following this, Robert Sherman's thoughts on discipleship in connection with the categories of king, priest, and prophet will be briefly presented as a supplement to Cooper's work. Finally, the broad contours of my own discipleship proposal will be presented.

A good place to begin in considering the theme of discipleship in the context of Matthew's Gospel is Ben Cooper's book *Incorporated Servanthood: Commitment and Discipleship in the Gospel of Matthew*. Cooper in his first three chapters surveys existing Matthean discipleship literature and asserts that two camps emerge, each with shortcomings. Redaction-critical studies, which Cooper groups together with historical-critical and author-oriented studies, tend to be so focused on biblical history itself that they do not sufficiently account for discipleship application today. For example, according to Cooper, Ulrich Luz emphasizes Christology and plot in Matthew in such a way that he largely only allows for minimal "transparency" of the disciples in the narrative so that Luz neither adequately shows what things were like for people and events in Matthew's bounded community nor provides much relevance or "allegorizing" for disciples today.[1] Alternatively, narrative-critical studies, which Cooper groups together with reader-oriented studies, tend to so focus on real readers today that they tend to be "essentially ahistorical." Such approaches make Matthew relevant today but often at the cost of making the Gospel one-sidedly allegorical, which can downplay Matthew's Christology.

The final chapter of Cooper's book summarizes his own pragmatic-critical approach that he sees as an extension of narrative criticism but integrating redaction criticism as well, thus seeking to bring together the two main approaches. Cooper sees Matthew teaching discipleship by encouraging commitment to God using a broad array of terms and themes. According to Cooper, Matthew wrote his Gospel knowing that the number and type of his readers would be unbounded, with Matthew writing in such a way as to maximize the subset of readers who would process the text compliantly. Matthew desired that post-resurrection readers

---

1. See further Luz, "Disciples in the Gospel according to Matthew," 98–128.

would be "drawn in" to stand alongside Christ and the disciples in the narrative in constructive empathy and then translate what they read to apply to their actual situation. Applying this pragmatic-critical approach to Matthew's text, Cooper finds that Matthew's eschatology provides the framework for understanding his Christology and, derivatively, his call to discipleship. Here earlier portions of Matthew speak of God's will and coming judgment, which creates tension in the narrative that ultimately can only be resolved by Christ at the end of the narrative, where Christ as Isaiah's Suffering Servant will suffer judgment for the human race. The victorious Suffering Servant thus earns the right to send out his disciples in the Great Commission (Matt 28:16–20) to follow a similar, yet dependent, suffering servant program of making new disciples themselves as Jesus lifts the limitations of their partial mission to Israel from Matthew 10. Cooper thus tends to advocate two distinct readings of Matthew, a christological reading marked by a realized eschatology and a discipleship reading marked by a future eschatology.[2]

As helpful as Cooper's work is, it lacks much discussion of the king, priest, and prophet categories that are central in Matthew, although Cooper's approach is certainly capable of integrating such views. Here Robert Sherman's book *King, Priest, and Prophet: A Trinitarian Theology of the Atonement* provides a helpful supplement to Cooper's work. In chapter 1, Sherman surveys some recent prominent works on the atonement, assessing how well each scholar balances an objective approach that focuses on Christ's life with a subjective approach that focuses on discipleship today. For example, from the existing literature Sherman finds most helpful Geoffrey Wainwright's book *For Our Salvation: Two Approaches to the Work of Christ*, where Wainwright looks at the offices of king, priest, and prophet using two sets of categories, objective ("christological") and subjective ("baptismal," "soteriological," "ministerial," and "ecclesiological").[3] Sherman in chapters 2 and 3 goes on to lay out the basic theological and

---

2. Wilkins, *Concept of Disciple in Matthew's Gospel*, 222, describes the complexity of discipleship in Matthew as follows, "The disciples are a positive example of what Matthew expects from his church, a negative example of warning, and a mixed group who are able to overcome their lackings through the teaching of Jesus. The historical disciples become a means of encouragement, warning, and instruction as examples." For other helpful discussions on discipleship see Wilkins, *Following the Master*, 25–38; Davies and Allison, *Matthew*, 2:647–52; Scaer, *Discourses in Matthew*, 9–70; and Broadhead, *Gospel of Matthew*, 17–23.

3. Sherman, *King, Priest, and Prophet*, 29, notes that Wainwright tends to blur the soteriology category between the objective and subjective poles.

scriptural underpinnings for his own views on Christ's work and discipleship. Sherman's views on these things are explicitly trinitarian in contrast to Wainwright's largely christological approach. Here Sherman sees the royal, priestly, and prophetic offices of Christ as applicable to discipleship, tying them to baptism, the Lord's Supper, and the life-giving Word, respectively, as well as to the Father, Son, and Holy Spirit, respectively.[4] Coordinating Sherman's conclusions with my findings from the previous chapter on the offices of Christ in Matthew and with Cooper's discussion, a discipleship reading of Matthew emerges where the first third of Matthew emphasizes royal discipleship and baptism, the middle third emphasizes prophetic discipleship and the life-giving Word, and the final third emphasizes priestly discipleship and the Lord's Supper.[5]

THE MOST PROMINENT FORM OF DISCIPLESHIP IN EACH THIRD OF MATTHEW

This section will look at the most prominent form of discipleship in each third of Matthew in more detail. Sherman argues that although the same basic king-prophet-priest categories hold for discipleship as for Christology, there are differences in how these categories apply to Christians today in comparison to how they applied to Christ. In what follows, the thought of Sherman on the discipleship form relevant for each third of Matthew will be summarized and critically appropriated, and then the discipleship form for that third will be analyzed in greater detail.

---

4. See Sherman, *King, Priest, and Prophet*, 151–68, 194–218, 241–61, and Wainwright, *For Our Salvation*, 121–86, for their conceptions of the practical relevance of discipleship in conjunction with the king, priest, and prophet offices.

5. For a similar connecting of the sacraments, atonement theories, and Christian sanctification, see also Sánchez, "Life in the Spirit of Christ," 7–14. Just, *Heaven on Earth*, 180–236, has a helpful discussion of the relationship between worship and discipleship, but Just only sees two main foci within a typical worship service, the service of the word and the service of the sacrament (the Lord's Supper). For me, liturgical elements like the invocation, opening hymn, confession and absolution, and the opening collect at the beginning of a service together constitute a distinct third liturgical time period that especially recalls a Christian's being brought into God the Father's family through baptism.

Matthew 1:1—9:34

Since the first third of Matthew (Matt 1:1—9:34) focuses on the Father and the office of king, Sherman's discussion of royal discipleship will be analyzed first.[6] Sherman begins by noting a couple of ways that the office of king differs for disciples in comparison to the office of king for Christ. First, since the fall into sin, disciples have original sin whereas Christ does not. Second, Christ's victory reestablished true human ontology for other human beings, whereas Christ himself has always had a stable ontology as the eternal Son of God. Disciples have not existed eternally but rather have entered the community of God through baptism and have been freed from the power of the devil and enabled to engage in spiritual warfare against him. One addition I would make to Sherman's discussion is that prayer is also an important part of disciples reflecting upon what God has done for them, both in baptism and in the past generally.[7]

Turning now to the Gospel of Matthew, Matthew 1–4 emphasizes royal discipleship in a way that recalls Christ's exercising the office of king in this place. In Matthew 1–2, just as the incarnation is arguably the Father's most prominent work in the life of Christ, conversion is the Father's most prominent work in a disciple's life. Whereas the beginning of Matthew emphasizes Christ's actual incarnation, in terms of discipleship the beginning of Matthew emphasizes such things as a disciple being given new birth at conversion, declared a newborn king, and placed into the community of God's people.[8] In Matthew 3, baptism immediately follows Christ's incarnation, teaching in correspondence to God's care for Jesus at his baptism that disciples are baptized following upon their conversion.[9] Similarly, in correspondence to Jesus's victory over the devil

---

6. Sherman, *King, Priest, and Prophet*, 157–68.

7. An individual Christian's baptism into God's family should be clearly distinguished from his or her continued life and worship. Baptism is an unrepeatable act, even as God's creation of the world and his sending of his Son into the world are. Nevertheless, baptism has an ongoing significance for a Christian. Prayer can be an important way for Christians to reflect on God's bringing them to faith and putting them in a position to lead the Christian life.

8. Besides Christ obviously being a newborn king in Matthew 1–2, Joseph and even Mary seem to be declared kings through their inclusion in the genealogy of kings and patriarchs (1:16). They are kings in spite of the fact that the genealogy also gives evidence that they are born into a human family bearing the marks of original sin.

9. Scaer, *Baptism*, 147–56, argues that people have faith prior to baptism because God has worked in their lives prior to baptism and exposed them to his Word, but after they are baptized they should put their trust especially in their baptism.

at his temptation, Matthew 4 teaches that a disciple is promised ultimate victory over the devil at the beginning of their faith life. Thus the first four chapters of Matthew strongly emphasize royal discipleship in general agreement with Sherman's definition of royal discipleship through such things as emphasizing conversion in the past, baptism, and the overcoming of the devil in connection with a *Christus victor* theme.

The Sermon on the Mount (Matt 5:1—7:27) also emphasizes royal discipleship in a way reminiscent of Christ's exercising the royal office in this place. Just as Jesus in the Sermon on the Mount reflects on the incarnation and God's preparatory work in his life, so too does the sermon further teach what God has done for disciples through conversion and baptism. For example, Jesus's third-person beatitudes (5:1-12) declare both Jesus himself and his disciples blessed by God. Furthermore, corresponding to Jesus reflecting on the Ten Commandments, disciples can reflect upon the fact that the Father by his grace has declared disciples blessed and justified in spite of original sin. But the sermon is not just about what God has done in the past, it also shows that God enables disciples to reflect upon and speak about what God has done for them, as can be seen in Jesus teaching the disciples to pray the Lord's Prayer together (6:5-15) and reflect on the Father's intimate care for them (6:25-34). Finally, corresponding to Jesus speaking about action in Matthew 7 (e.g., 7:12, 7:17, 7:21, 7:24), disciples in their silent and spoken reflections can ponder the Father's enabling and encouraging them to act authoritatively on his behalf. Thus in the Sermon on the Mount, royal discipleship is emphasized as disciples can reflect inwardly and outwardly on what God has done for them in the past and on the fact that he has enabled them to act authoritatively on his behalf.

The narrative material following the Sermon on the Mount (7:28—9:34) also emphasizes royal discipleship in a way that is reminiscent of Christ's exercising the royal office in this place. 7:28—9:34 shows that just as the Father empowers Jesus to perform a series of powerful miracles, so too does the Father help disciples to represent him through their works flowing from faith. These works are miraculous not in the sense that disciples do ostentatious powerful miracles like Jesus, but rather in the sense that God miraculously enables disciples to do works for others flowing from faith in spite of original sin (9:1-8) and the presence of the devil in the world (8:28-34). In 7:28—9:34, royal discipleship is emphasized as disciples can reflect on the fact that God has enabled them to act authoritatively on his behalf.[10]

Matthew 9:35—20:34

Turning now to the middle third of Matthew (9:35—20:34), in keeping with the middle third focusing on the Holy Spirit and the office of prophet, Sherman's discussion of prophetic discipleship will now be analyzed.[11] Sherman's discussion shows at least one way that the office of prophet differs for disciples in comparison with for Christ. Whereas Christ in his life was physically present with his disciples as history's greatest teacher, disciples today are reliant upon the Scriptures that testify to his teachings. But this doesn't mean that the Scriptures are a lifeless book. Rather Sherman emphasizes that the Holy Spirit utilizes the living Word: the Spirit in connection with the Scriptures works among Christians to empower them to live the Christian life and exemplify Christ's life among them. Here Sherman also emphasizes the Holy Spirit's work in worship to build up both the Christian community and individual Christians. And yet the *telos* of the Spirit's working is the Christian life as the Spirit provides Christians a new framework for their entire lives, a framework connected to their experiences, words, and deeds. One major place I part ways with Sherman here, similar to in the previous chapter, is that the Spirit's prophetic work in the life of a disciple corresponds chiefly with the present tense, not the future tense as Sherman holds.[12]

---

10. Cooper, *Incorporated Servanthood*, 66–121, 241–42, has Cooper's discussion of Matthew 1–9. My proposal agrees with Cooper's views on these chapters on such things as an Old Testament emphasis; God the Father's faithfulness; Matthew 5–7 teaching that the Father enables a disciple, like he enabled Jesus himself, to trust in and pray to him as well as proclaim who the Father is to the world; and Matthew 8–9 emphasizing God's helping his people. But my proposal tends to disagree by stressing God's initiative more than the choice and response of disciples. Furthermore, for Matthew 8–9, my proposal stresses God enabling disciples to do works flowing from faith, such as learning from Jesus as he does powerful miracles, whereas Cooper holds that these chapters teach chiefly about the faith of disciples.

11. Sherman, *King, Priest, and Prophet*, 250–61.

12. Wainwright, *For Our Salvation*, 121–35, contains Wainwright's chief discussion of the prophetic office. He summarizes by saying that Christians are taught and teach. But for him such teaching is not just about knowledge; it also includes concepts like trust and deeds. Here Wainwright can also cite Matthew 28:19 and use the language of being made a disciple and making disciples.

Jesus's second sermon and the following narrative (9:35—12:50) emphasize prophetic discipleship in a way that recalls Christ's exercising the office of prophet in this place. Here just as Christ through the power of the Holy Spirit reaches a new point in his ministry by sending his disciples out and beginning to train them for ministry, disciples today through the power of the Holy Spirit learn to actively send out and train others. There are two aspects of discipleship here. First, disciples are recipients of the work of other Christians whom the Holy Spirit has empowered to commission and train them. And second, the disciples in question themselves will train and commission other disciples. Returning to Matthew's text, whereas the disciples mainly followed and observed Jesus when he did a series of powerful miracles in 8:1—9:34, now disciples are sent out themselves (10:5) in order to serve the crowds that have been following Jesus through specific vocations (9:36–38) as well as reach new people (10:7). On the one hand, disciples today can identify here with the crowds, with those in the towns, or with the original disciples themselves who benefit from the apprenticeship of other Christians. On the other hand, disciples today are like Jesus himself and like the original apostles in their active capacity, sending out disciples for vocations of service, pastoral and otherwise.

Jesus's third sermon and the following narrative, Matthew 13–17, emphasize prophetic discipleship in a climactic way that recalls Christ's exercising the office of prophet in this place. Jesus's instructions about sowing the seed of the gospel (13:1–9, 24–30) and the kingdom's growth (13:31–33), teachings which are demonstrated in the feedings of the 5,000 (14:13–21) and 4,000 (15:32–39), illustrate that today's disciples are empowered to work hard in their vocations in conjunction with the church to help the church grow in size, help Christians in the church grow in their faith journey, and serve the world. Similarly, disciples in the church benefit from their fellow Christians working for them. Here we can further specify in connection with the parable of the sower that pastors proclaim the gospel through preaching, for example, and laity serve through witnessing and their other vocational gifts. The two feedings and some of the later material in the section, like Jesus's patience with his disciples when they struggle to understand the cross—both Jesus's and their own (16:21–28)—also illustrate that disciples today are to give an example to others and benefit from the example of their fellow disciples for the sake of growth in the church and mission. Here pastors in their vocations can train to feed people spiritually, and other disciples in their unique vocations can train to feed people in ways appropriate to their vocations, so that pastors and laity benefit from each other. Pastors and laity can also exercise the office of the keys in distinct ways and also benefit from this Word themselves (16:13–20).

Jesus's fourth sermon and the following narrative, Matthew 18–20, also emphasize prophetic discipleship in a way that recalls Christ's exercising the office of prophet in this place. Here there is a stress on the need for disciples to show mercy, bear with sins and weaknesses, and provide examples for one another and others. For example, after Jesus instructs the disciples to show mercy (18:1–4, 21–22), he puts this teaching into practice and gives the disciples an example by being merciful with them after they fail to follow his instructions (19:13–15; 20:20–27). Disciples today can learn from these things to be merciful to each other and others and provide a Christ-like example to them, even while disciples also seek to learn and benefit when their fellow disciples provide such an example for and to them. To this end, disciples can again benefit from the Word through utilizing the office of the keys (18:15–20). But in this second instance of the keys, the sin involved seems to be more grievous and treasonous as Jesus speaks specifically of multiple brothers dealing with the sin of a brother, whereas 16:13–20 spoke of the keys in the more positive context of Peter's great confession. Disciples today can learn from these things to go to great lengths to show mercy for even more grievous sins and take comfort that their fellow disciples are to strive to provide a similar Christ-like example to them. Thus whereas the beginning of the middle third of Matthew (9:35—12:50) seemed to emphasize especially empowerment by the Holy Spirit, Matthew 18–20 seems to emphasize the need to follow Jesus's example of sacrifice in the power of the Holy Spirit.[13]

---

13. Cooper, *Incorporated Servanthood*, 121–80, 243–44, has Cooper's discussion of Matthew 10:1—20:34. Here my proposal generally agrees with Cooper's on such things as Matthew 10 teaching a limited commission of the Twelve appropriate for their progress in training, a mixed response both by the disciples and by those outside of their group to this commission and mission in approximately chapters 11 through 16, and a call to bear with sin (or to bear a cross) in approximately chapters 16 through 20. Cooper also rightly sees in chapters 10–20 both the disciples being the objects of divine training as well as learning to train others themselves. My proposal differs somewhat from Cooper's on such things as clearly connecting Matthew 11–20 with Jesus's commissioning the disciples in the power of the Holy Spirit in Matthew 10, although Cooper does connect Matthew 10 with some of the later chapters within Matthew 11–20.

Matthew 21–28

Turning now to the final third of Matthew (Matt 21–28), in keeping with the final third focusing on the Son and the office of priest, Sherman's discussion of priestly discipleship will now be analyzed.[14] Sherman's discussion emphasizes one very important way that the office of priest differs for disciples in comparison with for Christ. Christ is the redeemer, and disciples are not, so disciples "should not be too quaking to identify ourselves with the character of Christ." Sherman sees two main aspects to the priesthood of disciples. First, priests today are beneficiaries of Christ's work, forgiven of all of their sins. Second, because of this forgiveness, disciples can have a clean conscience before God and a fresh start in leading a new life. Here disciples can look at justice differently, appreciating their own forgiveness and seeking reconciliation with rather than retribution against those who have wronged them. These things are focused especially in the Lord's Supper, which both forgives the worst of sins and encourages communion with others in anticipation of the eschatological communion of heaven. One major place I part ways with Sherman here is that a disciple's priestly work is oriented chiefly toward the future, not the present tense as Sherman holds.

The narrative material that begins holy week (Matt 21–22) emphasizes priestly discipleship in a way that recalls Christ's exercising the office of priest in this place. Here Matthew contrasts the qualifications of Jesus as the true priest with especially Jesus's opponents as false priests as Jesus has various debates with his opponents in the setting of the temple (21:12–17, 23). In this context the disciples are more recipients of the priestly work of Jesus who will be the true temple sacrifice than working priests themselves, although they are the latter as well. Disciples today can learn from these things to trust in Christ the faithful priest in their lives, such as through reflecting on his character and how he has exhibited this at the Lord's Supper and trying to witness to his character to others.

Jesus's final sermon (Matt 23–25) also emphasizes priestly discipleship in a way that recalls Christ's exercising the office of priest in this place. Here Matthew 23 continues to contrast Jesus's priestly qualifications with those of his opponents, now even more intensely than before through recording Jesus's statements of woes against the scribes and Pharisees. As the sermon continues, the apocalyptic language intensifies and the disciples' own faulty priestly qualifications emerge more clearly

14. Sherman, *King, Priest, and Prophet*, 210–18.

(24:1). The apocalyptic language points to a near future where Jesus will bear apocalyptic suffering (24:44), a more distant future where the disciples will testify about the gospel of Jesus (24:14), and a remote future, even the end of the world (25:31–46). Disciples today can learn from these things that their own character and sacrifices are lacking and that they need Christ's sacrifice for forgiveness, and to a lesser extent they can learn to witness to others about such things. Here they are encouraged to come to their Lord's Table and especially witness there how Christ's being a faithful high priest propelled him forward to prepare to sacrifice himself for the sins of disciples and even the sins of the whole world.

The passion narrative (Matthew 26–28) emphasizes priestly discipleship in a climactic way that recalls Christ's exercising the office of priest in this place. From the events surrounding the Last Supper, disciples can reflect on the great feast that Jesus instituted for them in spite of their betrayals of him. From the events surrounding Jesus's trial(s) they can ponder more deeply the severity of their sins and how this is depicted in the actions of Jesus's various opponents at his trial. And from the events connected to Jesus's death and resurrection, they can ponder their very worst sins and how in the final analysis there is no difference between them and the chief priests who led the effort to crucify Jesus; their sins caused Jesus's unfathomable suffering and sacrifice for them. They also can reflect on how through Jesus's death and resurrection they have been forgiven of all of their sins and restored to fellowship with him. Here disciples don't just have to think about such things but rather follow Christ's command and come to the Lord's Supper to receive Christ's body and blood for their forgiveness. Here they can appreciate that Christ continues to come to them over and over at his table, reckoning them priests in spite of themselves, and giving them hope for everlasting life with their fellow Christians gathered and the whole church in heaven and on earth.[15]

15. Cooper, *Incorporated Servanthood*, 180–239, 243–45, has Cooper's discussion of Matthew 21–28. Here my proposal agrees with Cooper's on seeing Matthew 21–28 as a distinct unit, which Cooper refers to as the "Coming of the Son of Man." It also agrees that disciples must first be beneficiaries of Christ's "Servant Program" that reaches its climax in Matthew 21–28 before they can take up such a program themselves. It also agrees that the work of Christ builds to a climax as holy week proceeds, as Jesus first pronounces judgment in the contest for authority, then teaches his disciples about his climactic work in his servant program, and then reaches its climax in the actual suffering and vindication of Jesus in his cross and resurrection. My proposal differs somewhat from Cooper's on being less optimistic over how well disciples can imitate Jesus in holy week, as my proposal sees Jesus's work at the cross as much less imitable than his prophetic work in the middle third of Matthew.

This section has looked at the most prominent form of discipleship in each third of Matthew in more detail. Each third of Matthew with its king-prophet-priest discipleship form is in basic agreement with the corresponding discussion of Robert Sherman, with the exception of associating prophetic discipleship with the present and priestly discipleship with the future. Thus the first third of Matthew in connection with royal discipleship emphasizes such things as a disciple's relationship with the Father, baptism, victory over the devil, baptism-rooted prayer and contemplation, and the Father enabling good works. The middle third of Matthew in connection with prophetic discipleship emphasizes such things as disciples' sending through the empowerment of the Spirit, proclamation and vocations, the office of the keys, and disciples' Christ-like examples of sacrifice and mercy. The final third of Matthew in connection with priestly discipleship emphasizes such things as disciples' contemplating Jesus as their faithful high priest and trying to witness to him, receiving forgiveness at the Lord's Supper for the sake of Christ's body and blood sacrificed at the cross, and celebrating at the Lord's table the hope of heaven together for the sake of Christ's sacrifice.

MUTUAL HIERARCHY AMONG THE THREE DISCIPLESHIP FORMS AND ITS PRACTICAL SIGNIFICANCE

The previous chapters have dealt with a mutual hierarchy framework and had uniqueness and dignity as the two main categories. The previous section emphasized that each third of Matthew emphasizes a unique discipleship form in connection with a unique king-prophet-priest category and a unique divine person. What about dignity among the discipleship forms? There were already hints of these things in the discussion of each third in the previous section. For example, even though priestly discipleship and forgiveness in Christ is emphasized in the final third of Matthew, this priestly discipleship also still fosters royal discipleship and prophetic discipleship. Thus in looking at the passion narrative, disciples not only ponder the Lord's Supper and the forgiveness of the worst of their sins for the sake of Christ, in a less prominent way they are driven to witness to the cross to others (prophetic discipleship) and remember that baptism has put them in a position to now be forgiven in a tangible way at the Lord's Supper (royal discipleship). Thus priestly discipleship does not stifle the other discipleship forms but rather serves them and leads to them. As important as such a discussion of the dignity of the two discipleship forms less prominent within each third is, it is beyond the scope of the present work. Instead, this section will look briefly at the interrelations among the three thirds of Matthew. Each third with its emphasis on one discipleship form will be shown to support the other two thirds with their discipleship forms, and this will be further illustrated through imagining if the discipleship form of Matthew in question were absent. Finally, diagram 4, which helps summarize and illustrate the mutual hierarchy of the divine persons in Matthew, will again be used to help lay out some of the practical significance of the mutual hierarchy of the discipleship forms in Matthew.

We begin by looking at how royal discipleship in the first third of Matthew helps foster prophetic discipleship and priestly discipleship as stressed in the middle third and the final third of Matthew, respectively. Here disciples being brought into God's family in conversion and baptism puts them into a position to and begins to equips them to prophetically serve God's kingdom, where they will train new disciples in connection with the Word even while continuing to be trained themselves (prophetic discipleship) as evident especially in the middle third of Matthew. Similarly, royal discipleship provides the ongoing necessary foundation for disciples to benefit from their destiny in Christ of being forgiven of sins and progressing toward eternal life in connection with the Lord's Supper.[16] The necessity of royal discipleship can also be seen in the fact that if royal discipleship did not exist to lead to the other discipleship forms, a disciple would lack assurance that they are a believer and hence lack an enduring identity as God's child, reducing prophetic discipleship to moralism and priestly discipleship to an undependable or secular forgiveness. To use a worship analogy, this would be like never knowing if one were welcome to enter a worship service to benefit from what is offered there.

Prophetic discipleship as stressed in the middle third of Matthew also supports royal discipleship and priestly discipleship as stressed in the first third and final third of Matthew, respectively. Here disciples are trained to train others in the Word, which enables them to live out their royal identity as the baptized children of God. Similarly, prophetic discipleship also enables disciples to propagate the church that will trust in Christ's forgiveness and anticipate its final destiny at the Lord's Supper. The necessity of prophetic discipleship can be seen in that it provides a

---

16. For more on the Lord's Supper as an ongoing movement toward eternal life, see Zizioulas, *Being as Communion*, 53–70.

separate space where disciples can struggle and grow in their vocations, where such partial victories and failures are less appropriate in the realms of royal discipleship and priestly discipleship where God's love and Jesus's forgiveness, respectively, ultimately are most prominent.[17] The necessity of prophetic discipleship can also be seen in that if prophetic discipleship did not contribute to the other discipleship forms, a disciple would have no purpose in the world, reducing royal discipleship to an individual relationship with God and priestly discipleship to forgiveness for sins committed only against God and not a fellow human being. To use a worship analogy, this would be like entering an empty church, giving oneself the Lord's Supper alone, and never serving others.

Priestly discipleship as stressed in the final third of Matthew also supports royal discipleship and prophetic discipleship as stressed in the first third and middle third of Matthew, respectively. Here the forgiveness of disciples' sins and the anticipation of eternal life at the Lord's Supper enable disciples to have tangible assurance that they remain God's royal, baptized children in spite of ongoing and even grievous sins. Similarly, priestly discipleship also enables disciples to receive the forgiveness and hope they need in order to continue in their mission to train and be trained by others in the Word. The necessity of priestly discipleship can also be seen in that if priestly discipleship did not contribute to the other discipleship forms, a disciple would feel threatened by sins and feel lacking in ongoing fellowship with God, reducing royal discipleship to a memory-based relationship with God with an uncertain future, and reducing prophetic discipleship to forming a community lacking in mercy and hope. To use a worship analogy, this would be like entering God's house and being trained in the Word with God's people but having no hope for a destination in the future.

Diagram 4 will now be considered again to help illustrate the mutual hierarchy of the discipleship forms in Matthew and bring out some of the practical implications of this. Recall that diagram 4 illustrates the prominence of the divine persons in Matthew's narrative:

17. For example, a Christian might struggle with a particular area of doctrine or a particular area of life, such as perhaps anger, greed, lust, etc. (see 15:19). All Christians will have some such struggle. Prophetic discipleship provides Christians a space to struggle with such things so long as they are open to the process of growing as Jesus's disciples in the power of the Holy Spirit. Various sins are engulfed in God's love and the forgiveness of Christ especially in royal discipleship and priestly discipleship, respectively, and we struggle to improve in the areas of sins especially in connection with prophetic discipleship and the middle third of Matthew.

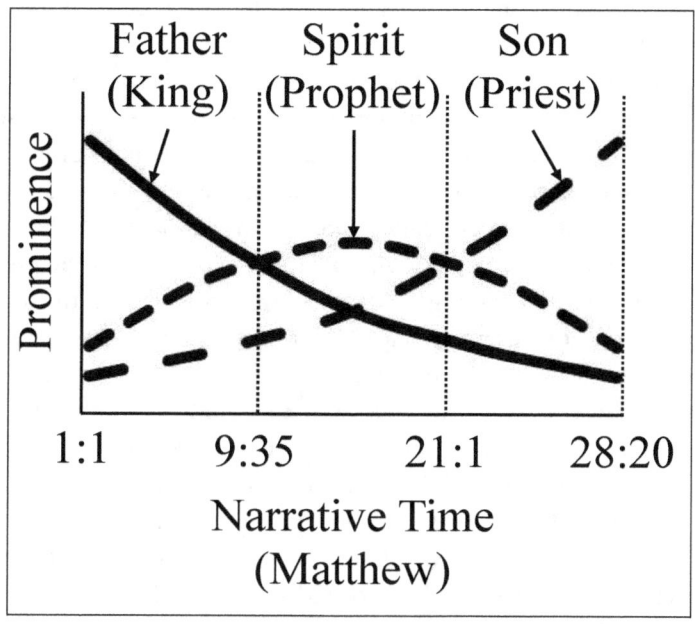

Diagram 4. The Prominence of the Divine Persons in Matthew

As has been said, diagram 4 looks at narrative time in the Gospel of Matthew and shows the prominence of the vocation of each divine person as the narrative proceeds. For the purposes of this chapter, diagram 4 also shows the prominence of the king-prophet-priest discipleship forms. Thus, royal discipleship is most prominent in the first third of Matthew, prophetic discipleship is most prominent in the middle third, and priestly discipleship is most prominent in the final third. Diagram 4 also suggests that the discipleship forms are always changing in prominence. For example, in the first third, as the narrative proceeds and more is discovered about royal discipleship, this discipleship form increasingly gives way to prophetic discipleship and priestly discipleship.

This diagram helps illustrate some of the practical significance of the discipleship forms in Matthew. Here it especially helps in the area of hermeneutics. Rather than needing to rely on proof texts scattered around the biblical narrative to understand discipleship matters like the sacraments and Christian vocation, diagram 4 shows that there is a relatively systematic presentation of such themes in the Gospel of Matthew. Diagram 4 provides a picture of how each third of Matthew emphasizes a unique discipleship form, while not excluding the other discipleship forms in that third, and while helping foster these other discipleship forms in the other parts of Matthew.

The mutual hierarchy of the discipleship forms in Matthew as illustrated in diagram 4 is important not just for the hermeneutics of discipleship but also for the associated practical matter of sermon preparation. In sermon preparation, a pastor could look at diagram 4 and have a map to help navigate where a pericope is situated in Matthew and what sort of discipleship themes to look for and preach on. Whereas in the previous chapter, diagram 4 helped provide a map for considering the story of Jesus's life, now it helps provide a map for how Jesus's life affects the lives of disciples today. For example, if a pericope for a given Sunday is from Jesus's fourth sermon (Matthew 18), a pastor could look at diagram 4 and see that since this sermon comes at the end of the middle third of Matthew, the Holy Spirit's work is most prominent, closely followed by the Son's work, with the Father's work less prominent. This means that the sermon might deal chiefly with Jesus training his disciples in the power of the Holy Spirit, even while recognizing that the latter stages of this focused training where Jesus calls on the disciples to seek true greatness and sacrifice for others (e.g., 16:24, 18:4, 20:28) is increasingly anticipating the need for the Son's sacrifice for sin on the cross (e.g., 16:21, 17:22–23, 20:18–19). Here the hearers of the sermon could be encouraged to sacrifice for others as they strive to follow Jesus's example in the Word, even while a slightly less prominent theme could be that disciples will often make mistakes and fail in this task and need Christ's forgiveness at the Lord's Supper.

Similarly, the mutual hierarchy of discipleship forms in Matthew as illustrated in diagram 4 also is potentially very helpful for the practical matter of mentoring disciples. For example, when a person new to the faith joins a congregation, a mentor could use diagram 4 to help them not only better understand the basic flow of Jesus's life, but also better understand the basic flow of their own life as a new disciple of Jesus. Here the pastor or other members of the congregation could show the new disciple that their walk with Christ begins with baptism, leads to a life of service and striving to emulate the life of Christ in the power of the Holy Spirit, continually receives forgiveness, and reaches for its destination in the Lord's Supper. The new disciple could be taught that this flow characterizes their life as a whole, as they have come into God's family in baptism, will live in the Spirit in connection with the Word, and will follow Christ to the great feast in heaven at death. The new disciple could also be taught that the flow of discipleship in diagram 4 also applies in a more existential manner to the various missions in their life, such as from beginning a day awaking in God's love to finishing a day in Christ's forgiveness, or such as from beginning a week awaking in God's love in worship to working in the power of the Spirit to resting in Christ's forgiveness at the next week's worship. As a disciple progressed in the process of discipleship, the more complex aspects of diagram 4 could be taught, such as that at any given point in the diagram, there are three separate discipleship forms in play. Thus diagram 4 could be very helpful for the practical matter of mentoring disciples.

This section has thus briefly shown that each third of Matthew by having its own distinctive discipleship emphasis is not a threat to the other two thirds but rather fosters their dignity. The three thirds with their distinctive discipleship themes require and complement each other in a dignified way. If any of the discipleship forms were missing, the theology of discipleship in Matthew would fall apart.[18] Finally, this mutual hierarchy of the divine persons in Matthew can be illustrated in diagram form, which helps bring out the great practical potential of mutual hierarchy in areas such as hermeneutics, sermon preparation, and mentoring disciples.

CHAPTER CONCLUSION

This chapter began by asking the question of whether there is a discipleship-centered reading of Matthew's Gospel that complements the christocentric reading from the previous chapter. The present chapter has argued for an affirmative answer to this question by building on the results from the previous chapter and analyzing the connection between

---

18. Wainwright, *For Our Salvation*, 172–86, in the conclusion to his book provides various brief sketches of potential practical and theological prospects of the offices of king, priest, and prophet. For example, Wainwright suggests that there may be a connection between the three offices working together and the biblical triads "way, truth, and life" and "faith, hope, and love." He also suggests that the three offices could be connected to three main time periods both within a worship service and in the church year. He also asserts that the three offices depend upon each other in a way that is fruitful for understanding the triad of the modern ecumenical movement: *leitourgia*, *martyria*, and *diakonia*. See also Sherman, *King, Priest, and Prophet*, 262–80, where Sherman in his concluding remarks similarly attempts to describe how the three offices work together.

the three thirds of Matthew and the royal, prophetic, and priestly discipleship forms. In the first section it looked at Ben Cooper's survey of discipleship in Matthew; Cooper's own pragmatic-critical approach that incorporates both a christocentric and a discipleship reading of Matthew; Wainwright's balancing of christocentric and discipleship concerns in looking at the king, prophet, and priest categories in Scripture; and Sherman's balancing of trinitarian theology and discipleship in looking at the king, prophet, and priest categories in Scripture. This survey then allowed me to briefly lay out my own trinitarian proposal for looking at discipleship in the Gospel of Matthew. The second section looked in greater detail at each of the three thirds of Matthew in connection with the royal, prophetic, and priestly discipleship categories, respectively. Finally, the third section looked at how the discipleship form most prominent in each third does not compete against the other discipleship forms most prominent in the other thirds but rather the forms complement each other and foster mutual dignity. In connection with each discipleship form being unique and yet fostering the dignity of the others, the mutual hierarchy of the discipleship forms in Matthew was evident in a systematic way at a macro-level and in a way that reflects the mutual hierarchy of the divine persons of the Trinity (Matthew 28:19). This mutual hierarchy of the divine persons in Matthew was illustrated in diagram form, which helped bring out the great practical potential of the mutual hierarchy among the discipleship forms in such areas as hermeneutics, sermon preparation, and mentoring disciples.

Conclusion

IN THE FIRST PARAGRAPH of this book, I noted that Social Trinitarians emphasize community as the ultimate ontological category for trinitarian discourse but tend to define community in a way that is arguably not the most desirable by advocating either an egalitarian or a hierarchical extreme view of community. I said that this book would advocate a third alternative for the sort of community present in the Trinity. Just as genuine teamwork is generally desirable in various human communities, the divine persons have a mutual hierarchy relationship with each other where each divine person has a unique hierarchy over the others, and yet each uses this hierarchy to serve the others in a dignified way. In proceeding thus, I intended to advocate a social model of the Trinity that maximally lives up to its name and to in a unique way show the harmony between systematic theology, exegesis, and practice. Now is the time to reflect on our attempt to accomplish these things.

The social trinitarian movement has much potential in contemporary trinitarian discourse. Social trinitarian proposals have made certain advancements beyond the person-oriented and unity (substance)-oriented trinitarian models that are often associated with the Eastern-Cappadocian and Western-Augustinian traditions, respectively. The reader will recall that person-oriented and unity (substance)-oriented models assert, respectively, the relative independence of the divine hypostases (in particular, the person of the Father as cause) and the one divine substance (understood as a sort of fourth entity or concept that logically precedes the divine persons) as the ultimate ontological category in trinitarian discourse. We have argued that Social Trinitarianism by positing community among the divine persons as the ultimate ontological category has the potential to account more adequately for the sociality of the divine persons than person-oriented and substance-oriented models do. That is, Social Trinitarianism has the potential to simultaneously account for both the uniqueness (stressed to a point in a person-oriented model) and dignity (a concern expressed to a point in a substance-oriented model) of the divine persons necessary for their fuller sociality.

Although social trinitarian proposals have much potential relative to the aforementioned trinitarian models, we have shown that social trinitarian proposals also often evidence a hierarchy-equality polarity or tension that causes them to not account adequately for either the uniqueness or the dignity of the divine persons (depending on whether the social trinitarian trajectory is hierarchical or egalitarian) and hence not live up to its communal name fully. We identified the field's inherent polarity at work in the following three areas: (1) its critique of other trinitarian models; (2) its understanding of the economic Trinity with particular emphasis on the incarnate life of the Son; and (3) its understanding of the immanent Trinity. This hierarchy-equality tension led to the need for a revised social model, in line with a mutual hierarchy framework.

A number of significant conclusions follow from my investigation. First, we have seen that Balthasar, as a representative of a hierarchical social trinitarian trajectory, generally accounts for the uniqueness of the divine persons but does not account adequately for their dignity. In all three areas of tension Balthasar emphasizes the Father's hierarchy over the Son, as well as the Father and the Son's hierarchy over the Holy Spirit, often portraying this hierarchy as oppressive in character. Balthasar rarely mentions the equality of the divine persons, and when he does it is redefined in a hierarchical manner. Here he does not account adequately for the dignity of the divine persons who are "oppressed" or the divine persons who "oppress" and thus does not account for the sociality of the divine persons as fully as otherwise possible.

Second, we have seen that Volf as a representative of an egalitarian social trinitarian trajectory generally accounts for the dignity of the divine persons but does not account adequately for their uniqueness. In all three areas of tension, Volf emphasizes the equality of the divine persons and portrays this equality in a way that homogenizes the divine persons and minimizes any hierarchy among them. This means that he does not account adequately for the hierarchical uniqueness of each divine person and thus does not account for the sociality of the divine persons as fully as otherwise possible.

Third, a mutual hierarchy social trinitarian critique of person-oriented and substance-oriented trinitarian models was able to effectively critique these other models in a balanced way. I critiqued Augustine's substance-oriented trinitarian model for making hierarchy and equality opposites and choosing equality in such a way that the uniqueness of the divine persons was not adequately accounted for. But my critique of Augustine could say more positively of him that he generally accounted for the dignity of the divine persons. This contrasted with the critiques of Augustine by Balthasar and Volf, which were intense and simplistic in their critiques by rejecting what they saw as Augustine's allegedly wrong-headed egalitarian and hierarchical trajectory, respectively. My mutual hierarchy critique of Zizioulas as an example of a person-oriented trinitarian model again critiqued him for tending to make hierarchy and equality opposites but in this case choosing hierarchy in such a way as to not adequately account for the dignity of the divine persons. This critique again contrasted with the corresponding critiques by Balthasar and Volf that tended to be simplistic and unnecessarily severe. In this way, my critique could simultaneously account for both the dignity, a concern of Augustine's and Volf, and the uniqueness, a concern of Zizioulas and Balthasar, of the divine persons that are necessary for a more balanced and consistently social critique.

Fourth, a mutual hierarchy social model of the Trinity accounted for both the uniqueness and dignity of the divine persons necessary for their true community in both the economic Trinity and the immanent Trinity. In reference to the economic Trinity, my proposal showed that in the Gospel of John, the divine persons have unique or differentiated vocations relative to one another in contrast to Volf's reading of the Gospel of John that accounts for the dignity of the divine persons but less so their differentiated vocations. My proposal also showed that in the Gospel of John the differentiated vocations of the divine persons are kenotic in such a way that the divine persons work together in a complementary and dignified way. This reading accounted for the dignity of the divine persons more adequately than Balthasar's hierarchical reading of John that accounted somewhat for the uniqueness of the divine persons but less so their dignity. My mutual hierarchy reading of John was also correlated to a different view of the immanent Trinity than in Balthasar and Volf. In my proposal each divine person in connection with their unique personal properties constitutes the others. This accounts for their uniqueness in contrast to Volf's egalitarian proposal where the divine persons are largely homogenized in their mutual relations. But my proposal also accounts for the dignity of the divine persons as they mutually constitute one another, with each divine person limiting his powers and giving space for the other divine persons to contribute. This contrasted especially with Balthasar's hierarchical view of the immanent Trinity that sees the constitution and relations between the divine persons as being hierarchical in a largely unilateral and oppressive way. In this way my mutual hierarchy proposal simultaneously accounted for both the uniqueness and dignity necessary for a more consistently social conception of both the economic Trinity and the immanent Trinity.

Fifth, my mutual hierarchy proposal made a significant ecclesiological contribution. It showed how Balthasar and Volf's trinitarian proposals were integrally connected to their hierarchical and egalitarian ecclesiological proposals, respectively. In both Balthasar and Volf's ecclesiology, because of the hierarchy-equality polarity in play, choices had to be made between laity and pastor and between congregation and larger church, with Volf consistently choosing the former in each pair and Balthasar the latter. Balthasar and Volf's systems also tended to choose church maintenance over mission. But my mutual hierarchy ecclesiological proposal, rooted in the mutual hierarchy of the divine persons, fostered a more consistently social conception of the church and its mission to the world by encouraging both distinctness and dignity in human fellowships in the image of the Trinity.

Finally, this book has made certain contributions to hermeneutics in connection with the mutual hierarchy of the divine persons. It has argued that the Gospel of Matthew has a systematic method for teaching the mutual hierarchy of the divine persons to the extent that Matthew is divided into three thirds, each emphasizing a distinct divine person and his work in connection with a king-prophet-priest category, even while the three thirds also serve each other and are complementary reflecting the mutuality of the divine persons. Similarly, the book has argued that royal, prophetic, and priestly discipleship forms are present in the three thirds of Matthew, respectively, in connection with the three persons of the Trinity. While distinct, these discipleship forms also support each other and foster mutuality among themselves in reflection of the mutual hierarchy of the divine persons. Finally, the mutual hierarchy among the three thirds of Matthew has significant practical potential in such practical areas as sermon preparation, Christian devotion, and mentoring disciples.

A brief discussion of suggestions for further study will conclude this book. Future study could look at the relationship between the mutual hierarchy of the divine persons and the doctrine of creation. For example, as the divine persons prepare to create, how does the hierarchical uniqueness of each divine person come into play and how does each divine person work to serve the others in the act of creation? Here it seems significant that the Father arguably creates as one who will be transcendent relative to creation, the Son creates as one who will become incarnate in that creation, and the Spirit creates as one who will mediate between the Father and the Son and who will be the sanctifier of human beings. At the other end of the spectrum, how is mutual hierarchy related to eschatology? For example, considering that the Son's response to the Father is associated with the end of the world (1 Cor 15:24), with the Spirit somehow mediating between them, might this have something to say about eschatological anthropology? Might human beings not only eternally benefit from the Father and Son's relations with each other but also as a fruit of this in the power of the Holy Spirit help mediate or magnify this relationship in some way? Future study could also look at how the mutual hierarchy of the divine persons could influence how we think about power in society—a topic often associated with Social Trinitarianism. A mutual hierarchy framework could critique rulers exercising a unilateral and oppressive authority over their subjects, even as it also could critique conceiving all members of society as equal to one another in such a way that no room is left for leadership or the unique strengths of the various members of society. Here a mutual hierarchy framework would seem to allow for the sort of leadership that is arguably necessary for life in an evil world, and yet it could also allow for citizens to have hierarchy over leaders in such a way that they might complement their leaders as well as serve as a check and balance to their exercise of power. Finally, as already alluded to in the book, future study could look at the possibility of the other Gospels besides Matthew having three thirds that involve mutual hierarchy with each other, as well as look at mutual hierarchy within each third of Matthew as well as within smaller pericopes.

Glossary

Dignity: A term that describes a divine person serving the other divine persons rather than oppressing them.

Economic Trinity: The divine persons considered in their relation to the world, especially beginning with the creation of the world.

Egalitarian Social Trinitarian: A Social Trinitarian who tends to polarize hierarchy and equality in trinitarian discourse and choose the latter over the former.

Hierarchical Social Trinitarian: A Social Trinitarian who tends to polarize hierarchy and equality in trinitarian discourse and choose the former over the latter.

Hierarchy: A term that refers to a divine person having a power over the other divine persons in connection with his vocation (in the economic Trinity) and personal properties (in the immanent Trinity).

Hierarchy-Equality Polarity: A false alternative of hierarchy versus equality (in the case of the Trinity, among the divine persons).

Hyper-Personal Monism: A view that heavily emphasizes the person of the Father in such a way that the other divine persons and all things are negated by being absorbed into him.

Immanent Trinity: The divine persons considered apart from their relation to the world, especially prior to the creation of the world.

Kenosis: A term pointing to a divine person limiting the exercise of his power relative to the others (and relative to creation), for example when the Son in his humiliation dwelt on earth and relied on the Father in heaven for various needs.

Mutual: A term associated with a divine person relating with the other divine persons rather than being isolated from them in some manner.

Mutual Constitution: A view where the divine persons each cause and form one another in the immanent Trinity, as opposed to one or some divine persons logically preceding others.

Mutual Hierarchy: A framework for the doctrine of the Trinity (and by extension other doctrines) that holds that each divine person in unique ways has hierarchy and power over the others, yet amid the exercise of power limits his power in a dignified way in order to serve the other divine persons and their dignity.

Perichoresis: A term associated with the unity or communion of the divine persons, such as through face-to-face encounter (circumincessio) or, as emphasized by Moltmann, for example, mutual indwelling (circuminsessio).

Person-Oriented Trinitarian Model: Also associated with an Eastern-Cappadocian trinitarian model, a view that stresses the category of person, in particular the person of the Father as cause, as the ultimate ontological category in trinitarian discourse.

Persons: Beings each with a center of consciousness that mutually affect each other as well as their environment.

Pre-Personal Monism: A view that heavily emphasizes the divine substance, whether conceived of as transcendent over the world or as immanent within the world, in such a way that the divine persons and all things are negated by being absorbed into it.

Processions: The generation of the Son and the spiration of the Spirit in the immanent Trinity.

Prominence: A term referring to how much a divine person's work stands out or is conspicuous at a given time in a biblical narrative. A human analogy for this is how in a play a character often stands out in connection with such things as being in the middle of the stage, having the spotlight on him or her, and speaking an important line.

Relation: A term that in Latin (Western-Augustinian) theology typically describes both a connection and a distinction between the divine persons and is typically subordinate to the divine substance. In

Greek (Eastern-Cappadocian) theology, a term that typically describes how the Son and the Holy Spirit interact with the Father as their cause and leader. In Social Trinitarianism, a central term describing the conscious interactions of the divine persons in community with each other.

Social Trinitarianism: A viewpoint associated with Jürgen Moltmann that holds to community as the ultimate ontological category in trinitarian discourse.

Sociality: A term that measures how well a viewpoint agrees with a social model of the Trinity and that for maximization requires both the uniqueness and the dignity of the divine persons.

Substance: A term that points to the one divine nature the three divine persons have in common or are (depending on the trinitarian model).

Substance (Unity)-Oriented Trinitarian Model: Also associated with a Western-Augustinian trinitarian model, a view that stresses the divine substance as the ultimate ontological category in trinitarian discourse; this view is sometimes associated with effectively positing the divine substance as a fourth entity conceptually separable from the divine persons and above them.

Uniqueness: A term that describes the divine persons being distinguished from each other rather than confused with each other.

Bibliography

Allison, Dale C., Jr. *The New Moses: A Matthean Typology*. Minneapolis: Fortress, 1993.
Augustine. *On the Holy Trinity*. A Select Library of the Nicene and Post-Nicene Fathers of the Christian Church: First Series 3. Peabody, MA: Hendrickson, 1994.
Awad, Najeeb. "Between Subordination and Koinonia: Toward a New Reading of the Cappadocian Theology." *Modern Theology* 23 (2007) 181–204.
Balthasar, Hans. *The Glory of the Lord: A Theological Aesthetics*. 7 vols. Translated by Erasmo Leiva-Merikakis. San Francisco: Ignatius, 1982–1991.
———. *Herrlichkeit: Eine Theologische Ästhetik*. 3 vols. Einsiedeln: Johannes, 1961–1969.
———. *Theo-Drama: Theological Dramatic Theory*. 5 vols. Translated by Graham Harrison. San Francisco: Ignatius, 1988–1998.
———. *Theodramatik*. 4 vols. Einsiedeln: Johannes, 1973–1983.
———. *Theo-Logic: Theological Logical Theory*. 3 vols. Translated by Adrian Walker. San Francisco: Ignatius, 2000–2005.
———. *Theologik*. 3 vols. Einsiedeln: Johannes, 1985–1987.
Barber, Michael. "Jesus as the Davidic Temple Builder and Peter's Priestly Role in Matthew 16:16–19." *Journal of Biblical Literature* 132 (2013) 935–53.
Basser, Herbert, and Marsha Cohen. *The Gospel of Matthew and Judaic Traditions: A Relevance-Based Commentary*. Brill Reference Library of Judaism 46. Leiden: Brill, 2015.
Bauckham, Richard. "The Holiness of Jesus and His Disciples in the Gospel of John." In *Holiness and Ecclesiology in the New Testament*, edited by Kent Brower and Andy Johnson, 95–113. Grand Rapids, MI: Eerdmans, 2007.
———. "'Only the Suffering God Can Help': Divine Passibility in Modern Theology." *Themelios* 9 (1984) 6–12.
Bidwell, Kevin. *The Church as the Image of the Trinity: A Critical Evaluation of Miroslav Volf's Ecclesial Model*. Eugene, OR: Wipf & Stock, 2011.
Boff, Leonardo. *Trinity and Society*. Translated by Paul Burns. Maryknoll, NY: Orbis, 1988.
Boxall, Ian. *Discovering Matthew: Content, Interpretation, Reception*. Discovering Biblical Texts. London: SPCK, 2014.
Brink, Gijsbert. "Social Trinitarianism: A Discussion of Some Recent Theological Criticisms." *International Journal of Systematic Theology* 16 (2014) 331–50.
Broadhead, Edwin. *The Gospel of Matthew on the Landscape of Antiquity*. Tübingen: Mohr Siebeck, 2017.

Brown, Raymond. *The Gospel according to John*. Garden City, NY: Doubleday, 1970.

Byrne, Brendan. *A Costly Freedom: A Theological Reading of Mark's Gospel*. Collegeville, MN: Liturgical, 2008.

Capdevila i Montaner, Viçens Maria. "El Padre en el Cuarto Evangelio." In *Dios el Padre*. Salamanca: Secretariado Trinitario, 1991.

Clark, David J., and Jan de Waard. "Discourse Structure in Matthew's Gospel." *Scriptura* (1982) 1–97.

Coakley, Sarah. "'Persons' in the 'Social' Doctrine of the Trinity: A Critique of Current Analytic Discussion." In *The Trinity: An Interdisciplinary Symposium on the Trinity*, edited by Stephen Davis et al., 123–44. New York: Oxford University Press, 1999.

Coker, Joe. "Peace and the Apocalypse: Stanley Hauerwas and Miroslav Volf on the Eschatological Basis for Christian Nonviolence." *Evangelical Quarterly* 71 (1999) 261–68.

Coloe, Mary. *God Dwells with Us: Temple Symbolism in the Fourth Gospel*. Collegeville, MN: Liturgical, 2001.

Cooper, Ben. "Adaptive Eschatological Inference from the Gospel of Matthew." *Journal for the Study of the New Testament* 33 (2010) 59–80.

———. *Incorporated Servanthood: Commitment and Discipleship in the Gospel of Matthew*. Library of New Testament Studies 490. London: Bloomsbury T & T Clark, 2013.

Corecco, Eugenio. "Ekklesiologische Grundlagen des Codex Iuris Canonici." *Concilium* 22 (1986) 166–72.

Cross, Richard. "Two Models of the Trinity?" *Heythrop Journal* 43 (2002) 275–94.

Crump, David. "Re-examining the Johannine Trinity: Perichoresis or Deification?" *Scottish Journal of Theology* 59 (2006) 395–412.

Davies, William. *The Setting of the Sermon on the Mount*. New York: Cambridge University Press, 1964.

Davies, William, and Dale C. Allison. *A Critical and Exegetical Commentary on the Gospel According to Saint Matthew*. 3 vols. International Critical Commentary on the Holy Scriptures of the Old and New Testaments. Edinburgh: T & T Clark, 1988–1997.

Davis, Leo. *The First Seven Ecumenical Councils (325–787): Their History and Theology*. Theology and Life 21. Collegeville, MN: Liturgical, 1990.

Del Colle, Ralph. "Communion and the Trinity: The Free Church Ecclesiology of Miroslav Volf—A Catholic Response." *Pneuma* 22 (2000) 303–27.

Denaux, Adelbert. "The Delineation of the Lucan Travel Narrative within the Overall Structure of the Gospel of Luke." In *The Synoptic Gospels: Source Criticism and the New Literary Criticism*, edited by Camille Focant, 357–92. Bibliotheca Ephemeridum Theologicarum Lovaniensium 110. Leuven: Leuven University Press, 1993.

Doyle, Dennis. *Communion Ecclesiology: Vision and Versions*. Maryknoll, NY: Orbis, 2000.

Dunham, Scott. *The Trinity and Creation in Augustine: An Ecological Analysis*. Albany: State University of New York Press, 2008.

Erickson, Millard. *God in Three Persons: A Contemporary Interpretation of the Trinity*. Grand Rapids, MI: Baker, 1995.

France, R. T. *Matthew: Evangelist and Teacher*. Grand Rapids, MI: Zondervan, 1989.

Fretheim, Terence E. *Exodus*. Interpretation, a Bible Commentary for Teaching and Preaching. Louisville: John Knox, 1991.

———. "The Reclamation of Creation: Redemption and Law in Exodus." *Interpretation* 45 (1991) 354–65.

Gibbs, Jeffrey. *Matthew 1:1–11:1*. Concordia Commentary. St Louis: Concordia, 2006.

———. *Jerusalem and Parousia: Jesus' Eschatological Discourse in Matthew's Gospel*. Saint Louis: Concordia, 2000.

Gieschen, Charles. "The Death of Jesus in the Gospel of John: Atonement for Sin?" *Concordia Theological Quarterly* 72 (2008) 243–61.

Giles, Kevin. *Jesus and the Father: Modern Evangelicals Reinvent the Doctrine of the Trinity*. Grand Rapids, MI: Zondervan, 2006.

Goetz, Ronald. "Karl Barth, Jurgen Moltmann and the Theopaschite Revolution." In *Festschrift: A Tribute to Dr. William Hordern*, edited by Walter Freitag, 17–28. Saskatoon, Canada: University of Saskatchewan, 1985.

Goulder, Michael. "Sections and Lections in Matthew." *Journal for the Study of the New Testament* 76 (1999) 79–96.

Grabbe, Lester. "The Law, the Prophets, and the Rest: The State of the Bible in Pre-Maccabean Times." *Dead Sea Discoveries* 13 (2006) 319–38.

Grenz, Stanley. *Reason for Hope: The Systematic Theology of Wolfhart Pannenberg*. New York: Oxford University Press, 1990.

———. *Rediscovering the Triune God: The Trinity in Contemporary Theology*. Twentieth Century Religious Thought, Volume I: Christianity. Minneapolis: Fortress, 2004.

———. *The Social God and the Relational Self: A Trinitarian Theology of the Imago Dei*. Louisville: Westminster John Knox, 2001.

Gresham, John. "The Social Model of the Trinity and Its Critics." *Scottish Journal of Theology* 46 (1993) 325–43.

Gruenler, Royce. *The Trinity in the Gospel of John: A Thematic Commentary on the Fourth Gospel*. Grand Rapids, MI: Baker, 1986.

Gunton, Colin. *The One, the Three, and the Many: God, Creation, and the Culture of Modernity*. Cambridge, UK: Cambridge University Press, 1993.

———. *The Promise of Trinitarian Theology*. Edinburgh: T & T Clark, 1997.

Gurtner, Daniel. *The Torn Veil: Matthew's Exposition of the Death of Jesus*. Society for New Testament Studies 139. Cambridge: Cambridge University Press, 2007.

Horrell, J. Scott. "The Eternal Son of God in the Social Trinity." In *Jesus in Trinitarian Perspective: An Intermediate Christology*, edited by Fred Sanders et al., 44–79. Nashville: B & H Academic, 2007.

———. "Toward a Biblical Model of the Social Trinity: Avoiding Equivocation of Nature and Order." *Journal of the Evangelical Theological Society* 47 (2004) 399–421.

Just, Arthur. *Heaven on Earth: The Gifts of Christ in the Divine Service*. St. Louis: Concordia, 2008.

Kärkkäinen, Veli-Matti. *An Introduction to Ecclesiology: Ecumenical, Historical and Global Perspectives*. Downers Grove, IL: InterVarsity, 2002.

Kennedy, Joel. *The Recapitulation of Israel: Use of Israel's History in Matthew 1:1—4:11*. Wissenschaftliche Untersuchungen zum Neuen Testament 2. Reihe 257. Tübingen: Mohr Siebeck, 2008.

Kim, Jae. *Relational God and Salvation: Soteriological Implications of the Social Doctrine of Trinity—Jürgen Moltmann, Catherine LaCugna, Colin Gunton*. Kampen: Kok, 2008.

Kloha, Jeffrey. "The Trans-Congregational Church in the New Testament." *Concordia Journal* 34 (2008) 172–90.

Kolb, Robert. "Luther on the Two Kinds of Righteousness: Reflections on His Two-Dimensional Definition of Humanity at the Heart of His Theology." *Lutheran Quarterly* 13 (1999) 449–66.

Köstenberger, Andreas. *Father, Son and Spirit: The Trinity and John's Gospel*. Downers Grove, IL: InterVarsity, 2008.

Leftow, Brian. "Anti Social Trinitarianism." In *The Trinity: An Interdisciplinary Symposium on the Trinity*, edited by Stephen Davis et al., 203–49. New York: Oxford University Press, 1999.

Linahan, Jane. "Experiencing God in Brokenness: The Self-Emptying of the Holy Spirit in Moltmann's Pneumatology." In *Encountering Transcendence: Contributions to a Theology of Christian Religious Experience*, edited by Lieven Boeve et al., 165–84. Leuven: Peeters, 2002.

Lohr, Charles H. "Oral Techniques in the Gospel of Matthew." *The Catholic Biblical Quarterly* 23 (1961) 403–35.

Lösel, Steffen. "Conciliar, not Conciliatory: Hans Urs von Balthasar's Ecclesiological Synthesis of Vatican II." *Modern Theology* 24 (2008) 23–49.

———. "Murder in the Cathedral: Hans Urs von Balthasar's New Dramatization of the Doctrine of the Trinity." *Pro Ecclesia* 5 (1996) 427–39.

———. "A Plain Account of Christian Salvation? Balthasar on Sacrifice, Solidarity, and Substitution." *Pro Ecclesia* 13 (2004) 141–71.

———. "Unapocalyptic Theology: History and Eschatology in Balthasar's Theo-Drama." *Modern Theology* 17 (2001) 201–25.

Luz, Ulrich. "The Disciples in the Gospel According to Matthew." In *The Interpretation of Matthew*, edited by Graham Stanton, 98–128. Philadelphia: Fortress, 1983.

———. *Matthew 1–7: A Commentary*. Hermeneia. Minneapolis: Fortress, 2007.

———. *Matthew 8–20: A Commentary*. Hermeneia. Minneapolis: Fortress, 2001.

———. *Matthew 21–28: A Commentary*. Hermeneia. Minneapolis: Fortress, 2005

Mancini, Will. *Church Unique: How Missional Leaders Cast Vision, Capture Culture, and Create Movement*. San Francisco: Jossey-Bass, 2008.

Mansini, Guy. "Balthasar and the Theodramatic Enrichment of the Trinity." *Thomist* 64 (2000) 499–519.

Moloney, Francis. *The Gospel of Mark: A Commentary*. Grand Rapids, MI: Baker Academic, 2012.

Moltmann, Jürgen. "God's Kenosis in the Creation and Consummation of the World." In *The Work of Love: Creation as Kenosis*, edited by John Polkinghorne, 137–51. Grand Rapids, MI: Eerdmans, 2001.

———. *The Trinity and the Kingdom: The Doctrine of God*. Translated by Margaret Kohl. Twentieth Century Religious Thought, Volume 1: Christianity. San Francisco: Harper & Row, 1981.

———. *Trinität und Reich Gottes: zur Gotteslehre*. München: C. Kaiser, 1980.

Mongrain, Kevin. *The Systematic Thought of Hans Urs von Balthasar: An Irenaean Retrieval*. New York: Crossroad, 2002.

Morosco, Robert. "Matthew's Formation of a Commissioning Type-Scene out of the Story of Jesus' Commissioning of the Twelve." *Journal of Biblical Literature* 103 (1984) 539–56.

Ngien, Dennis. *The Suffering of God according to Martin Luther's Theologia Crucis.* New York: P. Lang, 1995.

Nichols, Aidan. *Say It Is Pentecost: A Guide through Balthasar's Logic.* Washington, DC: Catholic University of America Press, 2001.

———. "The Theologic." In *The Cambridge Companion to Hans Urs Von Balthasar*, edited by Edward Oakes and David Moss, 158–71. Cambridge, UK: Cambridge University Press, 2004.

Norman, Ralph. "Problems for the 'Social Trinity': Counting God." *Modern Believing* 41 (2000) 3–13.

O'Donnell, John. *Hans Urs von Balthasar.* Collegeville, MN: Liturgical, 1992.

———. "The Trinity as Divine Community: A Critical Reflection upon Recent Theological Developments." *Gregorianum* 69 (1988) 5–34.

Olson, Roger. "Trinity and Eschatology: The Historical Being of God in Jürgen Moltmann and Wolfhart Pannenberg." *Scottish Journal of Theology* 36 (1983) 213–27.

O'Regan, Cyril. "Balthasar and Eckhart: Theological Principles and Catholicity." *The Thomist* 60 (1996) 203–39.

———. "Balthasar and Gnostic Genealogy." *Modern Theology* 22 (2006) 609–50.

———. *Gnostic Return in Modernity.* Albany: State University of New York Press, 2001.

———. "Von Balthasar and Thick Retrieval: Post-Chalcedonian Symphonic Theology." *Gregorianum* 77 (1996) 227–60.

———. "Von Balthasar's Valorization and Critique of Heidegger's Genealogy of Modernity." In *Christian Spirituality and the Culture of Modernity*, edited by Peter Casarella and George Schner, 123–58. Grand Rapids, MI: Eerdmans, 1998.

Pannenberg, Wolfhart. "God's Love and the Kenosis of the Son: A Response to Masao Abe." In *Divine Emptiness and Historical Fullness*, edited by Masao Abe and Christopher Ives, 244–50. Valley Forge, PA: Trinity Press International, 1995.

———. *Systematic Theology.* 3 vols. Translated by Geoffrey Bromiley. Grand Rapids, MI: Eerdmans, 1991–1997.

Photius, I. *St. Photius: The Mystagogy of the Holy Spirit.* Translated by Joseph Farrel. Brookline, MA: Holy Cross Orthodox, 1987.

Pitstick, Alyssa. *Light in Darkness: Hans Urs Von Balthasar and the Catholic Doctrine of Christ's Descent into Hell.* Grand Rapids, MI: Eerdmans, 2007.

Plantinga, Cornelius. "The Fourth Gospel as Trinitarian Source Then and Now." In *Biblical Hermeneutics in Historical Perspective*, edited by Mark Burrows et al., 303–21. Grand Rapids, MI: Eerdmans, 1991.

———. *The Hodgson-Welch Debate and the Social Analogy of the Trinity.* PhD diss., Princeton Theological Seminary, 1982.

———. "The Perfect Family: Our Model for Life Together Is Found in the Father, Son, and Holy Spirit." *Christianity Today* 32 (1988) 24–27.

Porsch, Félix. *El Espíritu Santo, Defensor de los Creyentes: La Actividad del Espíritu según el Evangelio de San Juan.* Salamanca, Spain: Secretariado Trinitario, 1983.

Quarles, Charles. *A Theology of Matthew: Jesus Revealed as Deliverer, King, and Incarnate Creator.* Explorations in Biblical Theology 11. Phillipsburg, NJ: P & R, 2013.

Rahner, Karl. *The Trinity.* New York: Herder and Herder, 1970.

Sachs, John. "The Holy Spirit and Christian Form." *Gregorianum* 86 (2005) 378–96.
Sánchez, Leopoldo. "Life in the Spirit of Christ: Models of Sanctification as Sacramental Pneumatology." *Logia* 22 (2013) 7–14.
———. *Receiver, Bearer, and Giver of God's Spirit: Jesus' Life and Mission in the Spirit as a Lens for Theology and Life.* Eugene, OR: Pickwick, 2015.
———. "Toward an Ecclesiology of Catholic Unity and Mission in the Borderlands: Reflections from a Lutheran Latino Theologian." *Concordia Journal* 35 (2009) 17–34.
Saward, John. "Mary and Peter in the Christological Constellation: Balthasar's Ecclesiology." In *The Analogy of Beauty: The Theology of Hans Urs von Balthasar*, edited by John Riches, 105–33. Edinburgh: T & T Clark, 1986.
Scaer, David. *Baptism.* Confessional Lutheran Dogmatics 11. St. Louis: Luther Academy, 1999.
———. *Discourses in Matthew: Jesus Teaches the Church.* St. Louis: Concordia, 2004.
———. "Homo Factus Est as the Revelation of God." *Concordia Theological Quarterly* 65 (2001) 111–26.
———. *The Sermon on the Mount: The Church's First Statement of the Gospel.* Saint Louis: Concordia, 2000.
Sherman, Robert. *King, Priest and Prophet: A Trinitarian Theology of Atonement.* New York: T & T Clark, 2004.
Sonnet, Jean-Pierre. *The Book within the Book: Writing in Deuteronomy.* Biblical Interpretation 14. Leiden: Brill, 1997.
Thompson, Thomas. *Imitatio Trinitatis: The Trinity as Social Model in the Theologies of Jürgen Moltmann and Leonardo Boff.* PhD diss., Princeton Theological Seminary, 1996.
———. "Trinitarianism Today: Doctrinal Renaissance, Ethical Relevance, Social Redolence." *Calvin Theological Journal* 32 (1997) 9–42.
Thompson, Thomas and Cornelius Plantinga. "Trinity and Kenosis." In *Exploring Kenotic Christology*, edited by Stephen Evans, 165–89. Oxford: Oxford University Press, 2006.
Turek, Margaret. *Towards a Theology of God the Father: Hans Urs von Balthasar's Theodramatic Approach.* Theology and Religion 212. New York: P. Lang, 2001.
Volf, Miroslav. "After Moltmann: Reflections on the Future of Eschatology." In *God Will Be All in All: The Eschatology of Jürgen Moltmann*, edited by Richard Bauckham, 233–57. Edinburgh: T & T Clark, 1999.
———. *After Our Likeness: The Church as the Image of the Trinity.* Grand Rapids, MI: Eerdmans, 1998.
———. *Allah: A Christian Response.* New York: HarperOne, 2011.
———. "Being as God Is: Trinity and Generosity." In *God's Life in Trinity*, edited by Miroslav Volf and Michael Welker, 3–12. Minneapolis: Fortress, 2006.
———. "Community Formation as an Image of the Triune God: A Congregational Model of Church Order and Life." In *Community Formation in the Early Church and in the Church Today*, edited by Richard Longenecker, 213–37. Peabody, MA: Hendrickson, 2002.
———. "Eschaton, Creation, and Social Ethics." *Calvin Theological Journal* 30 (1995) 130–43.
———. *Exclusion and Embrace: A Theological Exploration of Identity, Otherness, and Reconciliation.* Nashville: Abingdon, 1996.

———. "Introduction: A Queen and a Beggar: Challenges and Prospects of Theology." In *The Future of Theology: Essays in Honor of Jürgen Moltmann*, edited by Miroslav Volf et al., ix–xviii. Grand Rapids, MI: Eerdmans, 1996.

———. *Trinität und Gemeinschaft: Eine Oekumenische Ekklesiologie*. Mainz: Grünewald, 1996.

———. "The Trinity and Gender Identity." In *Gospel and Gender: A Trinitarian Engagement with Being Male and Female in Christ*, edited by Douglas Campbell and Alan Torrance, 153–78. London: T & T Clark, 2003.

———. "The Trinity Is Our Social Program: The Doctrine of the Trinity and the Shape of Social Engagement." *Modern Theology* 14 (1998) 403–23.

———. "Trinity, Unity, Primacy: On the Trintarian Nature of Unity and Its Implications for the Question of Primacy." In *Petrine Ministry and the Unity of the Church: Toward a Patient and Fraternal Dialogue*, edited by James Puglisi, 171–84. Collegeville, MN: Liturgical, 1999.

———. *Work in the Spirit: Toward a Theology of Work*. New York: Oxford University Press, 1991.

Volf, Miroslav, and Maurice Lee. "The Spirit and the Church." *The Conrad Grebel Review* 18 (2000) 20–45.

Von Speyr, Adrienne. *Kreuz und Hölle*. Einsiedeln: Johannes, 1966.

Wainwright, Geoffrey. *For Our Salvation: Two Approaches to the Work of Christ*. Grand Rapids, MI: Eerdmans, 1997.

Ward, Graham. "Kenosis: Death, Discourse and Resurrection." In *Balthasar at the End of Modernity*, edited by Lucy Gardner et al., 15–68. Edinburgh: T & T Clark, 1999.

Wheaton, Gerry. *The Role of Jewish Feasts in John's Gospel*. Society for NT Studies Monograph Series 162. London: Cambridge University Press, 2015.

Wilkins, Michael. *The Concept of Disciple in Matthew's Gospel as Reflected in the Use of the Term Mathētēs*. Supplements to Novum Testamentum. Leiden: Brill, 1988.

———. *Following the Master: Discipleship in the Steps of Jesus*. Grand Rapids, MI: Zondervan, 1992.

Witherington, Ben, III. *The Gospel of Mark: A Socio-Rhetorical Commentary*. Grand Rapids, MI: Eerdmans, 2001.

Yee, Gale A. *Jewish Feasts and the Gospel of John*. Zacchaeus Studies New Testament. Wilmington, DE: Michael Glazier, 1989.

Zizioulas, John. *Being as Communion: Studies in Personhood and the Church*. Crestwood, NY: St. Vladimir's Seminary Press, 1985.

———. *Communion and Otherness: Further Studies in Personhood and the Church*, edited by Paul McPartlan. London: T & T Clark, 2006.

Index of Names

ANCIENT

Anselm, Saint, 23, 27, 91
Aquinas, Thomas, 10, 23, 28, 32
Arius of Alexandria, 2–3, 46, 91
Augustine, Saint, 3–5, 21, 23, 26–31, 34, 36, 43–47, 49–51, 91, 183
Basil, Saint, 2, 3, 48
Bonaventure, Saint, 23, 25, 28
Cyril of Alexandria, 37
Dante, 28
Eckhart, Meister, 24, 26
Gregory of Nyssa, 24
Ignatius of Loyola, 26, 69
Irenaeus, Saint, 21–23, 30, 66–67, 71
Joachim of Fiore, 21–22, 28
Nicholas of Cusa, 24, 28–30
Photius, I, 27, 43
Pseudo-Cyril, 98
Pseudo-Dionysius, 24, 27, 29
Siger of Brabant, 28

MODERN

Allison, Dale C., Jr., 132–33, 138–42, 145–46, 148–54, 156, 165
Awad, Najeeb, 2–3
Bacon, Benjamin, 132–34
Balthasar, Hans, xiii–xv, xvii, 1, 6, 8, 12–15, 18–31, 41–43, 51–59, 68–72, 78, 84, 86–96, 100–103, 105, 109, 114–15, 117–18, 122–29, 182–84
Barber, Michael, 139, 142, 149–53, 155
Barth, Karl, 13, 22–23, 78
Basser, Herbert, 143
Bauckham, Richard, 78, 132, 143
Baur, Ferdinand Christian, 22
Bidwell, Kevin, 119
Boff, Leonardo, 2–3, 6–9, 82
Boxall, Ian, 149–51, 154
Brink, Gijsbert, xii, 5–6
Broadhead, Edwin, 165
Byrne, Brendan, 132
Capdevila i Montaner, Viçens Maria, 74
Clark, David J., 134
Coakley, Sarah, 5
Cohen, Marsha, 143
Coker, Joe, 66, 121
Coloe, Mary, 132
Cooper, Ben, 147, 164–66, 169, 171, 173, 180
Corecco, Eugenio, 117
Cross, Richard, 5
Crump, David, 83
Davies, William, 132–33, 138–40, 145–46, 148–54, 156, 165
Davis, Leo, 108
De Waard, Jan, 134
Del Colle, Ralph, 97
Denaux, Adelbert, 131
Doyle, Dennis, 118
Dunham, Scott, 43
Erickson, Millard, xiii, 3, 7–9, 108
France, R. T., 142
Fretheim, Terence E., 138–39, 141

Gibbs, Jeffrey, 141, 143, 147
Gieschen, Charles, 74
Giles, Kevin, 5
Goetz, Ronald, 78
Goulder, Michael, 140
Grabbe, Lester, 131
Grenz, Stanley, 6, 11, 13, 107
Gresham, John, xii
Gruenler, Royce, xiii, 3, 8–9, 49, 80–81
Gunton, Colin, 5, 7–9, 95–96
Gurtner, Daniel, 154
Hauerwas, Stanley, 66, 121
Hegel, Georg Wilhelm Friedrich, 22–23, 26, 28, 96
Horrell, J. Scott, xii, 6
Just, Arthur, 166
Kärkkäinen, Veli-Matti, 119
Kennedy, Joel, 138, 140
Kim, Jae, xii
Kingsbury, Jack, 132,
Kloha, Jeffrey, 116
Kolb, Robert, 126
Köstenberger, Andreas, 49
Krieg, Robert, 33
LaCugna, Catherine Mowry, 34
Leftow, Brian, 5
Lessing, Gotthold Ephraim, 28
Linahan, Jane, 78
Lochman, Jan, 6
Lohr, Charles H., 132, 135
Lösel, Steffen, 24, 69, 102
Luz, Ulrich, 132–34, 139, 143–44, 148, 151, 164
Mancini, Will, 125
Mansini, Guy, 14
Marx, Karl, 28
Michelet, Jules, 28
Möhler, Johan Adam, 22
Moloney, Francis, 132
Moltmann, Jürgen, xi–xii, xiv, 4–5, 8, 10–12, 16–19, 22, 64, 66, 78, 97, 99, 105, 156, 188–89
Mongrain, Kevin, 21–25, 30–31, 42, 69
Morosco, Robert, 144
Ngien, Dennis, 77
Nichols, Aidan, 14, 118

Nietzsche, Friedrich, 32
Norman, Ralph, 5
O'Donnell, John, 5, 13, 97
Olson, Roger, 12
O'Regan, Cyril, 14–15, 21–27, 30–31
Ostathios, Geevarghese Mar, 6
Pannenberg, Wolfhart, 2–12, 17–19, 48, 71, 74, 78, 95
Pitstick, Alyssa, 54–56, 59
Plantinga, Cornelius, 3, 6, 8, 43–47, 80
Porsch, Félix, 74
Quarles, Charles, 138, 142
Rahner, Karl, xvii, 4, 22–23
Ratzinger, Joseph, 16, 32–36, 39–41, 43
Rienzo, Cola di, 28
Sachs, John, 78, 94
Sánchez, Leopoldo, 113, 128, 166
Saward, John, 118
Scaer, David, 78, 140, 165, 167
Schelling, Friedrich Wilhelm Joseph, 28
Segundo, Juan Luis, 6
Sherman, Robert, 133–34, 136–48, 154–56, 158–59, 164–69, 172, 174, 179–80
Sonnet, Jean-Pierre, 131
Staudenmaier, Franz Anton, 22
Taylor, Vincent, 108
Thompson, Thomas, xii, xvi, 3, 6, 8, 66, 80
Turek, Margaret, 89–90, 94
Volf, Miroslav, xiii–xv, xvii, 1, 8, 12–13, 16–20, 31–43, 47–48, 50–53, 60–71, 78, 86–88, 95–101, 114–15, 117–24, 126, 128–29, 182–84
Von Speyr, Adrienne, 55–50
Wainwright, Geoffrey, 165–66, 169, 179–80
Ward, Graham, 78
Wheaton, Gerry, 132
Wilkins, Michael, 165
Witherington, Ben, III, 132
Yee, Gale A., 132
Zizioulas, John, 16–17, 32, 36–41, 43, 47–51, 118, 175, 183

Index of Scripture

OLD TESTAMENT

Genesis

1	138
1:2	139
1:26–27	102
2	138
2:15	153
3:23	153
3:24	154
37:25–28	150

Exodus

4:16	133
4:22–23	139
19:3	140
19:6	139
23:14–17	148
24:8	148
26:31	153
28	152
28:30	152
32:11–14	133
34:18–23	148

Leviticus

4	149
4:20	149
4:26	149
4:31	149
4:35	149
8:8	152
8:9	152
8:12	152
8:23	152
8:30	152
8:35	150, 153
9:23	133
10:1–3	133, 135
11–15	152
16:8–10	152
23	148
27	150
27:4	150
27:29	150

Numbers

3:5–13	153
27:16–18	143
27:21	152

Deuteronomy

17:8–20	153
17:14	137
17:15	138
31:14–15	156
31:23	156

Joshua

1:1–9	156

1 Samuel

10:1	152
10:19	137
15:21	151
15:23	151
16:1	152
16:13	139
17:23	151

1 Kings

1:38–40	139

Psalms

2:7	139
22	151
69	151

Isaiah

53	149
53:4–7	149
53:7	150

Zechariah

6:11	152

NEW TESTAMENT

Matthew

1:1—9:34	135, 137–42, 156–62, 167–69, 174–180
1–4	135, 138–40, 157–58, 167
1–2	167
1:1–17	136, 138
1:1	111, 159, 177
1:18–25	138
1:18	157
1:20	1423, 138–39, 167
2	138
2:4	147
2:13	157
2:15	138–39
3:2	138, 140
3:15	140, 157
3:16	157
4	167
4:1–11	139
4:1	157
4:2	157
4:17	132, 140
4:23	134
5:1—7:27	135, 140–41, 168–69
5:1–12	140, 168
5:3	140
5:8–9	140
5:10–11	140
5:35	140
5:48	140
6:25–34	168
6:33	140
7	168
7:12	168
7:17	168
7:21	168
7:24	168
7:28—9:34	135, 141–42, 168–69
7:28–29	142
7:29	140
8–9	134, 169–70
8:5–13	141
8:23–27	141
8:28–34	141, 168
9:1–8	141, 168
9:8	141
9:27–31	142
9:32–35	143
9:35—20:34	134–36, 142–45, 156–62, 169–171, 174–180
9:35—12:50	135, 143–44, 170–71
9:35—10:42	134, 143, 160
9:35—10:4	133–34
9:35	111, 134, 159, 177
9:36–38	143–44, 170
10:1	143
10:2–4	134
10:2	134
10:5	134, 170
10:7	170
10:16–20	143–44
10:19–20	143
10:38	148
10:40–41	143

11:1–2	144	21:45	147
12:31–32	144	22:15–22	146
12:39–40	143	22:23–33	146
13–17	135, 144–45, 170–71	22:34–46	146
13	145	23–25	135, 147, 172–73
13:1–52	134	23	147, 172
13:1–9	144, 170	23:16–22	147
13:14	144	23:23–24	147
13:17	144	23:25–28	147
13:24–30	144, 170	23:29–36	147
13:31–33	144, 170	24:1–2	155
13:35	144	24:1	146, 173
13:44–46	144	24:14	147, 173
13:57	144	24:44	147, 173
14:5	144	25:31–46	147, 173
14:13–21	144, 170	26–28	135, 148–57, 173
14:28–33	144	26:2	148
15:19	176	26:3	147
15:32–39	144, 170	26:5	148
16:13–20	171	26:6–13	151
16:18	144, 155	26:12	152
16:21–28	170	26:14–16	149
16:21	132, 147, 178	26:14	148
16:24	145, 148, 178	26:17–19	148
17:22–23	178	26:21	148
18–20	135, 145, 171	26:23	148–49
18	134, 145, 178	26:25	148
18:1–4	145, 171	26:28	148, 152, 154
18:4	178	26:29	148
18:6	145	26:34	148
18:15–20	171	26:47	147, 149
18:21–22	171	26:55	146
19–20	145	26:57	149
19:13–15	145, 171	26:59	147, 149
19:28	150	26:61	146
20:18–19	178	26:62–63	149
20:18	147	26:64	151
20:20–28	145, 171	26:68	149
20:28	178	26:69–75	149
21–28	134–36, 145–62, 172–80	27:1–2	150
		27:1	147
21–22	135, 146–47, 172	27:3–10	149–150
21:1	111, 159, 177	27:3	147
21:12–17	146, 172	27:11–26	150
21:13	146	27:11	150
21:15	147	27:12	147, 150
21:18–22	147	27:14	149–50
21:23	146–47, 172	27:15	148
21:42	155		

Matthew (continued)

27:18	150, 153
27:19	150
27:20	147, 149–50
27:25	150, 152, 154
27:40	146
27:41–43	153
27:41	147
27:42	151
27:46	149
27:51	146, 154–55
27:52–53	155
27:54	153, 155–56
27:59	152
27:60	155
27:62–66	156
27:62	154
28:2	155
28:11–15	155–56
28:16–20	156, 165
28:18	60, 96
28:19	49, 144, 161, 169, 180
28:20	111, 155, 159, 177

Mark

6:6	132
6:6b—8:38	132
8:31	132
15:34	63

Luke

9:51	131
24:44	131

John

1:1–3	73
1:6–8	75
1:6	76
1:10–11	46
1:14	46, 48
1:18	48, 73
1:29–34	75
1:29	79
1:32–33	76
1:32	83
1:36	79
3:16–17	71
3:16	48, 81
3:18	48
3:30	84
3:32	77
3:34	45
3:35	45, 81
4:23	75, 81
4:31–35	76
4:34	45
5:17	81
5:19–22	45
5:20	81
5:21–23	80
5:23	80
5:30	77
5:35	75
6	132
6:46	73, 77
6:63–65	76
6:63	83
7:1—10:21	132
7:16	65
7:18	65
7:39	74
8:26	77
8:38	77
8:40	77
8:47	77
10:11	79
10:14–15	45
10:17–18	79, 80
10:17	81
10:18	73
10:22—12:11	132
10:29	73
10:36	76
10:38	44, 98
11:33	83
11:38–42	81
12:16	74
12:23–24	74, 80
12:29	77
12:49–50	73
12:49	65
13:12–17	79
13:16	73
13:21	83

13:31–32	60, 66, 96
14:2	73
14:6	77
14:10–11	98
14:10	81
14:12	77
14:13	74
14:15–23	81
14:16–17	83
14:16	71, 75
14:17	77
14:24	65
14:26	44, 46, 71, 75
14:28	48
14:31	73, 81
14:38	73
15:1–17	74
15:9–10	81
15:10	73
15:12–13	84
15:13	79
15:15	77
15:20	73
15:26	44–45, 71, 75, 77
16:7	46, 75
16:13	74, 77, 81
16:14	45, 60, 80, 96
16:20	81
16:23–33	81
16:26	81
16:27	81
16:28	46
17	62, 77, 80, 83
17:1	60, 73–74, 96
17:5	74
17:14–15	81
17:21	44, 61, 67, 98–99, 102
17:22	45
17:26	81
19:19	79
19:26–27	79
19:30	83
20:12	84
20:17	73
20:21–23	75
20:21–22	82, 83

Acts

9:31	116

Romans

4:25	155
15:7	64

1 Corinthians

11:3	105
15:24	60, 96, 156, 185

2 Corinthians

11:13	143

Ephesians

4:11	143
5:21—6:4	105, 108

1 Timothy

5:17–18	143

1 Peter

2:25	143

1 John

4:7–17	48

Revelation

5:12	11

www.ingramcontent.com/pod-product-compliance
Lightning Source LLC
Chambersburg PA
CBHW070318230426
43663CB00011B/2170